Collector's Encyclopedia of American
COMPOSITION DOLLS
1900 – 1950
Identification and Values

Ursula R. Mertz

COLLECTOR BOOKS
A Division of Schroeder Publishing Co., Inc.

DEDICATION

This book is dedicated to Pat N. Schoonmaker, pioneer researcher of American composition dolls. Her unflagging enthusiasm for these wonderful toys has inspired many collectors. We thank her for her generous sharing of knowledge and friendship.

ACKNOWLEDGMENTS

No effort of this scope could ever be accomplished by one individual alone. Appreciation and many thanks are extended to all those who helped with pictures, information, or other support and encouragement.

The current values in this book should be used only as a guide. They are not intended to set prices, which vary from one section of the country to another. Auction prices as well as dealer prices vary greatly and are affected by condition as well as demand. Neither the author nor the publisher assumes responsibility for any losses that might be incurred as a result of consulting this guide.

Searching For A Publisher?

We are always looking for knowledgeable people considered to be experts within their fields. If you feel that there is a real need for a book on your collectible subject and have a large comprehensive collection, contact Collector Books.

Front cover: Mibs, $900.00+; Madame Alexander, $400.00; Jackie Robinson, $800.00; Peter Rabbit, $300.00; Madame Hendren, $450.00.

Back cover: Red Ridinghood, Grandma, and Wolf, $700.00; Nancy Lee, $400.00; Madame Alexander, $500.00.

Cover design by Beth Summers
Book design by Mary Ann Hudson
Photographs by Otto J. Mertz

COLLECTOR BOOKS
P.O. Box 3009
Paducah, Kentucky 42002-3009

Copyright © 1999 Ursula R. Mertz

CONTENTS

PREFACE

This book is intended to be a basic reference work on American-made composition dolls for collectors, researchers, and historians interested in all aspects of identification, history, production, and commerce.

Starting at the turn of the century, the trade in mass-produced American composition dolls developed from marginal to a major force that was to dominate the domestic market. Political events and a wealth of personal initiative and ingenuity were major factors in this development.

It is hoped that collectors will take the time to read the information presented in the chapters preceding the picture section. All technical aspects of production are discussed and are organized in such a way as to enhance the identification process. By reading the chapters on history and manufacture, many clues can be gleaned, invaluable in identifying and dating an unfamiliar doll and learning more about it.

This book also provides information on how to improve "purchase power." Easy to follow guidelines are given for evaluating the quality of a doll. Most importantly, tips on proper maintenance are provided.

Hopefully, frequent use of this book will help with all aspects of composition doll collecting and research, thus broadening appreciation of these unique dolls and promoting a better understanding of their special place in the history of American dolls.

HOW TO USE THIS BOOK

The Gallery of Dolls section of this book, beginning on page 34, is arranged alphabetically by manufacturer (name or subject, if a manufacturer is unknown). An index which is cross referenced will aid further with the identification of dolls.

For example, if the collector is trying to identify a doll with several heads that can be screwed on alternately and there are no identification marks on the doll or heads whatsoever, look under "M" in the index of "multiple heads." Page numbers indicated under this heading will have information on multiple head dolls.

HISTORY OF COMPOSITION DOLLS

The earliest traceable American-made, unbreakable composition doll was advertised in Butler Brothers catalog of 1899. Very little is known about the next ten years. It was not until 1909, when E. I. Horsman & Co. introduced Billiken, that American-made composition dolls gained in popularity. At the time, the trade was dominated by European imports of various types of dolls and centered in New York City. It followed that the new domestic dolls were offered for sale by the already established large importers and wholesalers such as George Borgfeldt & Co., E. I. Horsman & Co., and others. Smaller, new companies like Fleischaker & Baum (Effenbee, est. 1910) followed.

Various factors contributed to the development of American-made composition dolls. Modern psychology had popularized the idea of children's special needs. In Germany, women like Kaethe Kruse and others had developed and successfully marketed unbreakable dolls with soft cloth bodies. The women considered the commercially available offerings unsuitable for children. Kaethe Kruse dolls were soon imported to the United States. These developments may have spurred the search for an easier to handle, unbreakable doll. The advent of World War One definitely was a big factor.

Change came slowly. German and French dolls with porcelain heads and the faces of real children (so called character faces) were popular here and abroad around 1910, and more so the dolls with idealized features, called "dolly faces." The German industry had a long tradition of porcelain dollmaking and dominated the world market with their reasonably priced products. They saw no reason to change their manufacturing program. Besides, the Germans already had papier mache composition, celluloid, and metal heads on the American market that were well established.

A Russian immigrant by the name of Solomon D. Hoffman was granted a U.S. patent on a composition material for the manufacture of unbreakable dolls, called "Can't Break Em," in 1892. He was first to produce dolls made of this new material. After his death, the business was bought by Aetna. By 1910, Horsman had control of the entire output of this firm. Various other enterprises such as Denivelle and Ideal were experimenting with their own composition formulas.

By 1910, E. I. Horsman had Billikin and the Campbell Kids on the market. Both were very successful. So was the Uneeda Bisquit Kid, introduced by Ideal in 1914. The rapid expansion of the toy departments of mail-order companies also contributed to this rather successful start. They had large distribution systems and could place sizeable orders for dolls during the slow months of the year.

1914 saw the start of World War I in Europe. Soon, the supply of dolls from foreign lands was cut off, and the new American doll industry had a chance to fill the void with American-made, unbreakable composition dolls. Patriotism was heavily stressed in their advertising. Many of the early dolls were copies of German bisque character dolls. Most of these examples were 14" tall and produced on cloth bodies filled with cork or excelsior. The bodies were of American design. In addition, many companies sold dolly faced composition children on ball-jointed bodies and babies with bent limbs that were copies of German dolls. The Amberg firm called their ball-jointed child "Victory" doll.

By 1920, smaller companies such as the Averill Mfg. Co. had had a chance to establish themselves. Georgene Averill was a woman with brilliant ideas and promotional talents. In 1918, she introduced and promoted a new doll type with a composition head that would revolutionize the doll industry. It was the mama doll with the swinging legs (See Mama Dolls — An American Invention p. 8). For at least 20 years, this doll type was a staple of all American dollmakers.

During the twenties, many innovative new doll designers were at work such as Grace Storey Putnam, Joseph Kallus, and others. The most prolific designer of all time was Bernard Lipfert. He created Effanbee's Patsy, introduced in 1927. With her stylish bob, small mouth, and shapely legs, she became a trendsetter. Many companies would produce dolls that resembled Patsy.

The 1930s were dominated by another Lipfert creation, namely, the Shirley Temple doll. With her slimmer figure of an older child and her curly wig, this doll established a new trend. After her introduction, many dolls would to some extent resemble the Shirley Temple dolls. One cannot discuss the dolls of the thirties without mentioning Effanbee's Dy-Dee, a very successful all rubber drink and wet baby. In fact, an industry official in the mid-thirties estimated that the Quints, Shirley Temple, DyDee, and their "look alikes" accounted for about 60% of annual sales.

By the end of the thirties, the popularity of the mama dolls, the Patsies, and Shirley Temples had waned. Other celebrity dolls were on the market. Debutante costumes were prominently featured and sold well. By 1950, dolls made of the new plastic materials had been introduced, and the composition era had come to an end.

During this period of roughly 50 years, an amazing variety of dolls was produced. When one considers that some companies to this day and for decades have based their sales contingent on a very few doll designs, the period from 1910 to 1920 produced an unbelievable number of character dolls and is well worth exploring. Most of the mama dolls of the twenties and thirties were dolly faces types. Nevertheless, in their design was captured the charm of toddlers just learning to walk. They were dressed in the latest fashions, and quite a few can be found in original clothes. Who can resist the interesting character faces of the babies of the twenties and thirties? Each decade, in addition, produced untold novelty types made of composition.

In summarizing, one realizes that World War I was the most important factor contributing to the success of the American-made, unbreakable composition dolls. Unfettered by foreign competition, the new industry had a chance to develop. The disappearance of the European imports created such a demand for dolls that even very small enterprises had a chance to compete. Many of them did not survive beyond the war years, but they helped to invigorate the market place. By the early twenties, the new industry was well established and ready to successfully face the renewed European competition in the domestic and foreign markets. If the toy pages of the Sears Roebuck mail-order catalog were any indication of popular trends, by 1924, the domestic scene was dominated by American-made composition dolls. This popularity continued until the new plastic materials were introduced around 1950.

American-made composition dolls are unique. A new material had been invented that was truly native. While an American doll industry existed before the turn of the century, it was small in scope. Industrialization of domestic production coincided with the rise in popularity of the new dolls. Many creative and enterprising people participated in developing a new toy that met modern needs in most innovative ways, thus helping to make the American doll industry what it is today.

DOLLS MADE IN AMERICA
AS REPORTED BY FORTUNE MAGAZINE IN 1936
(WITH PERMISSION FROM TIME LIFE PUBLICATIONS)

Reports on the doll industry provide invaluable insights for today's collectors and researchers. The following is no exception.

"It looks like a good year for dolls," were the opening words of an article published in the December 1936 issue of *Fortune Magazine.* It was profusely illustrated with pictures of Shirley Temple, Dy-Dee Baby, and the Dionne Quintuplets, the stars of the season. Facts and figures for this report had been provided by Mr. James Fri, managing director of the Toy Manufacturers Association in New York City. According to him, retail sales for 1936 would probably amount to $22,000,000.00, including accessories. He arrived at this figure in the following manner: "Take the $8,000,000.00 wholesale business reported by forty-five makers of dolls, doll parts, and doll clothes in 1934, the year of the NRA code. Add 15% per year for estimated growth of business and you get $10,500,000.00. Add another $500,000.00 for doll hospital supplies and other accessories not listed in the 1934 census, making $11,000,000.00 business at wholesale, about 40% of it done in September, October and November. The average retail markup will double the sum to $22,000,000.00 for dolls Made in America."

It was assumed that about 12,000,000 dolls would be sold that year, not including novelties. The article went to great length to explain the difference between a doll and a novelty. A doll lamp or a pincushion, figurine or "dime store gimcrack that floats in baby's bath" were not considered dolls. In order to be considered a doll, the item should have been made of composition, rubber, or cloth, and have movable arms and legs. At the time, they considered a doll in the image of a little girl a character doll. A baby was a baby doll.

One could buy a doll for as little as twenty-five cents or a girl doll for as much as $40.00. In the latter case, most of it would be for her wardrobe. Most dolls sold were between $1.00 and $5.00 retail. In the category of dolls sold for over $1.00, the average price was $2.00 and $3.00. A mama voice did not increase the price, and it was pointed out that only dolls with soft bodies were reported as usually having swinging legs, and that, "in their fashion they can be walked."

Quality of dolls was also discussed. "Much of the difference between a good doll and a cheap one enters at the final stages of manufacture: a cheap doll will not have its seams polished down as thoroughly, its complexion toned up as smoothly, its features painted as carefully. Its clothes and accessories may be downright tacky."

Grace Storey Putnam's Bye-Lo Baby had started the doll business off on its first big sales cycle and Effanbee's Patsy set in motion the second such cycle. Not only did Patsy come dressed, she had a big wardrobe and started a new trend. It brought the customer back to the toy store between seasonal peeks for more doll clothes. Thus, a new branch in the doll business was started. Moreover, the wardrobe idea was credited with smoothing the path for the individualized accessory business.

Experience had shown that sales of a doll would slip noticably in her third year. This was not true for the Shirley Temple doll. She was introduced in 1934 and still going strong. To date, she had produced $3,000,000.00 worth of sales, making her the "queenliest seller in all doll history."

The information on the distribution of business among New York City dollmakers is particularly informative and insightful: "About fifty companies are engaged in making dolls, and there is a general belief that ten of them account for about 75% of the dollar volume. Figured another way, possibly 60% of the business goes to three lines of dolls and their imitators. The three are Shirley Temple, Dy-Dee, and the Dionnes. Their respective makers are Ideal Novelty & Toy Co., Fleischaker & Baum, and Alexander Doll Co. Their imitators (i.e., companies patterning dolls after them) are almost everybody."

The doll business employed about 4,500 workers, 2,800 in the New York City area "doll center from the beginning," and the remaining 1,700 were employed by four companies which had left New York City because of labor troubles. They were Regal, Freundlich, American Character, and Cameo.

A fairly typical report was that numerous small companies did an important percentage of the chain store trade. The doll business required mainly hand labor and employed a high porportion of contract labor.

It may be of some interest to doll collectors that unionized firms worked a 40 hour week. Wages ran from a $13.20 a week minimum for the lowest paid to $45.00 for the highest (first class eyes setter). At that point, Effanbee still was not unionized.

The doll industry claimed that they were not making scandalous profits. Margins were between five and ten percent for the larger manufacturers in 1935.

The mortality rate of companies was reported as fairly high, six or seven of them going out of business in a normal year. The total number of businesses did not change much: "There are always newcomers putting dolls together in some back room, watching the new ideas to see what will take hold and what won't."

Certainly, the foregoing facts, figures, and evaluations, as reported by *Fortune Magazine*, help doll collectors and researchers get a better understanding of the doll business in the 1930s.

MAMA DOLLS — AN AMERICAN INVENTION

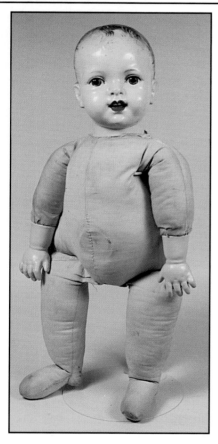

25", First Averill Mama Doll. Marks: none on doll. Ink stamp on cloth body (see Averill section). By January 1921, this doll was advertised as a mama doll. (Note extreme fading on this example.)

The trade reported that, once the mama voices had been introduced, dolls without one were difficult to sell. In order to move old stock, toy sellers added the voice boxes. One wonders, if this doll was involved in such a procedure, as a voice box was added after it left the factory. The machine sewn front seam was closed by hand stitching, after a crier had been inserted. The crier still works.

The mama dolls were such a unique and truly American invention, that no book about American composition dolls would be complete without paying special attention to their creation, development, and long-lasting success. Their simple design and construction filled the need for a doll that was easy to handle. Considering the fact that the toy business was extremely competitive and novelty features were usually soon forgotten, the mama dolls' staying power was phenomenal. These simply constructed toys, advertised as dolls that walked and talked, were the backbone of the American doll industry for at least two decades.

What is a mama doll? The *Coleman Encyclopedia* defined a mama doll as one with a two syllable voice that says "mama" and with a cloth body having swinging legs. The beginnings of an actual doll that walked and talked cannot be traced with quite the same certainty. Between 1915 and 1919, various firms advertised mama dolls, but additional information or examples have not been located. Around the same time, several companies advertised walking dolls. They did not have swinging legs but complicated walker mechanisms. Anyone familiar with some of these walkers knows that they were difficult to manipulate and usually didn't work that easily, if at all.

It was Georgene Averill of the Averill Manufacturing Co., of New York City, who created and introduced the new dolls with swinging legs in 1918. They had composition flange heads and hands wired to soft, cotton stuffed bodies with loose, stitched hip joints. When introduced, however, they had no voice boxes and were not called mama dolls. Mrs. Averill had been granted patent No. 1,269,363, on June 11, 1918, for a cloth bodied infant doll (stuffed with cotton) with loose joints. The patent pointed out that this special jointing would reduce cost. There was no mention of mama dolls in this patent but of "Life-Like" dolls. Curiously enough, the name "Life-Like" though later used extensively in advertising material, was not protected by the patent. It did cover "a doll foot provided with a heel portion ... to prevent slipping therefrom of a shoe or the like." These specially crafted heels are only found on Hendren dolls, another pointer for doll identification. The trademark "Madame Hendren Dolls" was introduced by the Averills in 1915, and was extensively used.

This ingeniously simple design of a soft cloth body with stitched joints was but one of Georgene Averill's contributions toward the success of the doll that would eventually be called the "mama doll." Madame Georgene, as Mrs. Averill was also called, had considerable talents as an innovative promoter.

MADAME HENDREN'S
"LIFE LIKE" BABY DOLL
Patented June 11, 1918.

A picture of this first mama doll was used in advertising from 1918 to 1921.

When her Life-Like dolls were introduced in 1918, Playthings reported "that the sales ladies in her Fifth Avenue shop love the Madame Hendren babies and try to teach them to walk." Teaching the dolls to walk was really quite easy. All one had to do was take them by the shoulders or under the arms, tip from side to side and move forward, and the legs would start swinging back and forth alternately. This was not difficult to do, and it really worked.

On another occasion Georgene Averill was reported to have had her sales assistants dressed as nurses or French maids to further the illusion of real children being handled rather than dolls. The trade was quite impressed with Madame Georgene's promotional prowess. A 1920 Playthings article encouraged retailers to emulate Madame Georgene's method of selling rather than just be "order takers."

In spite of these new efforts in design and promotion, sales were slow at first. It must be remembered here, that by 1919, the German dolls, which had been banished from the U.S. market during World War I, were back and competing vigorously with domestic products. Sales did pick up when mama voices were added to the dolls. These voice boxes were an American invention as well. A patent for such a mechanism was granted as early as 1915 to L. V. Aronson. In 1917, Burt E. Lloyd took out a patent for a talking doll of the mama type. Leo J. Grubman applied for and was granted patents for a sound-producing device in 1924 and 1926. According to the Colemans, a conglomerate of the three principal makers of voices for dolls licensed many doll markers to use their patented mama criers.

It is not clear when other manufacturers started making their versions of a mama doll. Certainly by 1922, firms such as Effanbee, Horsman, Ideal, and many others were heavily promoting their own creations and calling them mama dolls.

By now the demand for these new playthings had exceeded all expectations. It was reported in *Toys and Novelties* in 1923, that 80% of requests from merchants were for mama dolls. By 1926, all 23 members of the American Manufacturers Association made mama dolls, and they were heavily featured in trade journals and mail-order catalogs, such as Sears Roebuck and others.

While the lion's share of credit for the innovation of the mama dolls goes to Georgene Averill, other manufacturers made contributions that created variety and interest in the mama doll market. To mention just one example: Ideal's Vanity Flossy had a cupped hand designed to hold a mirror, and members of their Flossy Flirt line could roll their eyes and wink. Some dolls in this family featured limbs made of rubber, which made them even more life like.

Mama dolls were made with painted or sleep eyes, molded or real hair, composition or cloth limbs, and shoulder or flange heads. Eye catching novelties and child star dolls such as Baby Peggy were offered. The list of appealing mama doll creations is endless.

It is not known who invented the interchangeable legs which are frequently found on mama dolls. This type of leg has no big toe, but the foot has been rounded off in front, so that the manufacturer would no longer need to make a left and right leg. Interchangeable legs were used extensively by all doll manufacturers for a long period of time.

It seems that by 1926, the demand for the rather chubby mama dolls had slowed down. Georgene Averill's original Life-Like toddlers had been created to portray children about one year old and just beginning to walk. With the tremendous popularity of the mama dolls, their type of construction was used for dolls representing older children as well, but retaining the plumpness of the toddlers. Slimmer bodies and legs were now introduced. With this event, the original concept of the chubby, plump one-year-old toddler disappeared for the time being.

Even though Effanbee's very popular Bubbles and other successful dolls were on the market during the 1920s, the mama dolls were considered sales leaders by manufacturers and sellers.

Eventually, around 1928, mama dolls with jointed hips came on the market. They still had cloth bodies with mama voices but could not be made to walk so easily. However, they could stand by themselves. This new feature did not replace the original mama dolls with the stitched hip joints, and one can find identical heads on cloth bodies with mama voice and either jointed hips or swinging legs.

Most mama dolls were sold dressed. Fashionable, well styled clothes were also credited as having contributed to their success. As can be seen in the illustrations, mama dolls were offered in a wide variety of smart outfits. These clothes were made of good quality fabrics.

During the 1930s, the composition mama dolls had to share the limelight with a host of other dolls, such as the all-composition Patsy family, the rubber Dy-Dee Baby, and film star, Shirley Temple, to name but a few. The mama dolls endured and were still sold in the 1940s. Except for the shape of the legs, our present day, cloth-bodied babies still feature the very same construction as those famous mama dolls.

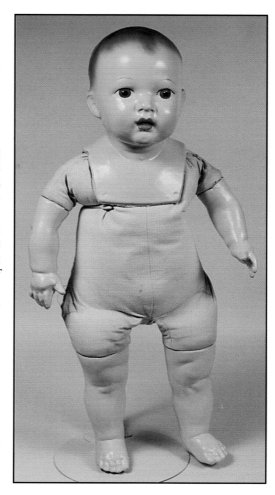

Second Mama Doll. 24" Wonder Mama Doll. Marks: none (can be positively identified from various large original ad illustrations in Playthings and Toys and Novelties from 1920 to 1923. Also see further information in Averill section.)

When compared with the first doll, various design changes have been made. A voice box was inserted during the manufacturing process, and the doll is called a mama doll. However, the emphasis in design is still very much of the Life Like aspect. Unfortunately, this doll is very faded, and this somewhat obscures the beautiful and realistic modeling of the face, but can be observed on neck, arms, and legs.

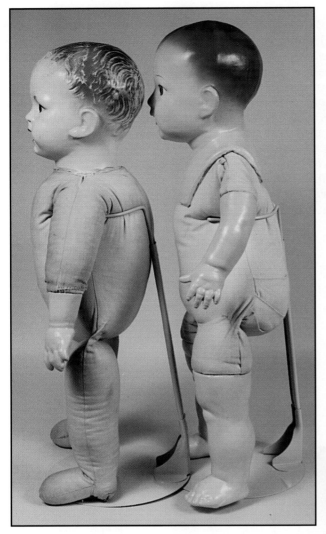

Side view of the first mama doll on the left and The Wonder Doll on the right. On the cloth foot, the special, patented heel is clearly visible. Note that on the left doll the legs are placed in the middle, whereas on the Wonder Doll the legs are placed in a frontal position, and the seat has been tucked. This well shaped rear allows the doll to sit more comfortably.

This Playthings ad from March 1922, was instrumental in positively identifying the unmarked Wonder Mama Doll. It also indicated that the dolls were sold as boys and girls with specific names. Available in sizes 20", 23", 25½", and 28".

Group of typical mama dolls from the 1920s. All original.

BERNARD LIPFERT
DOLL DESIGNER EXTRAORDINAIRE

When discussing American-made composition dolls, the picture would not be complete without mentioning the special position Bernard Lipfert occupied in this industry during the first 30 to 40 years.

The December 1936 issue of Fortune Magazine quoted Mr. Lipfert as saying with his heavy German accent: "Every doll that you see in the stores is born right here in this little basement (Mr. Lipfert's studio), without any mother, just a father." The father, of course, was Mr. Lipfert. At the time of the Fortune article, Mr. Lipfert had been in this country for almost 25 years and participated in the development of the early American doll industry. Born in 1888, he was a descendant of a German toy making family of four generations.

He was the creator of such dolls as Effanbee's Bubbles, Patsy, and Dy-Dee; Ideal's Shirley Temple; Alexander's Dionne Quintuplets; and many, many others. Mr. Lipfert did not have to go to the doll companies to peddle new designs. Important producers would come to his studio to discuss fresh ideas.

Starting with the Patsies, Mr. Lipfert introduced a new path in doll design. It was not the realism of a Bye-Lo baby that was catching on. Patsy was an abstract creation. With her bobbed, short hair style, tiny mouth, and big eyes glancing to one side, he had captured the spirit of a new and exciting modernity. Even though the Shirley Temple doll bears some resemblance to the real child star, it is the essence of her smile Mr. Lipfert had caught that was so appealing.

After World War II, Mr. Lipfert kept right on designing dolls for the new plastic medium, such as Ideal's Toni and Sparkle Plenty.

In the early 1940s, Mr. and Mrs. Lipfert moved to Westbury, Long Island, and Mr. Lipfert died there at age 86 on January 6, 1974.*

* For more personal information on the Lipferts see: "Bernard Lipfert, Father of the American Doll Industry" by Joan Amundsen. *The Antique Trader Weekly's Book of Collectible Dolls.* (The Babka Publishing Co., Dubuque, Iowa 52001, 1976)

MANUFACTURE OF COMPOSITION PARTS

In the early years and up to around 1916 (Ideal later), all makers used a glue-based composition that was very heavy and dense. Solomon Hoffman's and Aetna's (Horsman's) composition consisted of a mixture of 100 parts of glue and 25 parts each of glycerine, zinc oxide, and Japanese wax (Coleman I, pg. 413). The color of the material varied, from almost white for Horsman to brown for Ideal and a medium gray for Effanbee. Companies had their individual varying recipes which were kept secret. A piece of glue-base composition soaked in plain water overnight, became very rubbery and flexible, attesting to a high glue (gelatin?) content.

The early composition parts were produced by either a pouring process or the so-called "cold press" method. If a head was made by pouring into a mold, the surface will be totally smooth on the inside, with a mold seam on the outside only. If the head was produced by the cold press method, there will be many (6 – 8) lines visible on the inside, starting from a circle at the crown down to the neck edge.

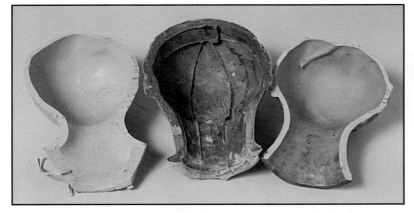

Front and back halves of three heads. From left to right: Horsman, Ideal, and Effanbee. Two heads were poured into molds, the middle one pressed into a mold. While the coloration for each head varies, all three were made of a dense, heavy mixture (see crosscut line).

When dry, the composition heads (and limbs) were dipped into a pink-tinted glue composition of thinner consistency. The parts were then airbrushed with oil paint. Some companies such as Denivelle did not use a dipped layer. Horsman, for example, seems to always have used a dipped layer.

While it is difficult to determine if the doll part was dipped or not when the doll it is in good condition, it is very easy, if the part has cracks that curl up at the edges. This is definitely a sign that the doll part was dipped in tinted glue composition and then spray painted. It is very important not to call this glue composition layer, paint, as it does not have the properties of oil paint. As the name indicates, its main ingredient is glue and the material is not waterproof but absorbs moisture when exposed. Since the glue composition layer and paper thin paint on top can have the same color, it is almost impossible to determine the condition of the paint. That is why composition dolls must never be washed, and good maintenance habits are very important.

Horsman was the only company who sewed their doll heads to the body (thread going through composition part) for both flared neck and shoulder heads. This is a good thing to remember when trying to identify an unmarked doll. If the head is actually stitched to the body, it was made by Horsman. (Also see note on special finish of early Horsman heads and limbs in Horsman section.)

Since glue-base composition was so dense and heavy, not many all-composition dolls were made, at least not large ones. A 12" baby made of glue composition weighed in at 20 ounces. Whereas a 12" baby of same construction made of the later wood pulp composition weighed only 12 ounces.

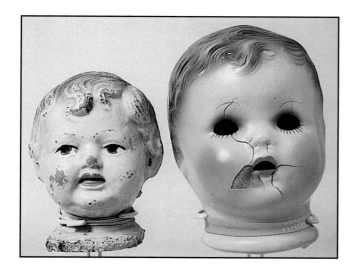 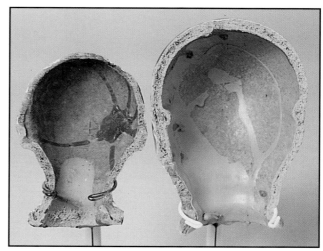

Early and late wood pulp heads.

As one can see from the surface of the cross cut, there is little difference in the texture and density of this material. The smaller head is an early one, probably a copy of a Kestner bisque head from before 1920. The larger head dates from the late 1930s and 1940s.

Not only was the early glue composition dense and therefore heavy, it was also cumbersome and time consuming to produce. By 1916 – 1918 a new material and manufacturing process was in general use. The main ingredient of the new material was ground up sawdust (also known as wood flour). A cross cut of this wood pulp composition looks very much like that of a Graham cracker, brown in color and porous in consistency. Parts made from this material were much lighter. The new process was called the "hot press method." Here, the composition dough was pressed into hot molds that dried very quickly, reducing production time immensely. Great quantities of dolls could now be produced. From then on, all dolls made by the hot press process would have the dipped glue composition layer and were spray painted.

Glue-base composition production did not stop abruptly, and some of the heavy composition heads can be found on mama dolls with cotton stuffed, very wide bodies. In fact, Ideal used their cold press, glue-base composition heads for their Flossy Flirt line right through the '20s. Vanity Flossy, illustrated in the Ideal section of the book, was pictured in the Sears & Roebuck catalog of 1927. She has a glue-base composition head.

Around 1935, another slightly different version of wood pulp composition was used for the tied-on limbs of cloth body toddlers. (No heads have been found made of this material.) Here, the sawdust was ground up even finer, as the individual fibers are very short, producing a less porous material (they too have a dipped layer under the paint). Other ingredients were changed as well, as a cross cut of this composition is whitish in color.

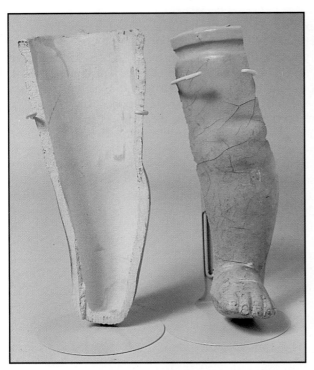
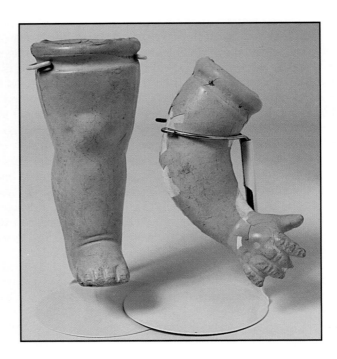

The third type of composition was introduced around 1935. It seems to be wood pulp, whitish in color, dense, with rather short fibers. It breaks more easily than parts made of the brown fiber mixture. No heads or bodies were made from this material, only arms and legs. Finishing of these limbs was handled as usual: dipped in syrupy, tinted glue composition and then spray painted. The photograph on the left shows front and back sections of a leg that has been cut in half (note white color and dense texture of cut edge). Limbs made from this material pretty much all have the same shape (photograph on right).

COPIES OF GERMAN BISQUE DOLLS

Around 1918 and for a short time, many American companies were copying German bisque dolls with ball-jointed bodies and babies with bent legs. This meant that molds were taken off the German heads and bodies for the production of all-composition American dolls. This is important to remember when examining the parts of a doll. If a German bisque head is found on a ball-jointed body made of wood pulp composition with a dipped composition layer, *it is not a German body.* The Germans made theirs of papier mache composition (gray color) that was dipped into a tinted plaster mixture and then varnished. (See separate chapter on doll bodies.)

A WORD ABOUT QUALITY

Although composition dolls of varying quality were offered throughout their duration, this did not mean that the basic composition mix was ever changed for this purpose. The difference in quality was in the finishing of the composition parts, the construction of the doll, and quality of clothing and wigs. This can be readily observed by checking on the smoothness and completeness of the dip layer and paint (no missed sections), smoothness of mold seams, quality and detail of painted facial features, etc.

BASIC BODY TYPES

We want to be able to check if the doll is in original condition. Knowledge about doll bodies can also help with the identification and dating of dolls that have no marks. Last but not least, knowing doll bodies in a historical context and being aware of various developments and achievements in the industry, will give us broader and deeper appreciation of our doll collecting hobby.

BODIES COPIED FROM GERMAN EXAMPLES

During World War I, when the supply of German bisque head dolly face dolls was abruptly cut off, American manufacturers tried to fill the void with copies made of all composition. Those American-made ball-jointed bodies were produced from about 1917 to 1920. To a lesser degree, the stuffed leather bodies with limbs of different materials and various types of jointing were also copied. Some of the all-composition baby bodies with bent legs were produced as well (heads copied also).

Though indistinguishable to the untrained eye, once familiar with production methods, it is not too difficult to tell a domestic product from the German-made one. The manufacturing process in both countries was very different. The Germans used either papier mache or papier mache composition, dipped in tinted plaster and then varnished (hence the yellowish discoloration not to be found on the copies). The American composition bodies and limbs were made of glue base (a very few) or wood pulp composition, dipped into a tinted glue-base mixture and then air brushed with oil paint. As discussed in the Manufacture of Composition Parts chapter, if bare of paint, the dipped glue composition layer may develop cracks that sometimes have formed rings around a limb, or have curled up edges. If such damage is discovered on the body of a bisque headed doll, it is definitely not of German manufacture.

Also, the grayish, dense look of the early glue base or later, brownish wood pulp composition material, identifies the body or limb as American-made and can usually be seen in the joints, where the dipping sometimes left small areas exposed.

Next to the yellowing, the most easily detected difference is in the construction of the neck socket on ball-jointed or baby bodies, for which the Germans always made a separate piece and glued it into place. On the American body, this neck socket is part of the body mold. Separately inserted socket cups were also used on some limb endings on the German product. Here again, the domestic equivalent was always molded in one piece. (Exception: The all-composition dolls sold by Mitred Box Co., around 1912 — see appropriate section.)

The left two dolls shown here have original ball-jointed bodies made of American wood pulp composition. On the leather body doll, the arms are made of wood, lower legs and hands of American composition.

Both German and American manufacturers used wood for the making of lower and sometimes upper arms and the ball for joints. However, the Germans dipped their parts into tinted plaster and varnished them. The Americans dipped into a glue-base mixture and then painted with oil paint.

By now it should be amply clear that it is not appropriate to use these bodies interchangeably. In other words, if a doll with a composition head now has a body assembly of German manufacture, or if a German bisque head is found on a slant hip ball-jointed body made in America (regardless of how desirable this body type is), this would greatly impair the value of a doll.

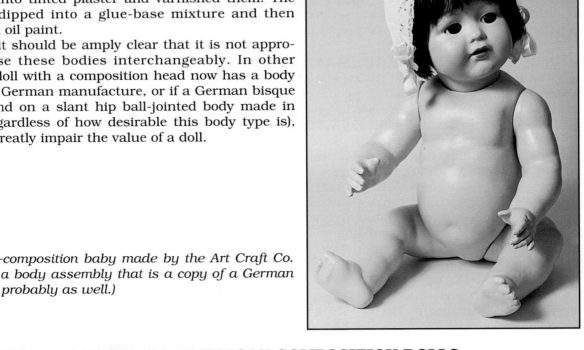

This 22" all-composition baby made by the Art Craft Co. of NY., had a body assembly that is a copy of a German type. (Head probably as well.)

CLOTH BODIES CREATED FOR AMERICAN COMPOSITION DOLLS

Right from the start, manufacturers tried their hand at new body designs. The large, already established firms like E. I. Horsman and Louis Amberg & Son were first to try new styles. While there had been doll bodies made of cloth and stuffed with sawdust before 1910, they had mostly adult features. They were long and thin and had pronounced waistlines. The idea of creating bodies with the proportion and shape of children was fairly new and, therefore, there was room for innovation. Also there emerged a growing awareness, that children should have easy to handle, lightweight toys, rather than stiff, heavy ones.

Group of composition dolls from the 1910 – 1920 period. Average size 14". Cork or excelsior stuffed cloth bodies with inside or outside disk joints, flange or shoulder heads, painted or sleep eyes, painted or real hair. Most of these dolls had closed or open/closed mouths. Some had stump cloth hands (no indication of fingers or thumbs). Some had molded composition boots. Others, such as the doll on the left, had black cloth boots that really were part of the leg casing.

16

When the E. I. Horsman Co. introduced the Campbell Kids in 1910, they were made with composition heads and hands and the new cloth bodies and limbs which were stuffed with shredded cork, making them light and shapely. Cardboard and metal disks were placed inside the limbs and body at jointing points and fastened with prongs. This made for a tight, but smoothly moving joint. This basic design was used by all makers during the next 10 years or so. The same type of bodies but with bent legs were produced for babies. With these new, cork stuffed cloth bodies American dollmakers had created a quality product that was good looking and serviceable. They were still being used by some manufacturers in the early 1920s.

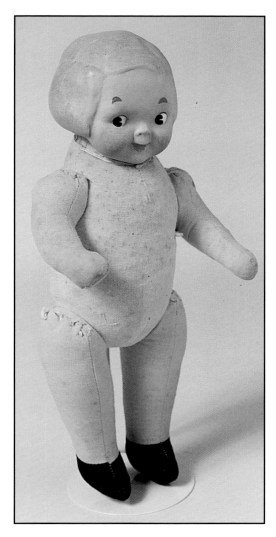

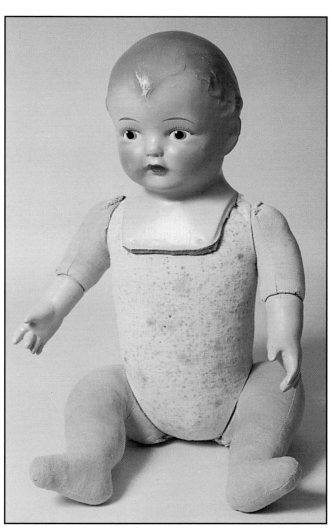

When the Campbell Kids were introduced in 1910, they were produced on the newly created and well designed cork stuffed bodies with inside hip and shoulder joints.

With these new, cork stuffed cloth bodies American dollmakers had created a quality product that was not only serviceable but also good looking.

Cheaper cloth bodies were available as well. They were stuffed with excelsior and had the cardboard or metal joint disks on top of the limb rather than within. This, of course, did not produce a body/limb assembly as visually pleasing as the one described before.

ALL-COMPOSITION BODY/LIMB ASSEMBLIES (1910 – 1920)

Since the early composition parts were made of glue-base composition which was rather dense and heavy, all-composition dolls, certainly not large ones, were not made in great numbers. Even when the much lighter wood pulp composition came into use during the latter half of the decade, not many all-composition dolls were manufactured.

MAMA DOLL BODIES

In 1918, Georgene Averill, of the Averill Manufacturing Company, was granted a patent for an improved infant body. This was a new cloth body with stitched, loose hip joints in a frontal position and a tailored heel, and was stuffed with cotton. They had tied-on composition half arms and later jointed, full composition ones. Soon, dolls with composition legs to above the knee were added to makers' lines. Eventually a mama voice was inserted into the body. This body type became so popular that it was used not only for infant dolls but older children as well.

The bodies of early mama dolls were rather wide and plump and by 1927 had fallen out of favor. Limbs and bodies of new designs were much slimmer. (When trying to date a mama doll, it is helpful to remember this information.)

At this point, the interchangeable legs were introduced. They had no big toe but their feet were rounded off in front. Their calves were not realistically shaped. If one has ever wondered if the legs might have been installed in the wrong position, examination of the toes will probably establish that one is dealing with a pair of interchangeable legs.

Around 1928, mama dolls with jointed hips were introduced. They had a right and a left leg. Their cloth bodies were firmly stuffed with cotton and nicely shaped. They could stand unaided, and when dressed, cannot be distinguished from an all-composition doll. Many had a separate shoulder plate with jointed neck, so that their heads could not only move from side to side but up and down as well. Since the ball of this neck joint was part of the shoulder plate, the joint was better hidden under the chin than on the German dolls.

Around 1935, another, distinct type of composition limb came into use for the mama dolls with stitched hip joints. They did have a right and left leg, and, therefore a big toe (see 21" Chuckles, next page, right). This feature too is an aid in dating dolls and checking originality. These limbs would be inappropriate for mama dolls from the 1920s.

Early mama dolls were very wide and plump, such as the doll on the left. By 1927, this type had become unpopular, and slimmer bodies were designed. With these slimmer bodies, interchangeable, slimmer legs came into use (doll on right).

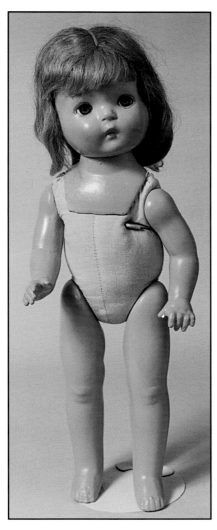

Around 1928, mama dolls with jointed hips were introduced. Their well shaped cloth bodies are stuffed firmly with cotton. When dressed, they are indistinguishable from all composition dolls. (Mama voice.)

This 21" American Character Chuckles features tie-on limbs used by many manufacturers. They were made of a special kind of composition and used over a long period of time. Effanbee's small Snoozie featured the legs (beginning in the 1930s), and Horsman's Sister and Brother, having these limbs, were marked 1937. Chuckles was advertised in 1942 and 1943.

For further information on the special composition material these limbs were made of, see photographs on page 14.

ALL-COMPOSITION DOLLS OF THE LATE 1920S, 1930S, AND 1940S

The year 1927 saw the very successful introduction of Effanbee's all-composition Patsy doll. She had a jointed head and the body contours of a young child i.e., no waistline and a slightly protruding abdomen. Her legs were slim but not as distinctly shaped as those of an older child and as the Shirley Temple dolls would have. Patsy definitely was a trend setter. Many Patsy look-alike dolls were produced by competing manufacturers with identical bodies. Other contemporary all-composition dolls also had this body style.

The Shirley Temple dolls were introduced in 1934 and were popular to the end of the thirties. Shirley Temple was six years old in 1934, and, accordingly, the Shirley Temple dolls had the body of a slightly older child than Patsy. There is an indication of a waist line with still slightly protruding abdomen but her legs are more shapely. Here again, after the introduction of the Shirley Temple dolls, other manufacturers would use this body shape for their all-composition children. With the appearance of the Mary Hoyer dolls in 1937 and similar types, the body/limb assemblies had again changed. They now featured even narrower waists and thinner legs.

Some all-composition babies were produced during the thirties and forties. Due to the tremendous success of Effanbee's all-rubber Dydee Baby and similar types, their numbers seem to have been fewer.

A few manufacturers had their own variations on the basic body types. They will be discussed when applicable under the company headings.

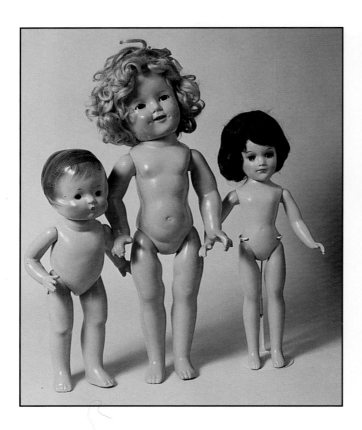
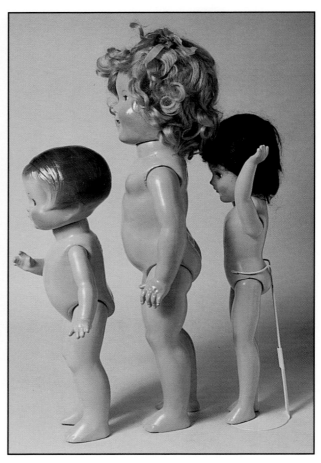

All-composition types of the late 1920s, 1930s, and 1940s. From left to right: 14" Patsy, 18" Shirley Temple, and 14½" Mary Hoyer.

EYES USED IN THE PRODUCTION OF COMPOSITION DOLLS

A very few early American-made composition dolls were outfitted with glass eyes. With the onset of World War I, the supply of glass eyes from Germany was cut off. Soon, American-made sleep eyes were introduced.

These new eyes had a sheet metal core formed into a half eyeball that was open to the back. This metal core was covered with a layer of celluloid. Pupil, iris, and white eyeballs had been lithographed onto the reverse side of this cover before mounting. Similar to under-glass painting, this technique gave the eyes some depth and also minimized the effects of scratching (eyelids were painted onto the surface). Patent #1,252,469 was issued to Samuel Marcus, of New York, New York, on January 8, 1918, for celluloid covered metal eyes.

In order to install the new eyes, the top of the head had to be removed and glued back. This presented no problem for dolls that were to have wigs but was more cumbersome for those with molded hair. The photo below, clearly shows how the eyes were mounted.

On the right, an eye assembly with reverse printed celluloid cover is illustrated. One cover has been removed to show construction (mounting hinge included). On the right can be seen a surface-printed pair of eyes.
Note: Patent No. 1,252,439 (application filed August 16, 1917), dated January 8, 1918, was issued to Samuel Marcus, of New York City, dealing with celluloid covered metal eyes.

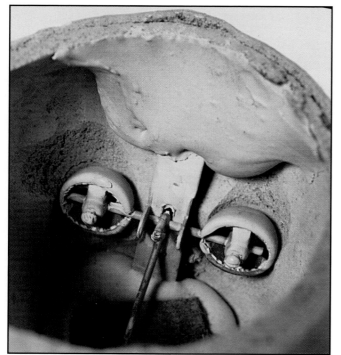

Early reverse printed and celluloid covered eyes and those which were surface printed on metal were mounted on the inside of the forehead with a lump of composition. (Note the different ways of mounting celluloid covered eyeballs on their horizontal rods — in this case, a small screw was used to hold them in place. In top photo on page 22, they have been clamped on.)

21

By the late 1920s, entirely surface-printed metal eyes were introduced. Even though these lithographed eyes were given a coat of varnish, they scratched more easily.

Sometimes it is difficult to tell which type of eye was used. By looking through the neck opening of the head and checking the back of the eyes, a definite judgment can be made. If the open, half eyeball has a sharp, narrow edge, it was surface painted. If the open eyeball has a wide, crimped edge, it is a celluloid covered one.

The Ideal Novelty & Toy Company was the first to introduce sleep eyes that could be set through the neck opening. Patent No. 1,149,858 was granted to I. A. Rommer, an employee of Ideal, in 1915. In order to mount the new surface-printed and varnished metal eyes, a protrusion was molded between the eye openings on the inside of the head. Each eye was threaded onto the ends of a pin that looked similar to a hairpin with both ends bent out at right angles. Pin and eye could now be inserted into a tiny hole at the temple on one side and the protrusion on the other.

If the back rim of the half eyeball is sharp and narrow, it is a surface printed on metal eye. If the rim has a wide, crimped edge, the eye is celluloid covered.

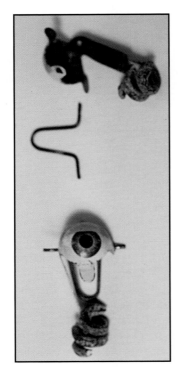

Bottom: Front view of Ideal sleep eye. Top: Rear view of Ideal eye. Note protrusions on top and bottom of half eyeball which prevent the eyes from flipping back into the head. The extension arm on the right accommodates a spiral counterweight. The mounting pin has been removed and is seen alongside (on the left).

The Ideal eyes were individually mounted. Note hairpin-type pins on which eyes have been threaded.

Each eye also had a long, narrow tongue extending on its right side which ended into a metal weight. Another unique feature of these very simple metal eyes was an extension lip on the bottom and top rim of the half eyeball. The upper lip kept the eye from turning too far when the doll slept, and the lower lip did the same when the doll was upright. These Ideal eyes never had real eyelashes but painted ones only. As can be seem in the illustration, their eyes were not completely round. The eye openings were cut in the shape of a narrow oval. These two features kept the eyes from staring, even though they had no real eyelashes.

Since the eyes had been mounted individually and were weighted, they could rock back and forth. Ideal took full advantage of this feature in their advertising and coined the phrase "She winks and she blinks." Ideal used these winking, blinking eyes until the early 1930s. Being familiar with these special Ideal eyes can be helpful in identifying unmarked dolls as to manufacturer.

Around 1925, another method of setting sleep eyes through the neck opening was invented. The construction of the eye assembly remained the same, i.e., weighted cross bar, with the eyes threaded onto the horizontal rod. But now, this assembly was held in place with an expandable metal slide the end prongs of which were pushed into the inner walls of the temples.

By the early 1930s so called "glass-like" doll eyes came on the market (the trade named them glassene eyes). They were made of celluloid as well. Those were the eyes that sometimes shatter and become cloudy. Here too a metal core was used for the open-to-the-back, half eyeball which was covered with a layer of celluloid. This layer was reverse painted for the white of the eyeballs, but the pink lid was applied onto the outside surface. The celluloid cover had a circular opening in the center. A lens of clear celluloid was inserted into this depression, representing iris and pupil. Black coloring for the pupil was applied to the back of the lens center. When seen from the front, the iris also showed soft rays. As with pressed glass, facets were molded into the reverse side of the iris which reflected light.

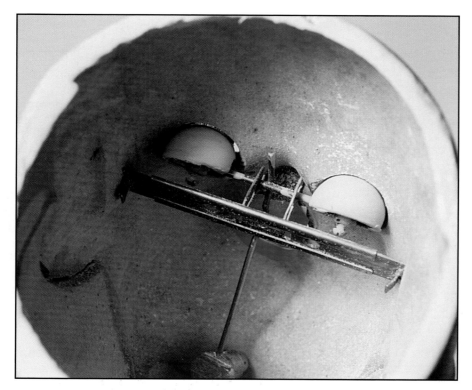

The expandable metal bar seen in this picture and used to hold the eye assembly in place, made it possible to set other than Ideal eyes through the neck opening. In this case the crown was cut off only to give a clear view of the construction.

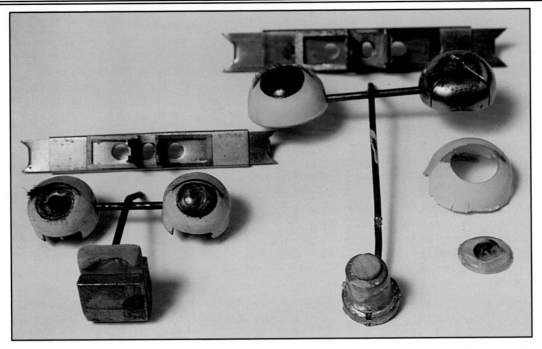

Left: A pair of surface-painted eyeballs with clear celluloid inserts is illustrated. (Extracted left lens not available, as it was shattered. Center depression left eye is rust covered.)
Right: A pair of eyes with celluloid cover that has been reverse painted and has an inset, clear celluloid lens, representing pupil and iris. The right eye has been taken apart to show construction. Both types of eyes were mounted with the expandable slide.
During the 1930s, both types of eyes were sold by the Margon Corp. of Bayonne, New Jersey.

Another version of these eyes had surface-painted metal eyeballs with a depression in the middle to accommodate the clear celluloid lens. This depression had also been painted white. The white background gave the iris more sparkle. Both types of so-called glassene eyes were installed with the expandable metal bar.

During the 1930s, the Margon Corporation of Bayonne, New Jersey, must have been a major supplier of the glassene doll eyes, as they advertised regularly in *Playthings* magazine, claiming: "MARGON lustrous, lifelike, moving eyes, recognized as the world's finest, have been the standard for dolls in all price ranges for over twenty-one years" (*Playthings*, February 1937).

On the much later (early 1940s) plastic lenses of doll eyes, the facets were molded into the iris more sharply and deeply and the background again painted white, making for really sparkling eyes. In addition, the plastic lenses had a colored line

This photograph shows the later (early 1940s) plastic lenses inserted into surface-painted metal eyeballs. More deeply and sharply molded facets on the backs of these lenses, together with a dark rim painted on the reverse side, rendered these eyes much more sparkly. Black coloring for the pupil was applied to the neck of the lens in back.

painted around the edge of the reverse side, which gave them even more depth. Even though these later plastic eye centers were set into a surface-painted metal eyeball, they don't seem to shatter like the earlier celluloid lenses.

Most metal eyes with plastic lens inserts were mounted into the head with clamps which were fastened to a protrusion molded to the inside of the head between the eye openings. The same eyes and mounting technique were used for the plastic dolls which followed around 1950.

At various times, composition dolls featured sleep eyes that could move from side to side. They were commonly known as flirty eyes. For this mechanism, the eyes were housed in a metal case, and hinged with a vertical rod. The weighted vertical rod of the eye assembly was also hinged. All three vertical rods were connected by a wire. When moving the doll from side to side, gravity would now shift the counter weight from side to side and the eyes with it.

With the exception of the Ideal winking/blinking eyes, all sleep eyes made for composition dolls were available with or without inset real eyelashes.

As can be seen, a wide variety of sleep eyes was created. Although this industry started out of necessity to replace the non-available German product, American manufacturers of doll eyes greatly contributed to the process of giving composition dolls an original, distinctive look.

Back view of mechanism with eyes that move from side to side.

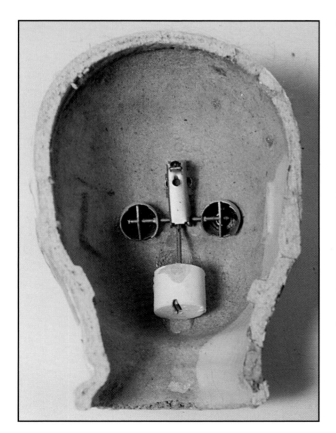

Most metal eyes with plastic lenses were clamped onto a protrusion inside the head.

IMPROVE BUYING POWER

Memorize the terms and look for these conditions whenever a composition doll is examined.

WHAT IS GOOD QUALITY IN COMPOSITION DOLLS? Nice, pink skin tone and rosy cheeks, smooth composition surface and mold seams, good modeling, competent face decoration, original wig, original or contemporary clothes.

WHAT ARE CLOUDY EYES? The celluloid iris of the doll eye has shattered and looks crackled.

WHAT ARE OILED EYES? Shattered doll eyes have been saturated with sewing machine oil or clear mineral oil to hide those cracks. This treatment restores some depth to the eyes. If the eyes look dark and a pupil is not discernable, the eyes have been oiled. Also check for oil damage. If there is discoloration around the eye openings, oil was handled carelessly. Oil is not supposed to touch the composition.

CRAZING — Fine lines in the paper thin paint. Acceptable, if not too obvious and there is no flaking.

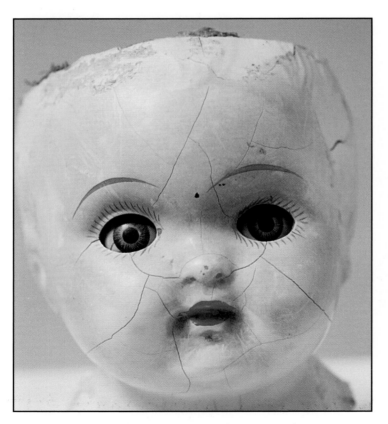

The condition on this head clearly exemplifies crazing.

26

FLAKING — The paper thin paint is coming off, a sign of dried out paint. Not acceptable in the face. Look for the beginnings of flaking in the depressions of the face, near the eye cuts, behind the ears. For dolls with dried out paint, proper maintenance is especially important.

On this head the subsurface is of a different color and flaking can be clearly observed. Note that the surface paint was applied in a very thin layer.

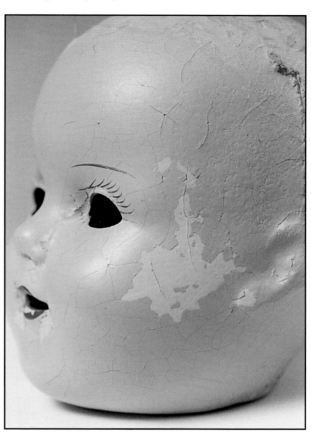

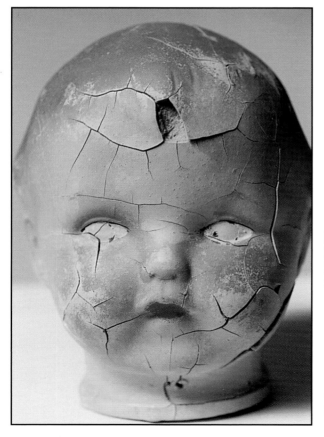

CRACKING — The intermediate composition layer has cracked (looks like thick paint but is not). Not acceptable in the face. Small amounts of it on limbs or body may be tolerated. Usually starts near the mold seams.

On this head a very advanced case of cracking can be studied.

27

LIFTING — The intermediate composition layer has separated from the base and left a hollow space. Look for it, particularly in the depressions of the face and behind the ears. Small amounts of it may be acceptable, but should not distort the features.

FADING — All composition dolls left the factory with a nice, pink skin tone and rosy cheeks. If the doll has no blush on the cheeks, it means she has faded. How much fading can be accepted is a very personal choice.

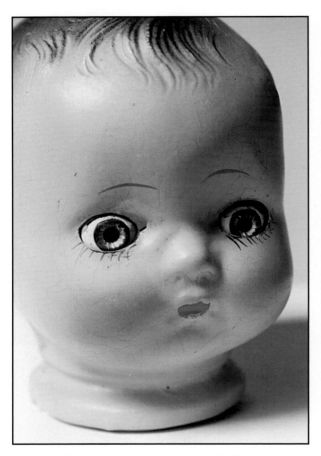

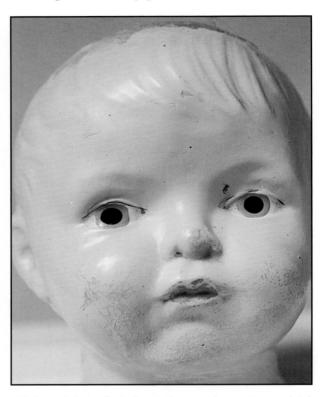

Note a hint of pink at the neck section which was not as exposed to light as the face.

In this face an extreme case of lifting can be studied. The subsurface near the right eye has lifted so high, that it is almost even with the nose and has started to crack. Note the rings in the nostrils, also a case of lifting.

WIGS — Great numbers of composition dolls are still to be found with their original wigs. A replacement should at least be a proper substitute, i.e., a human hair or mohair wig.

CLOTHES — Factory original, contemporary, or copies of original clothes.

TIPS ON MAINTENANCE

When discussing maintenance, one of the most often asked questions is: "What can I put on the doll to preserve her and keep the paint from drying out?"

The answer is that absolutely nothing must be put on the dolls. In the past, people have applied various substances in the name of preservation that have ruined otherwise perfectly sound dolls. Used were oils, creams, pastes, or lacquers, etc. All of these materials will in time get sticky or hard and/or turn yellow.

Successful maintenance of composition dolls is simple, as only two basic requirements have to be met: One must provide proper temperature/humidity conditions and keep the dolls away from direct sunlight or strong light. Room temperature should be 65 – 70° F. and the humidity approximately 45 – 55%. Simple temperature/humidity gauges can be purchased at hardware stores and are not expensive. More accurate hygrometers (humidity gauges) are available from museum supply stores. They are more expensive but worth having if the collection consists of more than a few dolls.

The temperature/humidity gauge seen on the right is available in hardware stores. The instrument on left is available from museum supply stores.

Of course, it is difficult to maintain even levels of temperature and humidity in the average home. As the weather changes, temperatures go up and down. This does not necessarily create problems, as long as the dolls are not exposed to sudden changes or drafts (open windows and sliding glass patio doors). When dolls travel, they should always be protected. At no time of the year should one walk out of the house with a doll under one's arm or put it on the back seat of the car as is.

Keeping an eye on humidity year round is most beneficial. Hot air heating systems with their constant movement of air are the worst offenders in terms of creating extremely dry conditions in winter. In such a case, it would be best to pack the dolls away or put them in cases when the heat is on. A glass of water in the doll case will assure that proper humidity is maintained (measure to be sure). By the same token, if the humidity constantly gets too high in summer, a de-humidifier should be installed. This can be done fairly easily in a basement.

Since all painted surfaces fade, composition dolls should not be permanently displayed in general living areas. The dolls can be used in decorating one's home. However, they should never be out longer

29

than a few months at a time (much less if they have original clothes and wigs). Even for these short periods, the dolls should not be exposed to direct sunlight or bright light.

It would be nice if every collector had a special room available for display purposes, which could be made safe for dolls. Homes do offer alternatives. A dry basement makes a wonderful doll room or storage area, as temperatures there are much more stable. Bedrooms can double as hobby rooms, as window shades can be drawn when they are not in use. If other living areas are used for permanent doll display, one might want to install ultraviolet light shields at the windows. Such shields are also available for fluorescent light tubes, as prolonged exposure to fluorescent lights is harmful as well.

Maintenance should even be thought about when buying a doll. A prospective purchase should always be checked for signs of dry paint. Small areas of flaking in the depressions of the face or behind the ears are telltale signs. The doll should be checked for cracks along seam lines and near joints etc. The ultimate goal should always be to buy a doll with the least amount of damage, as she will be the easiest to take care of and give the most pleasure in the long run.

Of course, there will be occasions when a purchase has more than a little damage. The doll may have been a rare find, very cheap, etc. Such examples can be rather stable for long periods of time if temperature/humidity conditions in the display or storage area are strictly observed. However, such dolls should be watched very closely.

Whatever the case, one should always be fully aware of present condition. This will prevent many unpleasant surprises. It will also establish a habit of immediately determining how much care a specific doll will need. Once these simple procedures have become routine, caring for composition dolls is easy.

FIRST AID & SMALL REPAIRS

All of us admire so-called mint dolls. Yet, most of the time, the dolls we buy need a little freshening or outright restoration. Rejuvenating a less than perfect doll can be a very satisfying and rewarding experience. However, haven't we all seen dolls where we wished the previous owner had not been so heavy handed? What are the hard and fast rules on the matter?

For new collectors, the first rule should probably be not to do anything until a little more experience has been gained. Looking at similar dolls and learning as much as possible about the example in question, such as its history, construction, and fashions of the period, will all help in doing a good job of restoration.

Preserving as much originality as possible should always be the main objective. Whatever we do should fit in, so that, hopefully, what we change will not be very noticeable. If a wig is replaced, for example, it should be done with a new wig of the same material. Before making such a decision, great pains should be taken to see if the old wig can be preserved. Separating strands of matted mohair with a wooden toothpick can do wonders in fluffing up a sparse, old wig. Clothes should be repaired rather than replaced. If a new dress is provided, it should be of the proper style and fabric weight. Prints should be in scale to the size of the doll. Synthetics such as nylon or permanent press fabrics should not be used.

Separating strands of matted mohair with a wooden toothpick can do wonders in fluffing up a sparse old wig.

SHOULDN'T THE DOLL AT LEAST BE CLEANED?

Composition dolls should not routinely be cleaned. The most desirable surface on a composition doll is one that has never been touched. It will have a matte finish and will not be shiny at all. If a doll is so dirty that she cannot be enjoyed in her present state, cleaning is an alternative. A composition doll should never be washed or even wiped with a damp cloth.

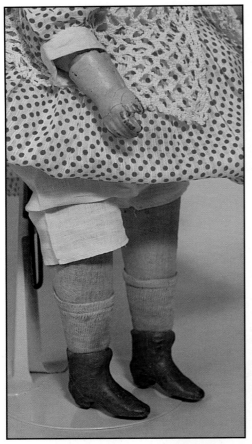

Renaissance Wax, made by Picreator Renaissance Products by Picreator Enterprises Ltd., London, and available from museum supply stores here in the United States, is currently being used by some museums for the cleaning of their composition dolls. In the past collectors have used such household items as Jubilee Kitchen Wax, Rally Cream Wax (a car wax), or cold cream to clean their dolls. One cautionary measure should be to always use a white cloth for cleaning and to check the cloth often while in use. If the white cloth at any time looks pink, one should stop immediately, as, obviously, the paint is being rubbed off.

If the doll has cloth legs that cannot be cleaned, why should the dress be snowy white again?

SHOULD THE CLOTHES BE WASHED?

Here, as in any other instance, common sense goes a long way. If the doll has cloth legs that are dirty and cannot be cleaned, why should the dress have to be snowy white again? Vacuuming can do wonders. However, a screen should be used to protect the fabric. (A screen can be very quickly made by pulling pantyhose over a stretched-out metal coat hanger.) Cotton fabrics may be washed with a neutral soap available from museum supply houses (unscented hair shampoo is an alternative as an interim measure). Minerals which are present in tap water are harmful to fabrics. For this reason, distilled water is recommended for washing doll clothes. To use rain water would be an alternative. Because of its acidity, vinegar cannot be used as a water softener for rinsing. Bleaches are also harmful to fabrics and should not be used.

HOW ABOUT REPAIRS?

This is the most difficult of all decisions and should never be rushed. If damage is extensive and a doll hospital is being considered, one should never pick one based on the claims of its owner. If fellow collectors don't have recommendations, one should at least ask the repairer to see a piece of work similar to the restoration to be done. One should constantly check in one's mind if the work suggested makes sense. Always ask for a written proposal. The main objective at all times should be to do as little as possible. If a composition part has a crack that is going to be repaired, the whole piece should not have to be repainted. Only the repaired area should be touched up. Make sure to ask if the repairer knows how to match paint and if he/she uses an airbrush for hair and cheeks. Hair and cheeks on composition dolls were airbrushed. It is almost impossible to duplicate the airbrush technique with a paint brush for the jobs mentioned.

HOW ABOUT SMALL "HOME" REPAIRS?

As has been pointed out in the chapter on maintenance, damaged dolls will be quite stable under proper maintenance and storage conditions. If the damage does affect structure, there are steps that can be taken. If, for example, the stringing on an all-composition doll exerts too much pressure and the mold seams have started to split, restringing with the proper tension can relieve the problem. If mold seams are open and too weak, some white glue may carefully be worked into the crack and the part strapped with wide rubber bands overnight, to allow the glue to harden. Cracks with upturned edges may also be filled with white glue. Painting should not be attempted by inexperienced practitioners. The rule of thumb here is that if the touched up area will be noticeable, it will probably not improve the looks of the repair. Since such jobs are not reversible, an inadequate touch-up will lower the value of the doll.

It is hoped that these few tips will be of help to collectors and increase the pleasure and satisfaction derived from freshening up a doll.

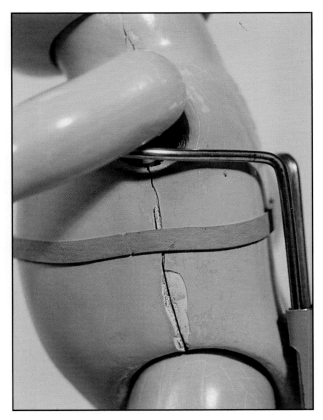

If mold seams have opened up, some white glue can be carefully worked into the crack and the part strapped with a wide rubber band overnight to let the glue harden.

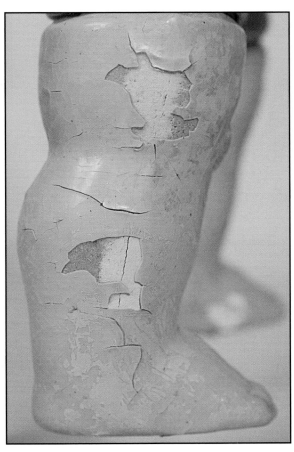

Cracks with upturned edges may also be secured with glue. (Carefully work small amounts of glue towards the loose edge.)

GALLERY OF DOLLS

This firm produced a general line of popular dolls. Their factory was expanded in 1930. In 1920, Davis & Voetsch are reported as distributors. In 1928, Kaufman, Levenson & Co., Salt Lake Hardware, and Vier Brothers are listed as distributors.

19". Marks: Acme Toy Co. 1920s.
Composition shoulder head and short arms. Cloth body, upper arms, and bent legs, jointed at shoulders and hips. Molded painted light brown hair and painted blue eyes. Open/closed mouth with molded tongue, re-dressed. $125.00.

15". Marks: ACME TOY CO. (Playthings, January 1927).
Composition flange head and hands. Molded painted blond hair. Tiny tin sleep eyes, closed mouth. Cloth body, arms, and straight legs with stitched hip joints. Re-dressed. $100.00 (fair).

24". Marks: Acme Toy Co. This is their Honey (Playthings, February 1928).
Was made in six sizes. Composition flange head, full arms, and bent legs to above the knee. Jointed at shoulders and hips. Cloth body and upper legs. Molded painted blond hair, gray tin sleep eyes, open mouth with two upper teeth, two dimples. Lower lip and tongue molded together. All original.
Note: Doll and clothes are of high quality, obviously designed to compete with such dolls as Effanbee's Bubbles and Horsman's Dimples. $350.00.

ALLIED-GRAND DOLL MANUFACTURING CO., INC.
BROOKLYN, NEW YORK

An ad in *Toys and Novelties* of March 1948, stated "Our 30th Year!" which would have meant that they were founded in 1918. Allied-Grand had two factories that produced inexpensive composition dolls. Illustrated ads from the late 40s show the typical, dolly faced 10" all-composition babies with bent legs, no neck joint, painted eyes and hair; one of them a black doll with three pig tails, the third a white toddler with straight legs. They also had a 14" all-composition toddler with sleep eyes and mohair wig. They consistently show the pig-tailed black baby in their ads. Their 1949 ads also featured a hard plastic baby (jointed shoulders and hips) and a hard plastic little girl jointed at the shoulders only (emphasizing that they had both, plastic and composition).

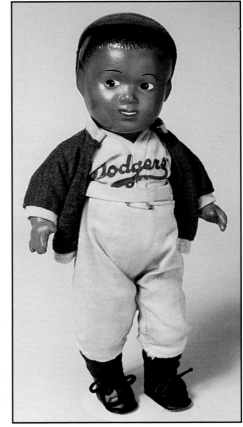

13", Jackie Robinson. Marks: none. See Playthings, March 1950.
All composition, fully jointed. Black hair is modeled in tight curls. Painted brown eyes to side. Open/closed mouth with white line between lips to indicate teeth. All original except for jacket which is a copy of the original. Original warm-up jacket had DODGERS on it, as seen on front of top. $800.00.

ARCADE TOY MANUFACTURING CO., INC.
58 CROSBY ST.
NEW YORK, NEW YORK

16". Marks: none (Playthings, August 1913).
Composition flange head with molded, light blue hat and white flower (red center). Molded painted blond hair and painted blue eyes, closed mouth. Composition lower arms. Cloth body and limbs, jointed with inside disks (body assembly is a proper old replacement). Re-dressed (photograph in the original ad shows the doll dressed in a striped sailor dress). $250.00.

ARCY TOY MANUFACTURING COMPANY
NEW YORK, NEW YORK

21". Marks: ARCY © 1914 (Playthings, August 1915).
Composition flange head, cloth body, arms, and bent legs, jointed with outside disks. Molded painted brown hair with molded loop for hair ribbon. Painted blue eyes, open/closed mouth, old clothes. Head has been restored. $150.00.

ARTCRAFT PLAYTHINGS CORPORATION
BROOKLYN, NEW YORK
1920 – 1921

This company produced ball-jointed composition children and bent limb babies, whose head and body part molds had definitely been taken from German bisque dolls. The dolls were of very high quality. Their July 1920 ad shows the baby doll seen in this section. Also illustrated is a little girl sitting in a bath tub, holding her nude dolly face, ball-jointed doll. Their dolls were definitely not waterproof. Such misleading advertising may help explain why so few of these very high quality dolls have survived.

22". Marks: Art Craft//N.Y.C. (Playthings, July 1920).
All composition, fully jointed, bent legs, dark brown human hair wig over metal pate. Dark brown glass eyes, open mouth with two upper teeth and celluloid tongue. Re-dressed. $350.00.

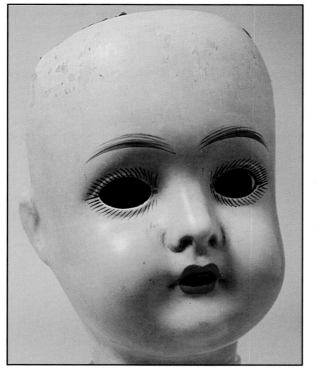

6", head only (should have ball-jointed body). Marks: Artcraft//U.S.A.//10.
Composition socket head, celluloid sleep eyes, open mouth with four upper teeth. Note well painted multi-stroke brows and painted eyelashes all around the eye opening. $50.00 head only.

ALEXANDER DOLL CO.
NEW YORK CITY

A 1926 article in Playthings reported on the creation of the Alexander Doll Company. Madame Alexander's (Mrs. Beatrice Berman) parents owned a doll hospital in New York City. At an early age, she and her three sisters sewed and sold doll clothes and later made cloth dolls. The earliest identifiable cloth doll produced by the Alexander Doll Company was an Alice in Wonderland, followed by the Little Women, representing the main characters of Louisa May Allcott's novel by the same name, and many others.

Throughout the 1930s and 1940s, the Alexander Doll Company sold a high quality line of composition dolls. The production of composition mama dolls may have started as early as 1927. Starting with her cloth dolls and throughout her career as a doll designer, Madame Alexander created many storybook characters, not only in an 8" size but larger as well. Regardless of size, clothes were made of excellent fabrics, well designed and executed. Unlike the mama dolls, these beautiful storybook children may have been played with less and used more as ornaments.

Madame Alexander also created character children such as Princess Elizabeth to represent the well known English princess and Margaret O'Brien of movie fame. These dolls were sold with other identities as well, and in that case are referred to by collectors as "Elizabeth face" or "Margaret face," followed by the name of their new identity.

Madame's greatest popular success was the Dionne Quintuplet dolls, which were produced in many sizes and styles. Her most enduring success, of course, were the 8" storybook children still being sold today.

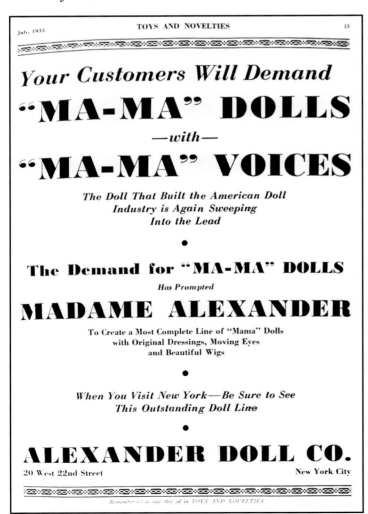

Full-page ad placed by the Alexander Doll Co. in Toys and Novelties, July 1933.

The ad makes it obvious that Madame Alexander vigorously participated in the mama doll market (possibly as early as 1927). Yet, Alexander mama dolls are practically invisible in today's collector market. Those examples that have been identified were unmarked but their clothes had Alexander cloth labels. Others have been seen marked "Fiberoid," with tagged Alexander outfits. In other words, once the tag has been removed or the clothes have been taken off, the identity is lost. This is probably the reason why so *few* Alexander mama dolls can be seen today.

There is no doubt in this writer's mind that the mama doll pictured here was sold by the Alexander firm. Her clothes particularly are of the highest quality in terms of materials, styling, and workmanship.

22". Marks: none (reported as Alexander).
Composition shoulder plate and swivel head, full composition arms and interchangeable legs to above the knee. Cloth body, stitched hip joints. Original blond human hair wig. Sleep eyes, open mouth with two upper teeth. All original. $250.00.

11". Marks: Madame//Alexander.
All composition fully jointed, painted black eyes, open/closed mouth. All original including white felt mittens with black tie strings. Pants have a same fabric tail attached in back. Accompanying ad by Playthings is dated November 1933.
Note that the Three Little Pigs pictured here were produced under license from Walt Disney on the occasion of Disney's Silly Symphony production. $500.00.

Full-page ad placed by the Alexander Doll Company (Playthings, October 1934).
Note: The Betty doll pictured is a fully jointed all-composition Patsy type, and this sewing set is advertised as an educational toy.

16". Marks: Baby Jane//Registered Mme. Alexander. 1935. All composition, fully jointed. Dark wig, brown sleep eyes, open mouth with four upper teeth. Re-dressed, replaced wig. Note: This is a portrait of child star Juanita Quigly, originally billed as Baby Jane. $500.00 (fair).

Dionne Quintuplets

The Canadian Dionne Quintuplets were born in 1934. The April 1935 issue of *Playthings*, reported that Madame Alexander had been granted an exclusive license to make quintuplet dolls. The first ones were marketed around the time of the quints' first birthday. The dolls met with great success and were subsequently issued in many sizes and variations. The quintuplet children had been assigned specific colors: yellow for Annette, green for Cecile, lavender for Emily, blue for Marie, pink for Yvonne. Madame Alexander used these color designations for the quintuplet dolls. The quint dolls also had name pins. Sometimes they wore bibs embroidered with their names and in their colors.

Due to the quints' popularity, many other companies sold groups of five dark-haired and dark-eyed dolls in matching outfits, most often in the 8" size. Due to the exclusive licensing agreement awarded to Madame Alexander, those sets could not be sold as Dionne Quintuplets.

7½". Marks: Alexander. All composition, fully jointed. Molded painted dark brown hair and painted brown eyes, closed mouths. All original including original box decorated with print created by Maude Tousey Fangel. Also included were long and short organdy dresses and slips, bibs, crocheted jackets, matching caps and booties. This was probably a special set created for a store like F.A.O. Schwarz in New York. Nancy and David Carlson collection. $2,000.00.

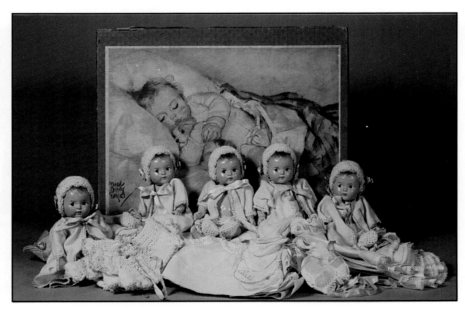

7½". Marks on heads: Dionne//Alexander.
Dress Tag: Genuine//Dionne Quintuplet Dolls//All Rights Reserved//Madame Alexander – N.Y.
All composition, fully jointed, painted eyes, closed mouths, brown mohair wigs over molded hair. Janet Shiely collection. $1,500.00.

7". Marks head: Dionne//Alexander Marks on back: Alexander.
All composition, fully jointed. Molded, painted dark brown hair and painted brown eyes, closed mouths. All original shirts, diapers, and individual name bibs. Original wooden bed. Bedding is a replacement. $1,500.00.

14". Marks: Dionne Quintuplet//Mme. Alexander (also tagged dress and original pin – Yvonne).
All composition, fully jointed, dark brown mohair wig over molded hair, brown sleep eyes, closed mouth. All original with original box and booklet. Emmy Lou DeHaven collection. $700.00 with box and tag.

41

14". Marks: Dionne Quintu-
plets//Mme. Alexander.
All composition, fully jointed. Molded painted brown hair with curly,
wavy hairline all around. Brown
sleep eyes, closed mouth. Re-
dressed. Original booklet.
$1,500.00 set.

These doctor and nurse dolls were created
to go along with the quintuplets.

Left: Dr. DaFoe.
14". Marks: none. Cloth tag: Madame//Alexan-
der// New York.
All composition, fully jointed. Gray mohair wig,
painted blue eyes, closed mouth. All original.
Right: Quintuplet Nurse.
13". Marks: none. Cloth tag: Madame//Alexan-
der// New York.
All composition, fully jointed. Blond mohair wig.
Brown tin sleep eyes, closed mouth. All original.
Doctor: $1,200.00 up.
Nurse: $700.00.

13". Marks: Jane Withers//Alexander Doll Co.
Tag outfit: Snow White//Madame Alexan-
der//NY//All rights reserved. All composition, fully jointed. Black mohair wig, brown
sleep eyes, closed mouth, all original. Note
special black slippers with bows on top.
Nancy and David Carlson collection.
$1,000.00 up.

19". Marks: none. 1937.
Pin: Jane Withers.
Tag: Authentic//Jane Withers//Doll — All Rights Reserved//Madame Alexander//New York. (Reverse: photo of Jane Withers.)
All composition, fully jointed. Brown mohair wig, sleep eyes, open mouth with four upper teeth. Was available in four sizes. All original. $1,500.00.

Portrait Faces

Several so-called portraits were produced, such as Princess Elizabeth and Margaret O'Brien. Those dolls were also sold with other, varying identities. The new names were specified on fabric tags sewn to their clothes. Wendy Ann was another popular example that was produced with many different identities. Collectors will soon learn to recognize the face, even when the doll is not marked with the Wendy Ann name.

16". Marks: Princess Elizabeth (on head).
All composition, fully jointed. Blond human hair wig, sleep eyes, open mouth with four upper teeth. All original including crown, pocketbook, silver shoes. $400.00.

13". Marks: 13 Pictured as tagged Princess Elizabeth in Rare and Hard to Find Madame Alexander Collector Dolls, McKeon, page 117.
All composition, fully jointed. Green sleep eyes, closed mouth. Human hair wig. All original.
Note: In this case, the Betty face doll was used to portray Princess Elizabeth. $400.00.

16". Marks: Princess Elizabeth//Alexander Doll Co.
Dress tag: Madame Alexander New York U.S.A.
Paper tag: Created by//Madame Alexander New York NY//USA.
All composition fully jointed. Blond mohair wig, brown sleep eyes, open mouth with four teeth. All original. $500.00.

13". Marks: none.
Dress tag: Flora McFlimsy//of Madison Square//Madame Alexander, N.Y. U.S.A.//All Rights Reserved.
All composition, fully jointed. Reddish blond human hair wig with short braid down back of head, green sleep eyes, open mouth with four teeth. All original. $650.00.

13". Marks: none on doll.
Dress tag: Flora McFlimsy//of Madison Square//Madame Alexander, N.Y. U.S.A.//All Rights Reserved.
All composition, fully jointed. Reddish blond human hair wig with short braid down back of head, green sleep eyes, open mouth with four upper teeth. All original. Nancy and David Carlsen Collection. $800.00 up.

15". Marks: Princess Elizabeth//Alexander Doll Co.
Apron tagged: McGuffy-Ana//All Rights Reserved//Madame Alexander — N.Y.
All composition, fully jointed. Blond human hair wig with braids, sleep eyes, open mouth with four upper teeth. All original clothes. $350.00.

11". Marks: none.
Dress tag: Madame Alexander//New York.
Ink stamp on shoe sole: Farmerette.
All composition, fully jointed. Blond mohair wig, blue sleep eyes, closed mouth. All original. $250.00.

9", Dutch Girl. Marks back: Wendy-Ann// Mme Alexander//New York. Late 30s.
Dress tag: Madame//Alexander//New York U.S.A.
Paper tag front: Created//by//Madame Alexander//New York.
Paper tag back: An//Alexander//Product// Supreme//Quality and//Design.
All composition, fully jointed. Blond mohair wig, painted blue eyes, closed mouth. All original. $150.00 (lifting in face).

9". Marks: Alexander//New York.
All composition, fully jointed. Blond mohair wigs, painted blue eyes, closed mouths. All original. $80.00 each (fair condition).

9". Marks: Mme. Alexander//New York.
Cloth tag: McGuffy Ana//Madame Alexander
N.Y. U.S.A.//Registered No. 350.781.
All composition, fully jointed. Blond mohair
wig with braids, blue painted eyes, closed
mouth. All original. $900.00.

13". Marks: Wendy Ann//Mme
Alexander//New York.
All composition, fully jointed, also
at waist. Brown sleep eyes,
closed mouth, blond human hair
wig. All original (old straw hat
may be Alexander). $400.00.

13". Marks: Wendy-Ann//Mme.
Alexander//New York (Playthings,
September 1938).
All composition, fully jointed including swivel waist. Molded painted
brown hair and painted blue eyes,
closed mouth. All original. $500.00.

Play set Mother and Me with suitcase and sets of extra clothes.
15", Mother. Marks: Mme. Alexander.
All composition, fully jointed. Blond mohair wig, blue sleep eyes, closed mouth.
9", Me. Marks: Mme Alexander//New York.
All composition, fully jointed. Blond mohair wig, painted blue eyes, closed mouth.
Extra matching sets:
White underwear combination, white socks, black shoes, white hankies.
Pink night gowns, panties, flower print robes, light blue ball gowns with matching half slips. Three sets of daytime dresses, one with navy blue tams. Three daytime sets labeled "Mother and Me" ball gowns "Mme. Alexander." Patent serial number 431.899, May 14, 1940 "Mother and Me." $1,500.00 up.

14". Marks head: Mme. Alexander.
Dress tag: Fairy Queen//Madame Alexander N.Y.
U.S.A.//All rights reserved.
All composition, fully jointed. Blond mohair wig,
brown sleep eyes, closed mouth. All original.
$400.00.

18". Marks: Mme. Alexander. Ca. 1941 – 1942.
(Described in Alexander catalog as Carmen
Miranda. See The Encyclopedia of Celebrity
Dolls, page 243, John Axe.)
All composition fully jointed. Black mohair wig,
decorated with bunch of fruit and feathers, blue
sleep eyes, closed mouth. All original. $600.00.

14". Marks on head: Madame Alexander//Sonja//Henie. Dress tag: Genuine//Sonja Henie//Madame Alexander N.Y. U.S.A.//All rights reserved. (Playthings, April 1939.) All composition, fully jointed. Original, blond mohair wig, brown sleep eyes, open mouth with four upper teeth. Original skating outfit and skates. $500.00.

GENUINE
"Sonja Henie" Doll
Madame Alexander, N.Y. U.S.A.
ALL RIGHTS RESERVED

19". Marks: Madame Alexander//Sonja//Henie (also see picture of dress tag). All composition, fully jointed. Blond human hair wig, brown sleep eyes, open mouth with six upper teeth. All original including box. Nancy and David Carlsen collection. $800.00 up.

*20". Marks on head: Mme. Alexander
(Playthings 1939).
Dress tag: Genuine Sonja Henie//
Madame//Alexander, NY, U.S.A.//All
Rights Reserved.
All composition, fully jointed. Blond
human hair wig, brown sleep eyes,
open mouth with six upper teeth. All
original including golden skate
boots. Skate blades missing.
$800.00 (should have skate blades).*

*16". Marks: Mame. Alexander.
Cloth tag: Baby McGuffy//Madame Alexander N.Y.
U.S.A.//All Rights Reserved.
Composition flange head, wired-on hands and bent legs to
above the knee, cloth body. Blond mohair wig over molded
hair, blue sleep eyes, closed mouth. All original including
rayon stockings and red leatherette one-button booties. (In
different outfit this doll was also sold as Little Genius.)
$400.00.*

20". Marks on head: Mme Alexander.
Cloth tag on dress: Pinky//Madame Alexander
N.Y. U.S.A.//All Rights Reserved.
Composition flange head, hands and bent legs
to above the knee. Stitched hip joints. Molded
painted dark brown hair and blue sleep eyes,
closed mouth. All original. $250.00 (faded).

18". Marks: Alexander//Doll Co.//Pat. No. 2171281.
Dress tag: Madame//Alexander//New York U.S.A.
Paper tag on slip: Jeannie Walker (Playthings May
1941).
All composition, fully jointed with walker mechanism.
Blond human hair wig, brown sleep eyes, closed
mouth. All original. $700.00.

14". Marks: none (Margaret O'Brien, Toys and Novelties, July 1946).
Dress tag: Madame//Alexander//New York, U.S.A.
All composition, fully jointed. Brown mohair wig with turned-up braids, gray sleep eyes, closed mouth. All original. $700.00.

18". Marks on head and back: Mme. Alexander. Clover leaf shaped paper tag on wrist.
All composition, fully jointed. Blond floss wig, gray sleep eyes, closed mouth. All original. $1.000.00 +.

The Portrait Dolls

Introduced at the March 1946, Toy Fair in New York City, they were also advertised in the November 1946 issue of *Playthings.*

In a feature article on Madame Alexander and her company, *Toys and Novelties* reported in their March 1947, issue that these exquisite portrait dolls had initially been intended by Madame Alexander as window display items only. Her idea had been that a dozen of these dolls plus a black velvet backdrop would make a very effective window display. The article went on to say that the toy buyers begged her to fill regular orders for these special portrait dolls and Madame relented.

The surprising success of these special composition dolls may have been the inspiration for the later 21" portraits that Madame Alexander created in hard plastic and vinyl.

This close-up illustrates how the Wendy Ann heads were customized for this special portrait series. As the new plastic sleep eyes had very white eyeballs, the upper part of them was painted brown, and that brown line extended onto the lower eyelid (where there usually is a red dot), thus reducing the prominence of those white eyeballs. A brown line was also drawn onto the movable lids right next to the real eyelashes. On top of the eye shadow, there is another soft, thick line (near the upper eye rim). There are some painted eyelashes at the outer, upper lid corners. They are of varying length. Eyebrows were painted with several connecting strokes in a steep arch, again, in a soft brown tone. The result of these modifications is a very adult looking face rather than that of a child. The beauty mark to the right of her mouth is in the shape of a half moon, by the left eye in the shape of a star.

21". Marks: none. Tagged on half slip: Madame Alexander//New York USA (Playthings, November 1946).
All composition, fully jointed. White mohair wig decorated with wreath of flowers and leaves. Grayish green sleep eyes, closed mouth. Two beauty marks. All original, including diamond stud earrings and ring on left hand, original nail polish. Shoes made of dress fabric. Pink cotton stockings to match slip. Original white cotton bloomers are trimmed with eyelet and small yellow ribbon bows, tie strings at waist. Necklace not original. $1,500.00 up.

21". Marks: none.
Tag on half slip: Madame Alexander//New York USA (Playthings, November 1946, this is Judy).
All composition, fully jointed. Dark brown mohair wig, brown sleep eyes, closed mouth. All original. Dress is faded. Taffeta fabric was originally light blue with pink trim. Pink short panties and half slip have lace trim and tie strings at waist. $1,000.00 (fair condition, faded).

11". Marks on head: Mme. Alexander (Playthings 1947).
Cloth tag dress: Bitsy//Madame Alexander//New York//All rights Reserved.
Composition flange head, hands, and bent legs to above the knee. Cloth body. Original dark brown mohair wig, blue tin sleep eyes, closed mouth. All original.
Note: Luxurious coat set made of fine pink wool fabric and lined. Matching mittens have real mink trim. $250.00.

11". Marks on head: Mme. Alexander (Playthings 1947).
Cloth tag on suit: Butch//Madame Alexander//New York//All Rights Reserved.
Composition flange head, hands, and legs to above the knee. Cloth body, arms, and upper legs, stitched hip joints. Blond mohair wig, blue tin sleep eyes, gray eye shadow, closed mouth. All original. $200.00.

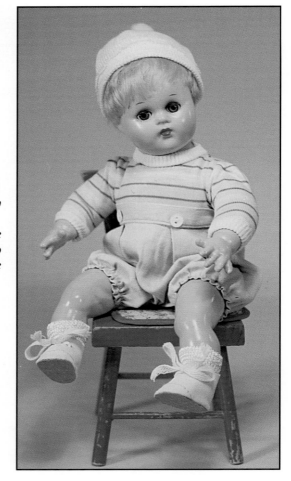

LOUIS AMBERG & SON
(FORMERLY HAHN & AMBERG)

The Amberg firm had been a large import house, jobber, and wholesaler of dolls and toys since 1878, in the Midwest and later in New York City. Being an established firm, they had the financial resources to start marketing American-made composition dolls on a large scale early on. The Denivelle Company as well as Ideal Novelty & Toy Co. produced dolls for Amberg. They were advertising their composition dolls as "they look like BISC and feel like BISC, but are guaranteed not to break." In 1910 they introduced their trademark "The Baby Beautiful Dolls of Character."

One of the other companies which was marketing American-made composition dolls on a large scale at that time was E. I. Horsman, and in the beginning Amberg was definitely trying to copy Horsman. In 1911 they were advertising Bobby Blake and Dolly Drake designed by Grace Drayton. Those two looked very similar to the Campbell Kids that Grace Drayton had done for Horsman. A March 1912, *Playthings* ad featured My Bully Bull Dog and Cunning Kitty Cat, both animals with composition heads and plush bodies, while Horsman had introduced Puppy Pippin and Pussy Pippin— of similar construction in 1911. Pussy and Puppy Pippin had cute Drayton faces, Bully Bull Dog had the realistic features of a bull dog.

Basically, the Amberg composition doll line developed pretty much the same way as that of other firms. In the beginning they copied German dolls and added their own models of basic children and babies. They also had a line of bisque dolls. Some models such as Baby Peggy and the Vanta Baby were available in composition as well as in bisque. Their most artistic creation, certainly, was Mibs, designed by Hazel Drucker and copyrighted by Amberg in 1921.

In 1930, the Amberg composition doll line was sold to E. I. Horsman.

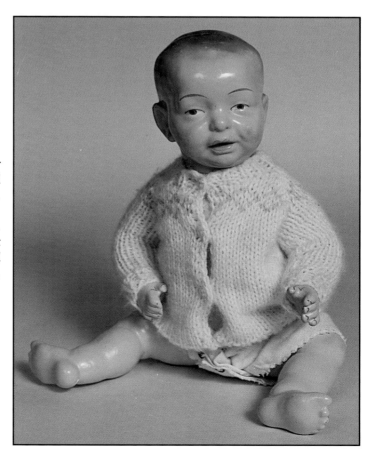

12". Marks: none. (See Hahn & Amberg later Louis Amberg & Son, of April 1910, Toys and Novelties, advertising this doll as Samson, Uncle Sam's First Born.) (K * R look alike.)
All composition, fully jointed with bent legs. Socket head has wooden base with hook screwed into it to hold the stringing. Molded painted brown hair and painted blue eyes, open/closed mouth, re-dressed. $250.00.

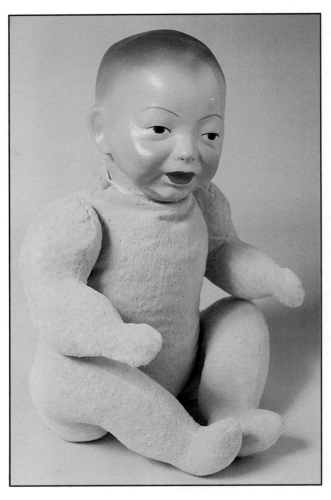

14". Marks: none (Dolly Strong – Velvet, Playthings, June 1910).
Composition head and pink velvet body and limbs, jointed with inside disks. Hair has hardly any modeling. Open/closed mouth. Head was totally restored and body casing has been washed.
Note: Mold for head was adapted from German Kammer & Reinhardt baby #100. $200.00 (restored).

18". Marks: none (K * R 100 look-alike).
See Playthings, July 1910, Baby Bumps — Trademark.
Composition flange head, cloth body and limbs, jointed with outside disks (stump hands). Faintly molded painted light brown hair and painted blue eyes. Open/closed mouth. Original romper. $250.00.

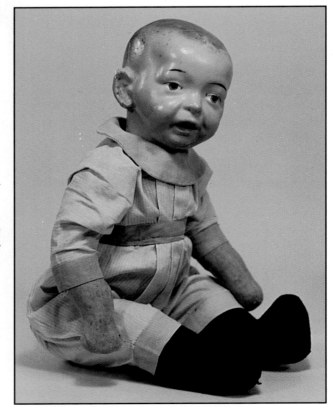

16". Marks: none.
See Hahn & Amberg ad in Playthings April 1910, showing K*R 100 copy baby with same stump hands and stitched finger and toe indications. Composition flange head, cloth body and limbs, inside joints. Painted hair (very little modeling), painted blue eyes. Open/closed mouth. Original romper. $125.00.

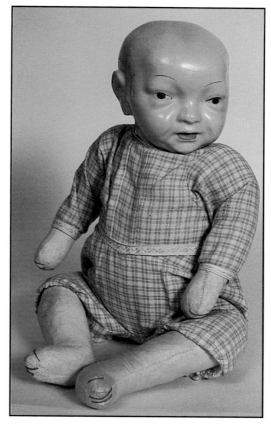

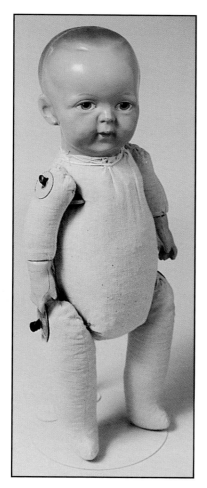

16", Dorothy Dainty. Marks: L.S. & S//414//1910.
Playthings, February 1912, designed by Jeno Jusko.
Flared composition head and short arms. Cloth body, upper arms and legs are contemporary. Molded painted hair with molded hair loop. Painted blue eyes, open/closed mouth with four painted upper teeth. Redressed. $250.00.
Note: "Dorothy Dainty, A Rare Advertising Doll." P. N. Schoonmaker, Doll Reader, Feb/Mar. 1982.

14". Marks: L.A. & S. 1911.
Composition flange head and short arms. Cloth body and limbs jointed with outside disks. Molded, painted brown hair and painted blue eyes, closed mouth. $150.00.

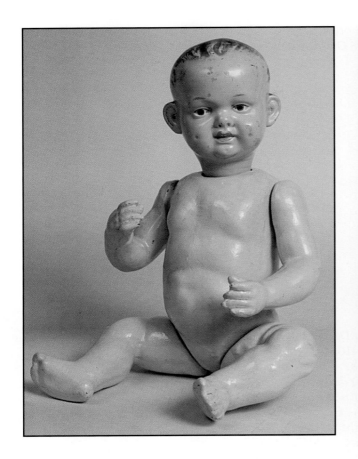 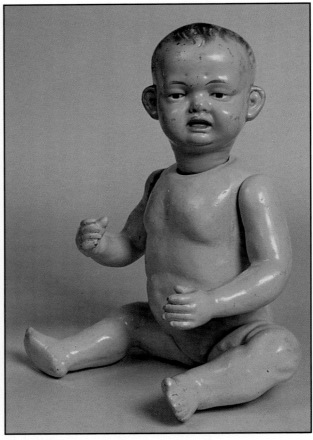

12". Marks: none (Playthings, April 1912: The Doll with Two Faces, Laughing and Crying).
All composition, fully jointed. Molded painted hair and painted blue eyes. Open/closed mouth with
molded tongue. On laughing side, two painted teeth. Has same socket head construction as
described for Samson Baby. $350.00.
Note: This doll is a copy of German Klay & Hahn bisque-headed two-face baby No. 159. (See Cieslik,
pg. 156 and 157, #953 and 955.)

19". Marks: L. A. & S. ©1912. Composition flange head, cloth body and limbs with stump hands and black cloth boots, stuffed with excelsior, jointed with outside disks. Old clothes. Similar doll with identical construction shown in Playthings ad of February 1914, a "Special Value (doll) For Between Seasons.") $80.00.

14", Sis Hopkins. Marks: none (Playthings, January 1912: Made by consent and approval of the original Rose Melville, Copyright Louis Amberg & Son).
Flared composition head with molded painted, pinned up braids and painted red hair ribbon. Two drill holes for real ribbons. Painted blue eyes, open/closed mouth. Cloth body and limbs, jointed with inside disks. Stockings and black boots are part of leg casing. Old dress. Head has been restored except for eyes. $350.00 (restored).

Note: Rose Melville, 1873 – 1946. made her debut in 1889 in a play called Zeb, in which she played the hayseed Sis Hopkins. This was so successful that she developed a vaudeville sketch along the lines of this same yokel. In other words, she became Sis Hopkins and played nothing else until her retirement in the 1920s.

12". Marks: L. A. & S. ©1915 (Copy of identical German bisque-headed doll marks: 2/O D #47// Heubach//Germany).
Composition flange head and short arms, cloth body and limbs jointed with inside disks. Black cloth boots are sewn in. Molded painted brown hair and painted blue eyes. Closed mouth. Old clothes. $250.00.

13½". Marks: 494.
This is one of The Pouty Pets, Real Live Children.
See Toys & Novelties, July 1915.
Composition flange head and short arms, cloth body, upper arms, and bent legs, jointed with inside disks. Molded painted brown hair and painted blue eyes. Closed mouth. Dress may be original. $280.00.

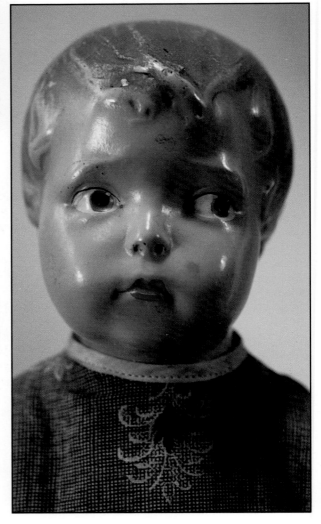

14½". Marks: 494.
This is one of The Pouty Pets, Real Live Children.
See Toys & Novelties, July 1915.
Composition flange head and lower arms, cloth body, upper arms, and full legs, jointed with inside disks. Molded painted brown hair and painted blue eyes, closed mouth. Old clothes. Collection of Gladys Brown. $300.00+.

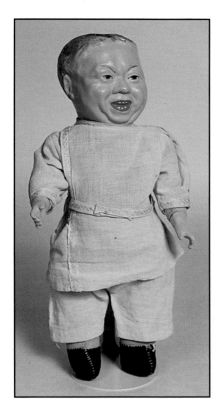

*11", John Bunny. Marks: none.
See Playthings, March 1914.
Copyright F. W. Reichenbacher.
Composition flange head and
short arms. Cloth body and
limbs, jointed with outside disks.
Molded painted brown hair with
middle part. Blue painted eyes.
Open/closed mouth with three
upper and three lower teeth.
Black cloth boots are sewn on.
Original outfit. $400.00.*

*13". Marks: none.
Cloth label: Charlie Chaplin
Doll//World's Greatest Come-
dian//Made exclusively by
Louis Amberg & Son N. Y.//
By special arrangement of
Essanay Film Company.
Composition flange head and
short arms, crude, excelsior
stuffed body/limbs, jointed,
with outside metal disks.
Huge, black cloth shoes are
part of leg casing. All original.
$600.00.*

*15". Marks: 784 (See Coleman II, pg.
33, #102. Head is shown as marked
©1916 L. A. & S.).
Composition flange head, appropriate, old cloth body/limb assembly
with lower composition arms, jointed
with inside disks. Molded painted
hair and painted blue eyes,
open/closed mouth with two upper
painted teeth. $125.00.*

*13". Marks: L. A. & S.//218.
Composition flange head and hands, cloth body
and limbs (straight legs), jointed with inside
disks. Molded, painted hair and painted blue
eyes, closed mouth. Re-dressed. $125.00.*

*14". Marks: none.
Box label: Amberg Dolls//The World's Stan-
dard//Made in USA — This is Skookum, Made
under exclusive license from the Northwestern
Fruit Exchange — National Advertisers of
Skookum Apples. (Playthings, December 1916).
Composition flange head and short arms, cloth
body and limbs jointed at shoulders with
inside disks and at hips with outside disks.
Molded painted black hair with two short
braids tied with red ribbon. Back of head has
a hole drilled to hold feather. Painted black
eyes, closed mouth. Clothes seem to be original
including leather moccasins.
13" woman has identical head modeling and
construction as Skookum. Clothes probably not
original. $250.00. each.
Note: No information is available on this doll.
Since she has identical modeling to Skookum,
it is assumed that she was intended as a mate
for him and was also sold by Amberg.*

17". Marks: none. Ca. 1919. (See Composition Dolls/II, P&P Judd, pg. 14. Identical head pictured on all original walking doll with cloth legs.)
Composition flange head, cloth body and limbs, jointed with outside disks. Molded painted, brown hair, painted blue eyes, closed mouth, re-dressed. $125.00.

Two walkers 30" and 21". Marks: L. A. & S//1919 (T&N, June 1919: patented June 11, 1918, No. 1,269,056. Made in sizes 20" and 28", ten styles).
Composition heads, full arms and ball-jointed legs mounted on wooden platform. Cork stuffed cloth bodies. Both dolls have same head mold. While large doll has a shoulder head, painted hair and eyes and an open/closed mouth, the smaller one has a flange head, human hair wig over molded hair, tin sleep eyes, and an open mouth with two molded painted teeth. 30" – $300.00; 21" – $200.00.
Note: Dolls were also advertised in Sears Roebuck catalog of 1921, in 19½", 22½", and 28½" sizes, stating that "the two larger sizes are full jointed, entirely of strong light weight composition. The smallest size has neatly shaped stuffed legs."

Display ad. Playthings, 1918, advertising their Amkid doll, seen in this section (note leather body with pin jointed knees and ball-jointed arms).

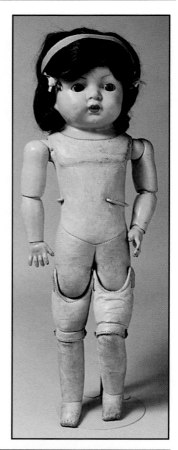

19". Marks: none (Amkid Doll – Playthings, 1918 – 1920). Composition shoulder head, leather body and legs with pin joints at hips and knees. Ball-jointed wooden arms and composition hands. Gray celluloid sleep eyes, open mouth with two upper molded, painted teeth. Old mohair wig. (Doll is recognizable in Amberg ad.) $250.00.
Note: Lower legs are leather with stitched toe indications.

24". Marks: none. But has identical head as Amkid doll Playthings, 1918 – 1920.
Composition shoulder head and arms to below elbow. Oilcloth body and limbs with stitched hip and knee joints and inside jointing at shoulders. Gray celluloid sleep eyes (eye mechanism stamped 1918). Open mouth with two upper molded painted teeth. Original dark human hair wig. $200.00.

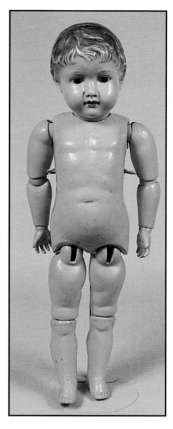

19". Marks: L. A. & S. Composition socket head on ball-jointed body. Molded painted brown hair and painted blue eyes. Open/closed mouth with four painted teeth. Old, American-made ball-jointed body is not original to this head. $250.00.

11". Marks: none. (Her name is Happinus. Playthings, February.1 1918.)
All composition, jointed at shoulders and hips (no neck joint). Molded painted hair with depression to hold hair ribbon. Painted brown eyes, closed mouth. Original dress. $200.00.

15". Marks head: L. A. & S//40.
Composition socket head on ball-jointed body. Original mohair wig, gray sleep eyes, open mouth with four upper teeth. Re-dressed. $250.00.
Note: Bodies usually marked Amberg//Victory//Doll. This doll's body is not marked.

20", Baby Peggy (Montgomery). Marks: none (Play-things, July 1923).
Composition shoulder head and tied-on lower limbs. Cloth body with stitched hip joints (no shoulder joints). Molded painted black hair and painted brown eyes, three highlights on iris. Multi-stroke eyebrows and heavy painted lashes. Wide, smiling mouth with four painted teeth. $700.00.
Note: Head is molded slightly to the left (wigged Peggy to the right). Original combination and dress.

20", Baby Peggy (Montgomery). Marks: none (Playthings, July 1923).
Composition shoulder head and lower arms, Cloth body, upper arms and legs, stitched hip joints. Brown mohair wig over bald head. Identical facial decoration to molded hair Peggy. Re-dressed. $700.00.
Note: Head is molded to her right (molded hair Peggy's to the left). Baby Peggy starred in 150 short comedies for Century Studio and three feature length films for Universal in the early twenties.

16″. Marks: none.

Mibs, a Phyllis May Dolly, created by Hazel Drukker and copyrighted in 1921 (Playthings, May 1921).

Composition shoulder head with head turned to the right, composition arms to above the elbow, and specially designed composition legs which are pin jointed. Cloth body. Molded painted light brown hair, painted blue eyes, closed mouth. Original dress with matching panties (not tagged but illustrated in ad mentioned above). $900.00 up.

Note: Under her old shoes Mibs has molded shoes that are not painted. In the ad she is shown with molded painted black shoes and white socks.

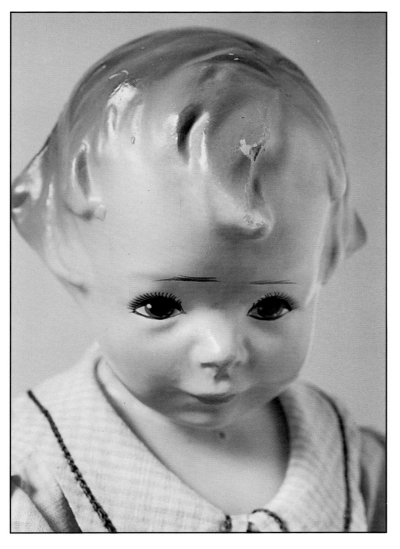

14" Marks: L. A. + S.//1924 this is Sunny Orange Maid (Playthings, July 1924). Collection of Sherryl Shirran.

Composition shoulder head (molded cap) short arms and legs to above the knee. Cloth body and upper limbs with stitched shoulder and hip joints. Squeaker in body still works. Painted blue eyes, closed mouth. All original. $600.00.

16". Marks: Vanta Baby//Amberg.
Dress tag: Vanta Baby//Trade Mark Reg.//An Amberg Doll.
Diaper tag: Vanta//Trade Mark Reg.
Paper tag: Vanta Baby//Known To Every//Woman Everywhere//Amberg Dolls//The World Standard.
Composition shoulder head and limbs, cloth body, jointed at shoulders and hips. Molded painted blond hair and blue tin sleep eyes. Open/closed mouth with two painted upper teeth. All original. All clothes tie on, no pins, snaps, buttons. Arlene and Don Jensen Collection. $400.00.

8" pair. Marks: L.A. & S. ©1928.
All composition, fully jointed, including
waist. Molded painted hair and painted
brown eyes. Closed mouth. Molded painted
white socks and black shoes. Re-dressed.
$350.00 pair.
Note: McMasters Auction Catalog 12/8/93 –
Original tag read: Amberg//The Teenie Wee-
nies//Weenie Line//Trade Mark Reg.//The
Golden Anniversary.

13". Marks: Amberg//LA & S ©1928.
All composition, fully jointed. Molded painted
yellowish hair, brown eyes to side, small,
closed mouth.
All original dress tagged: An Amberg Doll
With//Body Twist//all, all its own//Pat.
Pend. Ser. No. 320,018 (but doll does not
have a twist waist).
Alongside: Papier mache head with identical
face, different hairdo, no marks. $250.00;
$35.00, head.

13". Marks: Amberg//LA & S ©1928.
All composition, fully jointed. Molded, painted hair
with staple for hair loop and three vertical curls in
back. Painted brown eyes to side, very small
closed mouth. Re-dressed. Identical papier mache
head, except has molded hair bow (no marks).
Doll, $200.00; head only, $35.00.
Note: Playthings ad Feb. 1929, shows an insert
drawing of a doll with face and molded hair bow
identical to that of the papier mache head.

3½", papier mache head only.
Marks: none.
(Amberg had identical composition doll.)
$40.00 head only.

14". Marks: Amberg//Pat. Pend.
//L.A. & S. ©1928.
Dress label: An Amberg Doll With
A//Body Twist//all, all its own!
Pat. Pend SFR No. 320.016.
All composition fully jointed. Also
has a swivel joint at waist. Mold-
ed painted blond hair and paint-
ed light brown eyes (gray eye
shadow). Closed mouth. $500.00.

14". Marks: Amberg//Pat. Pend.//L.A. & S. ©1928.
Cloth tag: An Amberg Doll With A//Body Twist//all, all
its own!//Pat. Pend. SFR No. 320.016.
This is Peter Pan. See Playthings, February 1929.
All composition, fully jointed with additional swivel joint
at waist. Molded painted brown hair and painted light
brown eyes and eye shadow, closed mouth. All original
including shoes and socks.
Metal pin is not original to doll: "Peter Pan//A Paramount
Picture." $600.00.

AMERICAN CHARACTER DOLL CO.
NEW YORK

The American Character Doll Co. was founded in 1919, and in 1923 they started to use "Petite" as a name for their line of dolls. They were not a very innovative company. The 1920s were the decade of the character babies, and American Character had Happy Tot, a baby reminding one of Effanbee's Bubbles. Their Botteltot looked somewhat more unique. Neither one achieved the popularity of the other character babies on the market. Sally, a look-alike child to Effanbee's Patsy introduced in the early 1930s, met with more success. Puggy was probably their most unique creation in composition. He was introduced at the time of Effanbee's Skippy. According to the trade ads, American Character carried a basic line of mama dolls and babies. They may not all have been marked, as few are seen today. (Montgomery Ward carried their mama dolls in 1927.)

Rubber drink and wet babies had a large market share during the early 1930s. In the *Playthings* issue of June 1933, American Character reported on the opening of their own New Rubber Doll Factory, claiming that they had been the first to introduce rubber dolls. Their all-rubber drink and wet babies never seem to have been as successful as Effanbee's DyDee Baby. They would have better luck later on with their Tiny Tears, a drink and wet baby with a hard plastic head that actually had tear ducts and a rubber body and limbs. In the August 1936 *Playthings* issue they introduced a Sally Jane. She was made of a similar rubber composition as the I-De-Lite doll (seen in the Ideal section). They called it their Paratex doll. She came in sizes of 15", 17", 19", and 22".

An insurance policy was issued with each doll, guaranteeing that "little mothers" could wash their dolls without damaging them.

American Character may not have been a very innovative company during the composition period. But whenever they chose to create variations, they did it with flair and always produced well dressed, high quality dolls.

Full-page ad placed by American Character Doll Co. — Toys And Novelties, January 1921.

One of the earliest ads placed by American Character, it shows a line of baby and stiff-leg chubby dolls. The babies have dolly and character faces, the latter looking very similar to Kestner #211 (a German bisque headed doll). The chubby dolls show Kestner characteristics as well. The babies have painted hair or mohair wigs, painted or sleep eyes.

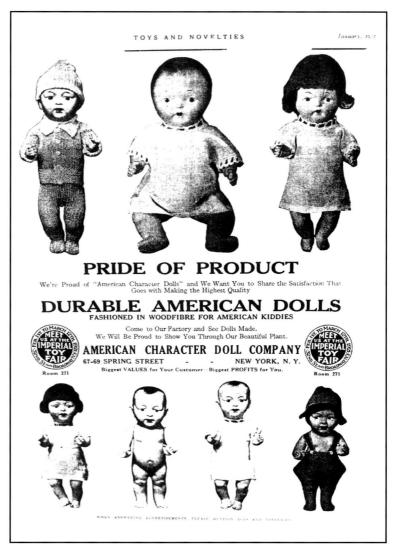

22". Marks: American Character//Doll Co.
See various ads Playthings 1924 – 1925.
Composition shoulder head, lower arms and legs,
cloth body and upper limbs. Full, blond mohair wig,
blue tin sleep eyes, closed mouth. All original except
for hair bow. $200.00.

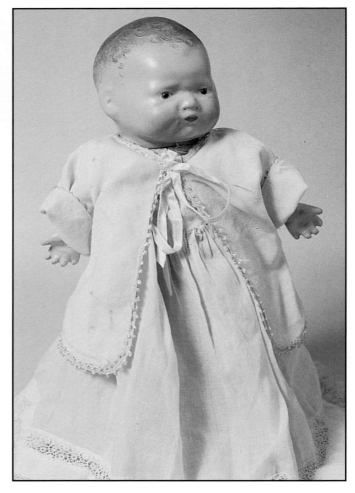

11", Baby (see Toys and Novelties, Sept.
1925).
Marks: Baby//Petite.
Composition flange head and hands, cloth
body and full, straight legs. Molded painted
blond hair and blue eyes, closed mouth. Re-
dressed. $125.00.
Note: Also sold as twins.

13". Marks: Petite//America's Wonder Baby Dolls. Dress tag: Botteltot//Reg. U. S. Pat. Off//A Petite Doll (Playthings, May 1926).
Full-composition shoulder plate to below the arms, full-composition arms, right hand molded so that it can hold a bottle. Cloth body and bent legs, jointed at shoulders and hips. Molded painted blond hair and gray tin sleep eyes, open mouth. All original except for bonnet. $200.00.
Note: On this 13" doll, it is the right hand holding the bottle.

16". Marks: Petite//America's Wonder Baby Dolls Dress tag: Botteltot//Reg. U. S. Pat. Off//A Petite Doll (Playthings, May 1926).
Full-composition shoulder plate to below the arms, full-composition arms, left hand molded so that it can hold bottle. Cloth body and bent legs, jointed at shoulders and hips. Molded painted blond hair and gray tin sleep eyes, open mouth. All original. $300.00.
Note: On this 16" doll, it is the left hand which is molded so that it can hold a bottle.

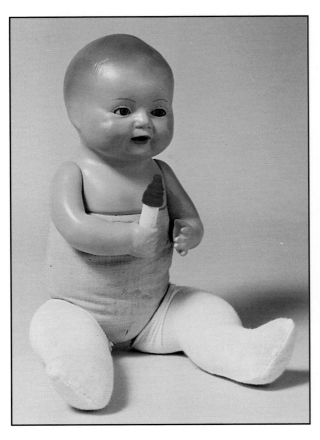

13". Marks: Petite//American Character Doll Co. This is Happy Tot (see illustrated ads Playthings, March/July 1927).
Full-composition shoulder plate, composition arms, cloth body and bent legs, jointed at shoulders and hips. Right fist is molded so that it can hold a bottle (bottle is a replacement). Slightly molded, painted hair, gray tin sleep eyes, open mouth, no teeth (composition parts on this doll have been restored). Happy Tot was sold in four sizes, with straight or bent legs. It was made with or without bottle. $125.00.

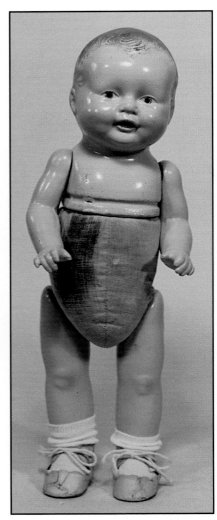

13". Deep shoulder plate marks: Petite//American Character Doll Co. — This is Happy Tot (see Playthings March 1927, showing bent leg as well as straight leg Happy Tot).
Composition head with full shoulder plate, arms, and legs, lower cloth body stuffed and glued into the shoulder plate rather than wired on, as usual. Molded, painted blond hair and painted blue eyes. Open/closed mouth with molded tongue and two molded, painted upper teeth. $100.00.
Note: This doll was also used to create Lucky Aviation Kid. An article in Playthings of July 1927, reported that American Character's Lucky Aviation Kid greeted Charles Lindbergh when he arrived in New York. The article was accompanied by a picture showing the doll dressed in aviator's outfit (surrounded by four mama dolls) and mentioned that it was created so that the trade could profit from the interest in aviation due to the Lindbergh publicity.

12", Spanish Dancer and Matador (Playthings, August 1929).
Both marks: A//Petite Doll."
Girl's dress tagged: Campbell Kid// Permission Campbell Soup Co.//A Petite Doll.
Boy's clothes tagged: Puggy//A Petite Doll.
All composition, fully jointed. Molded painted hair and brown eyes, closed mouth. $500.00 each.

12" pair. Marks: A//Petite//Doll.
Both doll's clothes are tagged: Puggy//A Petite Doll.
All composition, fully jointed. Modeled painted blond hair and painted blue eyes, closed mouth. All original. Nancy and David Carson collection. $500.00+ each.

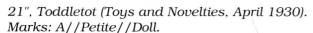

21", Toddletot (Toys and Novelties, April 1930).
Marks: A//Petite//Doll.
Composition flange head and wired on limbs, cloth body. Molded painted blond hair with S-curve curl in front. Gray tin sleep eyes, open mouth with two upper teeth and metal tongue, two dimples in cheeks. All original. $350.00.

23" and 20". Both marked on head: Petite. Paper tag front: Petite Dolls//Trade Mark //From Head to Feet You'll Love Petite. Paper tag back: How do you do, My name is "Petite" Don't you think I'm very Sweet. Composition swivel heads on shoulder plates and composition limbs, fully jointed. Cloth bodies. Human hair wigs, brown sleep eyes. Open/closed mouths. All original. $500.00+ each.

Full-page ad placed by American Character Doll Co. in Playthings October 1934.
As this ad indicated, American Character tried to create a movie tie-in for their doll. Surely not by accident, the doll is wearing a polka dotted dress that is very similar to Shirley Temple's universally recognized outfit.

October, 1934 **PLAYTHINGS**

SHIRLEY JEAN RICKERT and her PETITE doll, "Sally-Joy". Shirley's next picture is with Jack Holt, in "I'll Fix It" for Columbia.

SALLY'S in the MOVIES

• Millions of children will see Sally-Joy in her new picture with Shirley Jean Rickert and every girl will want a doll like this. It has character, reality, charm, appeal. Typical Petite doll quality and Value.

• She'll be a Xmas leader in leading stores the Country over.

AMERICAN CHARACTER DOLL CO., Inc., 20 East 17th St., N. Y.

Two Sally dolls with cloth torsos. 19". Marks: none on doll. Only dress and paper tag. 14". Marks on head: Petite//Sally. Composition heads, shoulder plates and limbs, fully jointed, cloth bodies. Molded painted brown hair and brown mohair wig. Gray tin, sleep eyes and closed mouths. All original. Nancy and David Carlson collection. 14", $250.00+; 19", $350.00+.

12". Marks: Sally//A//Petite// Doll (American Character). Dress label: A Lovable Petite Doll //Sally (Playthings April 1931). All composition fully jointed. Molded painted brown hair and painted, brown eyes, closed mouth. All original. $200.00.

Two Carol Ann Beery dolls, 16" and 19". Marks on both: Petite//Sally (on head) Petite (on back). All composition, fully jointed, blond and red mohair wigs and gray and brown eyes, closed mouths. All original. Nancy and David Carlson Collection. $500.00+ each. Note: The special hair style with braid across top of head made her into Carol Ann Beery. She was the daughter of Wallace Beery, the actor, and as a small child was seen in some minor movie parts.

19". Marks on head: Petite //Sally.
Dress tag: A Lovable Petite Doll//Sally Joy (See Playthings May 1931 and July 1934). Composition shoulder plate, head, and limbs. Cloth body, jointed at shoulders and hips, original, blond human hair wig, green celluloid sleep eyes, closed mouth. All original outfit. $350.00.

24". Marks: Petite//Amer. Character Doll Co.
Dress tag: A Lovable Petite Doll//Sally Joy.
Composition shoulder plate, head, and limbs, cloth body, jointed at shoulders and hips. Blond human hair wig, gray celluloid sleep eyes, open mouth with four upper teeth. All original. $400.00.
Note: Even though this doll has a different head mold with open mouth and dimples, her dress tag reads "Sally Joy," same as for the doll in orange felt coat. Sally Joy mentioned, but this version not pictured in Playthings May 1931, and July, 1934. This doll may be later than the Patsy-type Sally and crafted to more closely resemble the popular Shirley Temple by Ideal.

19". Marks on head: Petite// Sally (George Washington).
All composition except for arms, which are made of rubber, fully jointed. White mohair wig over molded hair, gray tin sleep eyes, closed mouth. All original. Nancy and David Carlsen collection. $400.00+.
Note: This doll was created on the 200th birthday of George Washington in 1932.

18". Marks: Am. Char. Doll (this is Chuckles, see Playthings, January 1943).
Composition flange head and tied-on lower limbs. Cloth body and upper limbs, stitched hip joints. Gray sleep eyes and open mouth with two upper teeth. All original with tag. $400.00.

Full-page ad (Toys and Novelties, August 1947). Besides Little Love and Chuckles on the left and right respectively, this ad features a skater doll. Her upturned nose is very recognizable, thus helping to identify the two unmarked dolls on page 84.

16". Marks: Am. Char. Doll (Playthings, August 1942 – January 1943. The baby's name is given as Little Love).
Composition flange head and hands, cloth body and limbs. Molded, painted brown hair and brown sleep eyes. Closed mouth, re-dressed. Came in three sizes. The ad stated that the doll was a replica of a two-month-old infant. $150.00.

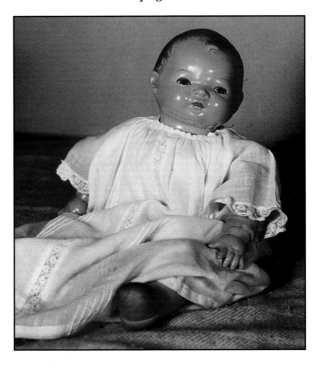

18." Marks: none.
See Toys and Novelties, August 1947.
All composition, fully jointed. Brown mohair wig, blue sleep eyes, closed mouth. Clothes are homemade but were obviously made for this doll. Consists of bra, panties, full slip, and gown. $250.00.

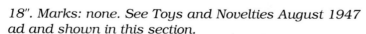

18". Marks: none. See Toys and Novelties August 1947 ad and shown in this section.
All hard plastic, fully jointed. All original. Janet Siegel collection. $250.00+.
Note: Even though doll is made of hard plastic, it is included here for completeness sake and to show that it was made of composition as well as hard plastic.

AMERICAN DOLL COMPANY

While at least small pieces of information have been uncovered about most American doll manufacturers and sellers, some enigmas remain. Such an enigma is the company which used the Am. Doll Co. mark and sold the dolls shown on the following pages.

Apparently, two basic head molds were used over a long period of time, a boy's with slightly curly hair and a girl's with a marcelled hairdo (their faces were identical). The baby came later and was obviously created when Grace Storey Putnam's Bye-Lo was so popular during the mid-20s, as it closely resembles that doll. It is not as frequently seen as the children. The infants pictured here are marked only Honey Child, but the Judds in their *Compo Dolls*, Vol. II, reported on a Honey Child that in addition was marked: "Am. Doll Co.//Copyr. 1926." The baby at one time had been seen in an identical blue, long dress, with a cloth label advertising Weatherbird Shoes.

All-composition parts were made of the wood pulp type. All, except for the large mama dolls, have decal eyes. This is very unusual. The American Doll Company children (and babies) are the only composition dolls with decal eyes ever seen. Their features and molded hair are very distinctive, and, therefore, the dolls are easy to spot, even when a wig has been put over the molded hair as in the case of the large mama dolls, and the small girl with the molded, unpainted shoes who, at one time, must have had a wig.

The body construction varies from cheap cloth stuffed with excelsior and jointed with outside disks to better fabric stuffed with cotton with stitched hip joints for the large mama doll. Unusual are the papier mache bodies with the blue and pink molded shoes and socks, another feature that has never been seen anywhere else before.

The original clothes on some of the dolls and the slim mama doll body give further clues for a time frame. Since all white, long little girls' dresses were not fashionable anymore in the 20s, the girl in the white dress may be from slightly before 1920. Slim mama dolls were not introduced until 1927. One can, therefore, assume that the American Doll Company was active in the late teens and during the 1920s.

It is hoped that by calling attention to the special features of these dolls and doing a small comparison study, this will eventually lead to further discoveries regarding this mysterious company.

25". Marks: Am. Doll Co.
Composition shoulder heads and full arms, pin jointed. Cloth bodies and legs are stuffed with excelsior and also pin jointed with outside metal disks. Black sewn in cloth boots. Molded painted yellowish/brown hair, blue decal eyes, closed mouths. Boy re-dressed. $200.00 each.

Three dolls of varying sizes with identical shoulder heads.
Marks: Am. Doll Co.
The two dolls in foreground with unpainted hair originally would have had a wig. Girl's dress is original, other two dolls re-dressed. Girl has cloth body stuffed with excelsior and stitched hip joints. Note molded shoes and socks that have never been painted. Sizes 25", $200.00; 21", 80.00 (fair condition); 18", $100.00.

Marks: Am. Doll Co.
23", boy with blue molded shoes.
24", girl with pink molded shoes, molded, marcelled hair.
Both are identically constructed. For description see "body" pictures. Girl all original, boy re-dressed. $300.00 each.

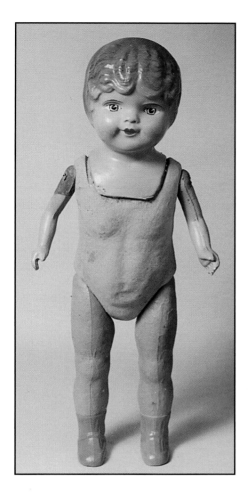

Composition shoulder head and arms, papier mache body and legs with molded Mary Janes and socks painted all one color. Pin jointed at shoulders, hips with elastic. Mama crier inserted in back. Molded painted light brown hair, blue decal eyes, closed mouth.

Note: All, except for the large mama doll, have these short, pin-jointed arms.

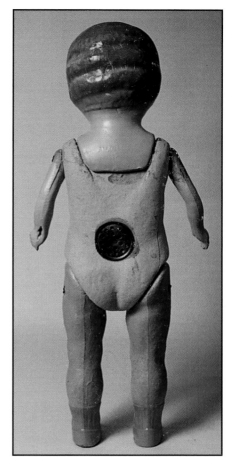

Front.   *Back.*

25" pair of Mama Dolls. Marks: none.

Composition shoulder heads and full arms. Composition legs to above the knee, cloth bodies. Jointed at shoulders, stitched hip joints. Brown mohair wigs over molded hair. Doll on left: painted eyes and closed mouth, original outfit. Right doll: Sleep eyes and open mouth with four upper teeth, original underwear, socks, and shoes. Homemade, old dress came on doll. $200.00 each.

Note: Both dolls have identical modeling of hair (under wig) and features as boys in this section.

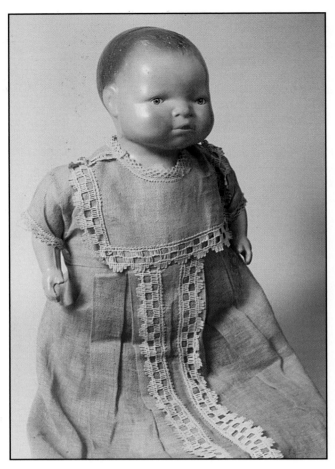

17". Marks front shoulder plate: Honey Child (The Judds in Compo Dolls, Vol. II report on a Honey Child whose back shoulder plate in addition was marked: "Am. Doll Co.//Copr. 1926").
Composition shoulder head and full arms, pin jointed. Cloth body and straight legs, crudely stuffed with excelsior. Stitched hip joints. Molded painted reddish hair, blue decal eyes, closed mouth. Original, long pink dress and white slip. $200.00.

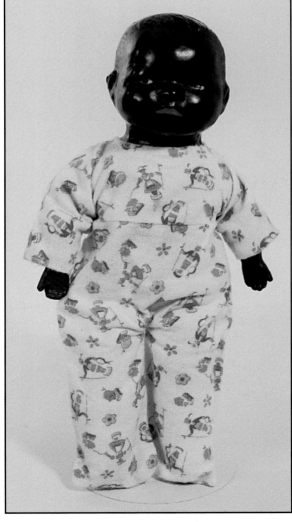

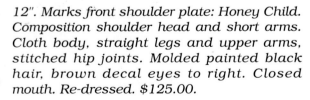

12". Marks front shoulder plate: Honey Child. Composition shoulder head and short arms. Cloth body, straight legs and upper arms, stitched hip joints. Molded painted black hair, brown decal eyes to right. Closed mouth. Re-dressed. $125.00.

ARRANBEE DOLL COMPANY
NEW YORK CITY
1922 – 1958

This firm carried a general line of good quality composition baby and mama dolls during the 1920s. A bisque headed baby, introduced in 1925, called My Dream Baby or Dream Baby, was very successful. In the 1930s their many good quality "look-alikes" of popular composition dolls stand out. The name Nancy was used for at least three different types of all-composition girls. Likewise the name "Dream Baby" was used as a trademark and included several different faces. Other dolls were marked ARRANBEE or R. & B.

The Arranbee Company was purchased by Vogue in 1958, and their name and product line discontinued in 1960. Virgil Kirby, brother-in-law of Georgene Averill, was plant manager until it was sold to Vogue. Ruby Hopf, sister of Georgene Averill, was the chief designer for this company for many years.

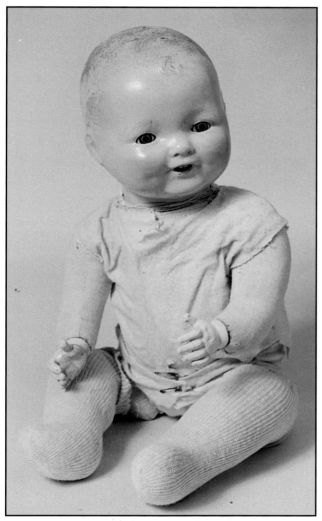

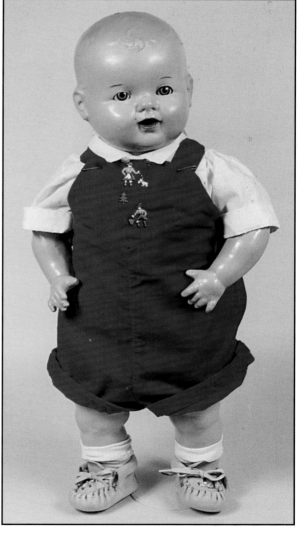

16". Marks: ARRANBEE. 1920s.
Composition flange head and rubber hands, cloth body, arms, and bent legs, jointed with inside disks at hips and shoulders. Molded painted blond hair and blue tin sleep eyes. Open mouth with two molded/painted teeth and celluloid tongue. Flannel west, diaper, and cotton stockings may be original. $50.00 (fair).

22". Marks: Dream Baby.
Composition flange head, tied on arms to above the elbow and legs to above the knee. Stitched hip joints. Molded painted blond hair, gray metal sleep eyes, open mouth, metal tongue with two upper teeth. Re-dressed. $125.00.

14". Marks: Kewtie.
All composition, fully jointed. Molded painted light brown hair, blue tin sleep eyes, closed mouth. All original with trunk and extra clothes (incomplete). $250.00.
Note: Same doll as 15" Martha Washington, (painted eyes).

15", Martha Washington.
Marks: Kewtie.
Dress tag: Nancy//An Arranbee Doll.
Dress fabric print: Figures of soldier on white horse, and banner imprinted: Washington; a circle imprinted: 1732.
Box label: R & B//Quality//Doll//Nancy Lee// 2101.
All composition, fully jointed. White mohair wig over molded blond hair, closed mouth, painted blue eyes. All original. $250.00.
Note: Pairs of dolls clad in colonial costume were produced on the occasion of George Washington's 200th birthday in 1932.

12". Marks: Nancy (See Playthings, February 1933). All composition, fully jointed. Molded painted light brown hair and painted blue eyes. Closed mouth. Hard trunk measurements: 6x6½x13." Set also includes two extra dresses, sun suit, jacket and tam, pajamas. $250.00.

12" pair, George and Martha Washington. Both marked on back: Arranbee//Doll Co. Dress tag: Nancy//An Arranbee Doll. All composition, fully jointed, white mohair wigs over molded, unpainted hair. Painted blue eyes, closed mouths. All original. These dolls were offered on the occasion of George Washington's 200th birthday in 1932. $200.00 pair (restored). Note: The heads of both dolls have been restored.

6½". Marked: R & B//Doll Co. (Ink-U-Bator Baby, see Playthings, November 1936). All composition, fully jointed, bent legs. Painted brown eyes and hair, closed mouth.

Round tag attached to blanket reads "RandB Quality Dolls //My//Dream//Baby//Like A Tot Of Your Own."

Complete set included oxygen tube, rubber hot water bottle, stethoscope, nurse's cap, organdy dress, underwear, organdy bonnet, knitted booties, blanket, and pillow. Each doll was dressed in flannel diaper and knitted shirt. Top of incubator has temperature gauge on the left. Collection of Mary Lu Trowbridge. $250.00.

16". Marks: ⊗ *(Playthings, July 1936).*
Paper tag: Nancy//RandB//Quality Doll.
Same markings on original box, plus Style No. 234, blue, Toska.
All composition, fully jointed. Blond human hair wig. Green glassene sleep eyes, open mouth with four upper teeth. All original including umbrella. $350.00.

9", Bo Peep. Marks: none. 1930s. All composition, fully jointed. Molded painted brown hair, painted blue eyes, closed mouth. All original costume including staff, shoes, socks, and small bonnet. $125.00.

15". Marks: none. 1940s. All composition, fully jointed. Dark brown human hair wig, brown sleep eyes, closed mouth. All original. $200.00.
Note: Identical 18" doll has been examined which was dressed in identical outfit of a different color. She was marked R & B.

21". Marks: R & B (Little Angel Baby), (Playthings, October 1940).
Composition flange head, full arms and bent legs to above the knee. Jointed at shoulders, stitched hip joints. Molded painted dark brown hair, brown sleep eyes, closed mouth, old clothes. $150.00.

14". Marks: none.
Tag: Nancy Lee//An//R & B//Quality Doll.
All composition, fully jointed. Blond mohair wig, brown sleep eyes, closed mouth. All original. Peggy Millhouse collection. $450.00.

19". Marks: Nancy (Playthings, October 1946).
All composition, fully jointed. Blond human hair wig with braids. Gray sleep eyes, open mouth with four teeth. All original including shoes and socks. $350.00.
Note: The nicely finished combination underwear can double as sunsuit.

14". Marks: none (Toys and Novelties, August 1949).
Paper tag: Nancy Lee//An//R & B//Quality Doll.
All composition, fully jointed. Blond mohair wig, blue plastic sleep eyes, eye shadow, closed mouth. All original. $400.00.

THE AVERILL MANUFACTURING CO.
NEW YORK CITY
1915 – 1930S

Paul Averill, Inc. 1920 – 1924
Madame Georgene 1920 – 1927
Georgene Novelties 1920 – 1930 and later

In 1924, Georgene Averill was superintendent of Borgfeldt's toy department (Coleman II, pg. 60).

The Averill Manufacturing Company was started in 1915. As can be seen from the above, they operated under various names, and it is difficult in some instances to discern the reasons for these simultaneously existing firms. From 1920 – 1924, for example, Paul Averill, Inc. advertised the Wonder Dolls. In 1924, The Geo. Borgfeldt Co. was given exclusive rights for the sale of this line. From then on, these dolls were produced by Borgfeldt's K & K Doll Factory. After the 1924 date, the Paul Averill, Inc. name no longer appeared on advertising. It is, therefore, assumed that the Paul Averill, Inc. company's sole purpose of existence was to make and distribute the Wonder Dolls.

In the collection of the Strong Museum library in Rochester, New York, are original photographs of an Averill factory, a rather large two-story corner structure. A sign on the roof read "Averill Manufacturing Corp., The Home of Madame Hendren Dolls." On the same pages, various stages of manufacturing can be seen, including the dipping process, which leads one to assume that the composition parts were actually manufactured on the premises. Unfortunately, no date or address survived with these photographs. The majority of dolls pictured in this file seemed to be from the mid-20s.

As many others, the Averills were a family business. Paul Averill and his wife Georgene (nee Hopf, also called Madame Georgene), were the principal owners. Their daughter Maxine and several brothers of Georgene's were involved in various capacities and at various times. The inter-relationships in the doll business were very complex, and the Averills were no exception. It is quite clear however, that Paul Averill was the business manager of this firm and Georgene Averill its creative force.

The earliest dolls advertised by the Averill Manufacturing Company were dressed in felt costumes and represented Dutch children, Indians, and cowboys. The very first Dutch children had bisque or celluloid heads. Soon, Madame Georgene bought composition character heads from various American companies for those little folk in felt costumes.

The trade name for their line was Madame Hendren Dolls. It was introduced in 1915 and used in the promotion of almost all of their dolls. The Averill Manufacturing Co. also based advertising slogans on this trademark, such as "Hendrenize Your Doll Department" (*Playthings*, July 1930).

As reported in a separate chapter, Madame Georgene was the creator of the new American babies called Lyf-Lik (Life-Like) and later mama dolls. Their immense success had a major influence on doll design and promotion industry wide, particularly during the 1920s.

Besides the many composition dolls created by Madame Georgene for the Averill Company and pictured in the following section, she also designed the famous Bonnie Babe. Bonnie Babe had a bisque head and an American-made mama doll body with composition limbs. In 1924, she created Prize Baby and a line of mama dolls for Geo. Borgfeldt & Co. Some of these mama dolls had bisque heads as well. The bisque heads were made in Germany. In 1927, Sunny Girl was introduced. This doll had a celluloid head made by Rheinische Gummi- und Celluloid-Fabrik (the German turtle mark firm) and an American-made mama doll body/limb assembly.

Throughout their existence the Averill Company made many cloth dolls such as Johnny Gruelle's Raggedy Ann and Andy and those designed by Grace Drayton and other artists. The Averills were partners to numerous licensing agreements. (Available information has been placed with the pictures of relevant dolls.) In October of 1931, they collaborated with the E. I. Horsman Co., Inc. on a radio advertising campaign.

In 1922 they registered the slogan "Madame Hendren Talking and Walking Doll" and incorporated the picture of a doll in their trademark.

In 1924, a new finish called Hendrenite was announced. Many Averill dolls have been thoroughly examined. Their finish does not seem to differ from that of other composition dolls of the day. If there was a difference, it may just have been in the brand of oil paint used in the final air brushing of the composition parts.

In conversation with Harriet Flanders, creator of Little Cherub and an employee of the Averills from 1932 until about 1940, she reported that she did not remember many composition dolls at the Averill factory during her tenure. She had been hired to paint faces for Raggedy Ann and Andy, cloth quintuplets and, others.

By 1949, Madame Georgene Averill had retired to California and was advertising a vinyl headed doll called Bi-Bye Baby (see various ads in *Toys & Novelties* in 1949). This doll was marketed by Fleischaker Novelty Co., Venice, California.

While the Averill Company became less prominent during the 30s and later, Georgene Averill's contributions in the areas of design and advertising certainly had a revolutionary and long-lasting impact on the industry.

Three Dutch Children.
13" girl. Marks: 72.
14" boy. Marks: 34.
20" boy. Marks: R. T. Mfg. Co.
All have flared composition heads and short arms. Cloth bodies, upper arms, and legs, jointed with outside disks. Molded painted hair and eyes, closed mouths. All original except large boy. 13", 250.00; 14", $250.00; 20", $200.00.
Note: Outfit of large boy came on ball-jointed body with remnants of celluloid head attached. (Only the outfit was for sale at the time, not the ball-jointed body.) Since Georgene Averill did buy composition character heads from other firms and dressed them in felt costumes, this doll was chosen to wear the unusually large outfit.

11". Marks: none.
Composition flange heads and short arms, cloth body and limbs (sewn-in black cloth boots), jointed with outside disks. Molded painted light brown hair, painted blue eyes, closed mouths. All original. $125.00 each.

13". Marks: Trion Toy Co. (Identical outfit: Playthings, June 1916).
Composition flange head and short arms, molded painted blond hair and painted blue eyes, closed mouth. Cloth body and limbs jointed with outside disks, black cloth boots are part of the leg casing. All original except cap. $125.00.

12", Indian. Marks: none on doll.
Cloth tag: Mme. Hendren//Character Doll.
Composition flange head and short arms. Cloth body, upper arms, and legs, jointed with outside disks. Molded painted black hair and painted brown eyes, closed mouth. All original. White doll, $80.00; Indian, $100.00.
Note: The accompanying white doll has the identical head (no original clothes). It is not clear if this head was used exclusively by the Averill firm.

9", 12", and 18", 1916 – 1924.
Two smaller dolls not marked.
Cloth tag: Madame Hendren//Character Doll//Costume Patent, May 9, 1916.
18", Marks: A.M. c Co. (Averill Mfg. Comp.).
Two smaller dolls have flange heads and cloth bodies, jointed with outside disks. They date from around 1916.
The 18" doll is a typical mama doll with composition shoulder head and arms, all cloth body and swinging legs. Black cotton wig over molded hair, painted brown eyes, open/closed mouth. Small, $150.00; Large, $250.00.
Note: Mama doll with identical, white head was advertised by Averill in Playthings, October 1924. The large Indian is assumed to be from that date. All original.

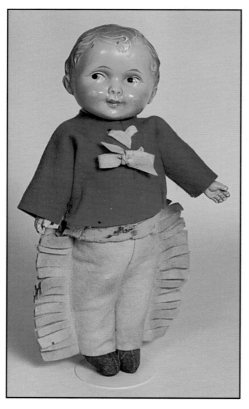

13", Cowboy. Marks: none (Playthings, June 1916).
Composition flange head and short arms. Cloth body and limbs, jointed with outside disks. Black sewn on cloth boots. Molded painted brown hair and blue eyes, closed mouth. All original. $150.00.

12", WWI Soldier, Yankee Doddle Kid. Marks: none (Playthings, May 1917).
Composition flange head and short arms. Cloth body, upper arms, and full legs, jointed with outside disks. Molded painted brown hair and blue eyes, closed mouth. Sewn in black cloth boots. All original uniform including belt and holster. $200.00.

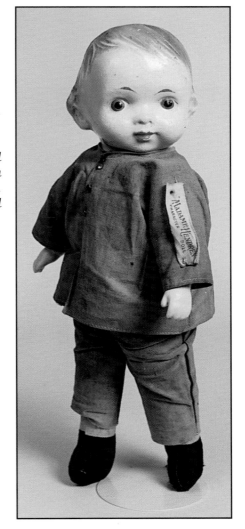

12", *Preparedness Kid. Marks: H.C.Q. (Playthings, July 1916).*
Tag on sleeve: Madame Hendren//Character Doll. Composition flange head and short arms, jointed with outside disks, cloth body and limbs. Black sewn in cloth shoes. Molded painted hair and blue eyes, closed mouth. Original clothes. Hat, belt/holster, and leggings missing. $80.00 (very faded).

13", *Boy in Blue Velvet Costume, 1916.*
Marks: H. C. Q. (Identical mark and head as Preparedness Kid. May have been dressed and sold by Georgene Averill.)
Composition flange head and short hands. Straw stuffed cloth body and legs, jointed with outside disks. Molded painted black hair with individually formed human hair curls glued on top. Human hair mustache and goatee. Head and hands painted brown. Brown painted eyes, closed mouth. Clothes all original, including black oilcloth booth and chain with ornament. $150.00.

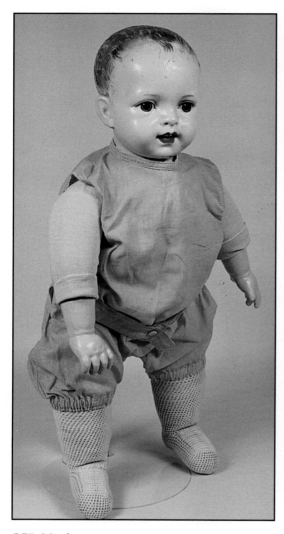
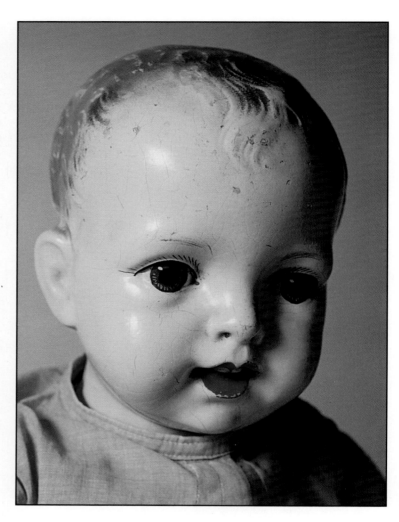

25". Marks: none.

Body has ink stamp: Madame Hendren Life-Like Doll//Patented June 11, 1918.

Composition head is made of early and heavy glue base composition (weights almost 2 pounds). Short composition arms. Cloth body and legs stuffed with cotton. Stitched hip joints. Molded painted brown hair and brown eyes. Irises have rays painted on them. Open/closed mouth with two upper molded, painted teeth. Foot has tailored heel. Old romper. $250.00 (very faded).

Note: This is the first Mama Doll created by Mme. Georgene. It can be recognized in several trade journal illustrations (not yet called a Mama Doll).

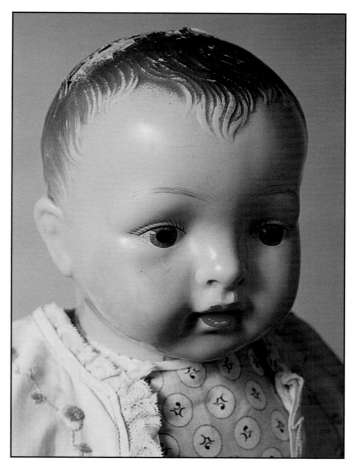

22". Marks: none.

Body stamped: Madame Hendren Life-Like Doll//Patented June 11th, 1918.

Composition flange head and short arms. Wide cloth body and limbs stuffed with cotton. No shoulder joints, stitched hip joints. Molded painted light brown hair and blue eyes, open/closed mouth. Clothes are original to the doll. $250.00.

Note: The head of this doll is made of the much lighter wood pulp composition, but same mold as "first doll."

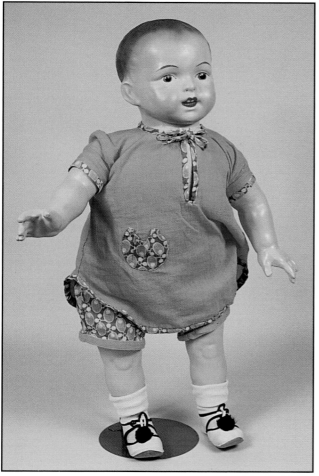

24". Marks: none.

Composition flange head, unusually well modeled arms and legs. Cloth body and upper limbs, stitched hip joints. Molded painted brown hair and painted blue eyes, open/closed mouth with two molded/painted upper teeth. Re-dressed. $250.00.

Note: A February 1921 Playthings ad showed this doll (wigged) and the following announcement: "By arrangements with the manufacturers and designer of 'Madame Hendren Life-Like doll': We have secured a license to manufacture dolls under patent 1,269,363." This had been placed by American Bisque Doll Co.

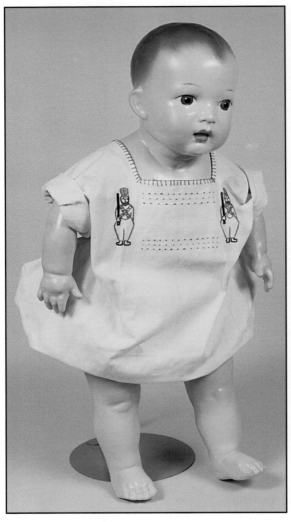
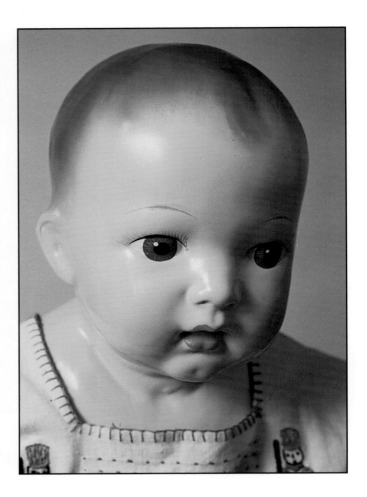

24". Marks: none. This is the Wonder Mama Doll introduced in 1920 (Playthings, November 1920). Composition shoulder head and limbs tied on to cloth body (stuffed with cotton). Faintly molded, painted brown hair and painted blue eyes. Irises have white rays painted onto them. Open/closed mouth. Old child's romper. Note excellent modeling of limbs and neck area. Doll came dressed as boy or girl, with painted hair or wig. $250.00.

In February 1922, Playthings reported that "Paul Averill, Inc. had no small compliment paid their line of Wonder Dolls when they were recently chosen for a feature act in 'Tangerine', the reigning musical comedy hit of the metropolis.... Ten young ladies dance with the 'Wonder Dancing Dolls' while singing the song hit of the show, 'Atta Baby.'

In Playthings of January 1923, Geo. Borgfeldt & Co. announced that they had made exclusive arrangements with Madame Georgene for the sale of The Wonder Dolls.

17", Early Mama Doll.
Marks on head: GEM (inside horizontal diamond).
Body stamped: Madame Hendren's//Life Like Doll//
Patented: June 11, 1918.
Composition flange head and lower arms, cotton stuffed cloth body and legs. Molded brown hair and blue eyes, closed mouth. $150.00.

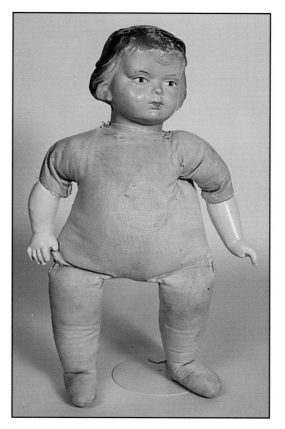

16", Early Mama Doll. Marks: none. See Playthings, April 1923 showing U-Shab-Ti doll (has identical head as this mama doll). Also see patented tailored heel and seams along side of leg.
Composition shoulder head and lower arms. Cloth body and full legs stuffed with cotton, with stitched hip joints. Cloth body has the typical wide shape of the early mama dolls. Molded painted brown hair and painted blue eyes. Open/closed mouth with white line between lips for teeth. $200.00.

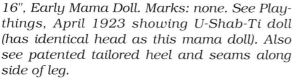

18", Early Mama Doll. Marks:
Composition flange head and limbs. Cloth body stuffed with cotton. Molded painted brown hair, blue eyes, closed mouth. Identical body construction and composition hands as GEM girl. May have been sold by Averill. $150.00.
Note: Has white rays painted on irises. Also was available with sleep eyes and wig.

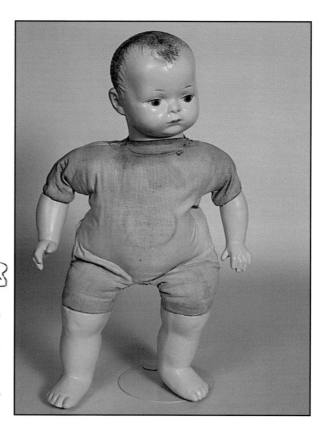

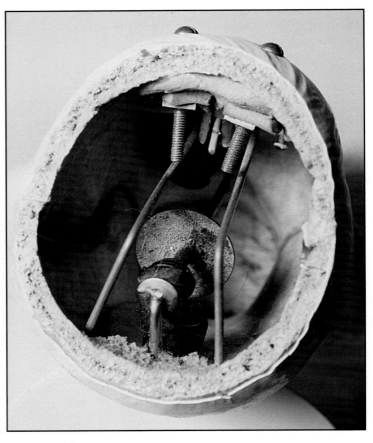

16", Rock-a-Bye Baby.

Marks: none. Pictured in Sears & Roebuck catalog from 1921 to 1924. Came in three sizes: 14", 16", and 18".

Composition shoulder head and short composition arms. Cloth body, straight legs and upper arms stuffed with cotton. Three criers have been inserted into body: one large one going through from front to back, two smaller ones, one at each hip. Brown mohair wig, gray tip sleep eyes, open/closed mouth. Appropriate old outfit. Special sleep eye mechanism inside head mounted with two screws to forehead. In addition to the regular sleep eye assembly a weight has been installed on a diagonally mounted rod. When the doll is rocked from side to side in a horizontal position, the weight moves out of the way of the eye assembly's counterweight and the eyes will close. i.e., when the doll is put in a horizontal position, the eyes do not close until the doll has been rocked from side to side. Shipping box could be made into a cradle for the doll. $250.00 (fair).

18", Pinky Winky. Marks: none. (Designed by Georgene Averill, sold by Pinky Winky Products Co., Inc.) (Playthings, September 1924.)
Celluloid mask face, cloth head, body, and limbs, stitched joints. Molded painted dark brown hair. Celluloid eyes with floating disk (pupil/retina), painted lashes around the eye opening with red dots. Closed mouth, three dimples. Re-dressed. $200.00 each, $40.00 small.
Note: Limbs of doll on right have been oil painted. Small doll is a Nelke product and a baby rattle. (Coleman, Doll World, Sept/Oct 1994, Vol. 2/#2.) Though not made of composition, this is a rare doll and included for completeness sake.

22", Dolly Record (Toys and Novelties, July 1922).
Marks, ink stamp on body: Genuine Madame Hendren Doll.
Composition shoulder head, arms to below the elbow and legs to above the knee, cloth body upper arms and legs, with stitched hip joints. Record player in body that is wound on her side. Funnel speaker open to front. Blond human hair wig, blue/gray celluloid sleep eyes, open mouth with tongue and two upper teeth. All original including shoes and socks and six records. $600.00 (in working order with six records).

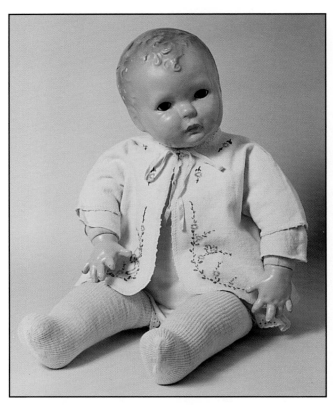

24". Marks: A.M. Co. (Averill Manufacturing Co.).
Ink stamp on body: Genuine//Madame Hendren
//Doll//424 (Playthings, April/November 1924).
Composition flange head, hands to above the
wrist. Cloth body and bent full-cloth legs. Molded
painted blond hair, brown sleep eyes, closed
mouth, re-dressed. $300.00.
Note: Doll is almost identical to Horsman's Baby
Horsman. For this baby, a few curls have been
changed, and it has sleep instead of painted eyes.

13". Marks: Am © Co. (This is Lullabye Baby,
Playthings, March 1925).
Ink stamp on body: Genuine//Madame
Hendren//Doll//314//Made in USA.
Composition flange head and hands. Cloth body
and limbs. Slightly molded light brown hair, blue
tin sleep eyes, closed mouth. $100.00.
Note: A Lullabye Baby of a different mold was
produced in composition as well as in bisque (see
Playthings, July 1925).

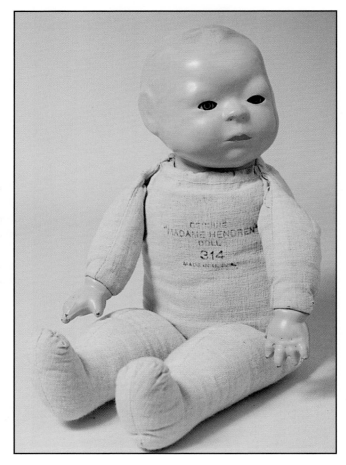

15". Marks: none.
Ink stamp on body: Genuine//Madame Hendren//Doll// 216.
Paper tag, front: Genuine Madame Hendren Doll.
Paper tag, back: Genuine//Madame Hendren//Wauck-an-Tauck Doll (Lloyd's Patent Voice)//To operate voice, hold doll in position lying on back, then turn completely over.//Made in U.S.A.
Composition shoulder head, arms, and legs to above the knee. Jointed at shoulders, stitched hip joints. Cloth body. Brown mohair wig, blue tin sleep eyes, closed mouth. All original. $300.00.

15". Marks: none.
Metal coin, front: Madame Hendren//Talking and Walking Doll.
Metal coin, back: Good Luck//Keep This Coin And Good Luck Will Follow You (lettering around cross with bent arms and four good luck symbols).
Composition shoulder head and lower arms, cloth body, upper arms, and legs, stitched hip joints. Blond mohair wig with bangs and short styling (no curls). Painted blue eyes, closed mouth. All original. $300.00 (faded).

13", Whistlers. Patent date: February 2, 1926. Marks: none on heads, ink stamp on cloth body mostly illegible (Mme. Hendren).
Left: Composition flange head and full arms.
Right: Composition shoulder head and full arms, both have cloth bodies and legs. Bellows and steel springs installed in legs. When legs are pushed upward, the bellows emit a whistling sound. Left, $300.00; right, $200.00.
Note: Different head molds. Left doll has puckered molded eyebrows and lips. For right head a stock dolly face mold was used. No puckered mouth. A hole was drilled into his mouth to indicate that he is a whistler.

14". Marks: Madame Hendren Doll. (This is Snookums; see Toys and Novelties, November 1927).
Composition head and upper body to under the arms is one piece. Full composition arms, cloth body and legs. Jointed at shoulders, stitched hip joints. Molded painted blond hair. Hole has been drilled into top of head to accommodate a tuft of real hair. Painted blue eyes, open/closed mouth with lower and upper molded painted teeth. White dolls have been re-dressed. Brown doll is all original. Note that brown doll does not have tuft of hair.
George McManus created the cartoon strip "The Newlyweds" for the New York World in 1908. Snookums was their baby. In 1927, Snookums was the star in Stern Bros. and Universal Picture Corp. comedies, "The Newlyweds and Their Baby." Sunny McKeen played the baby, and the doll is a portrait of Sunny McKeen. It is a very good likeness.
Note: See the earlier Snookums doll sold by E. I. Horsman. White dolls, $250.00 ea. (heads restored); black doll, $150.00 (heavy lifting and touch-up in face).

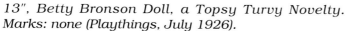

13", Betty Bronson Doll, a Topsy Turvy Novelty. Marks: none (Playthings, July 1926).

Composition shoulder heads and arms, jointed at shoulders. Brown mohair wigs glued directly to scalp (no wig cap). Crown of head had been cut off and glued back for insertion of eyes. Gray tin sleep eyes, with real and painted lashes. All original (not crown). $250.00 (some restoration).

Note: Betty Bronson was a young actress who, at the time, played leading roles in Peter Pan, and the picture A Kiss For Cinderella. Averill had exclusive license for a Cinderella doll.

*Illustrated ad from Playthings, March 1928.
Apparently, this baby had an inflatable torso.*

*28". Marks: Madame Hendren. Ca. 1928.
Dress tag: Madame Hendren//Dolls//
Everybody Loves Them.
Composition shoulder head and arms, composition legs to above the knee. Cloth body
and upper legs, jointed at shoulders and
hips. Original human hair wig, gray tin
sleep eyes, open mouth with two upper
teeth. Old shoes. $450.00.*

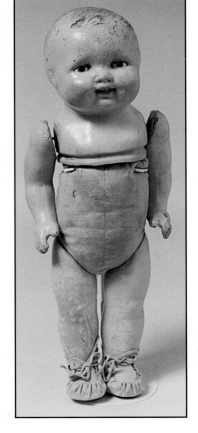

*12". Marks: Madame Hendren (in script).
Full composition shoulder head and limbs,
jointed at shoulders and hips. Cloth body
with mama crier. Molded painted light
brown hair and painted blue eyes.
Open/closed mouth with two upper, molded
painted teeth. $80.00 (fair condition).*

14". Marks: ©//By//Grace Corry.
Ink stamp on body: Genuine//Madame Hendren//Doll//60//Made in U.S.A.
This is Little Sister as pictured in Playthings, July 1927, wearing same dress (seen with Little Brother, wearing white blouse and button-on, short pants). Doll was sold in other outfits and given various names. Also came with all composition legs, jointed at hips. Composition shoulder head, arms and legs to above the knee. Cloth body and upper legs, jointed at shoulders, stitched hip joints. Molded painted blond hair and painted blue eyes with eye shadow, closed mouth. All original. $450.00.

14". Marks: ©//By//Grace Corry. Ca. 1928.
Body has faint Mme. Hendren ink stamp that is illegible.
Composition shoulder head and full arms. Cloth body and legs with stitched hip joints. Light yellow cotton yarn hair over molded hair. Painted blue eyes, closed mouth. Molded composition Dutch shoes. All original outfits. (Clothes have been turned inside out.) $300.00 each (some repair in faces).

22". Marks: Madame Hendren//Doll. This is Baby Brite (see Playthings, May 1928). Composition flange head and limbs, cloth body. Molded painted blond hair and gray celluloid sleep eyes, open mouth with two upper teeth. All original clothes. $350.00.

13". Marks: G. G. Drayton/©.
Ink stamp on body: Genuine // Madame Hendren// Doll//814 G//Made in USA.
Paper tag: Genuine Madame Hendren Doll (in circle)// SIS//Trade mark registered//Design Patented//Dolly Dingle//by G. G. Drayton.
Composition shoulder head and lower arms. Cloth body, upper arms and legs, stitched hip joints. Molded, painted reddish brown, curly hair with five woolen, reddish brown pigtails inserted into drill holes and tied with green silk ribbons. Black eyes, closed mouth. $350.00.
Note: It is assumed that this is another portrait of the character Sis, played by comedian, Rose Melville over a long period of time. (See earlier Sis doll in the Amberg section.)

13" pair. Marks: *G. G. Drayton//©. They are Dolly and Bobby (see Toys and Novelties, September 1928).*

Composition shoulder head, and limbs, jointed at shoulders and hips. Cloth body. Boy has molded painted brown hair and brown eyes, girl has blond hair and blue eyes. Closed mouths. Original hair bow and clothes. Old shoes and socks. Playthings, August 1928: "A New Sensation in Novelty Dolls, Dolly and Bobby, The famous DRAYTON cartoon kids — new members of the Madame Hendren Family."

Toys and Novelties, Aug. 1928, pg. 94, "While the dolls are sold separately, the Averill Manufacturing Company, who created them, are endeavoring to help the stores boost their unit of sale by packing the dolls, where sets are ordered, in a beautifully lithographed double box." $350.00 each.

14". Marks: none (Playthings, February 1929).
All composition, fully jointed. Unlike other composition dolls where the ball part of the neck joint is part of the body, this doll has a socket head. Molded painted brown hair and brown eyes. Closed mouth. Clothes are an original Effanbee Patsy outfit. This doll does not have a ball-jointed waist. $350.00.

Note: This doll was sold by several companies, and unless there are markings of some kind on the doll, she is almost impossible to place as to seller. The doll was sold by Horsman as Boots (separate waist joint ball) Hendren as Dimmie and Jimmie, by Maxine as Mitzi, and was illustrated in the 1929 Sears catalog as Tootsie. She was sold with or without a waist joint, and all seem to have had a socket head. Available advertising (Averill/Hendren and Sears catalog) does not mention the waist joint, yet Hendren dolls have been found with jointed waists (see Pat Schoonmaker article in Doll News, June/July 1982).

11". Marks: none.
Has tailored heel. Assume it is Hendren (Averill). Composition flange head, cloth body and limbs, stitched joints. Molded painted light brown hair and blue eyes. Open/closed mouth with white line for teeth. Dress may be original. $50.00.

17" girl in aviator outfit. Not marked, all original. Composition shoulder head and tied on limbs, cloth body stuffed with cotton. Painted blue eyes and medium brown molded hair, open/closed mouth. (Identical head often seen on marked Mme Hendren dolls.) Clothes consist of undershirt, panties, girdle, bra, silk stockings, oilcloth shoes, leggings, and jacket. The latter trimmed with real fur, aviator cap, and goggles. Beige wool pants with real leather belt, pink crepe silk blouse. $400.00 (some touch-up to face).

 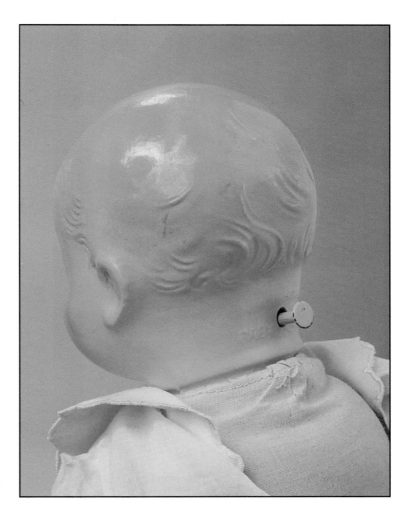

20", Baby Hendren (so marked on head), ca. 1930.
Body stamped: Head Protected by//Patent (illegible).
Original bib embroidered: Baby//Hendren.
Composition flange head and tied on limbs. Cotton stuffed cloth body. Gray tin sleep eyes that can be closed with doll in upright position by pushing a lever in back of neck. Open mouth with two upper teeth, molded hair. Clothes may be original, bonnet is a replacement. Bib embroidered Baby Hendren.
$350.00.

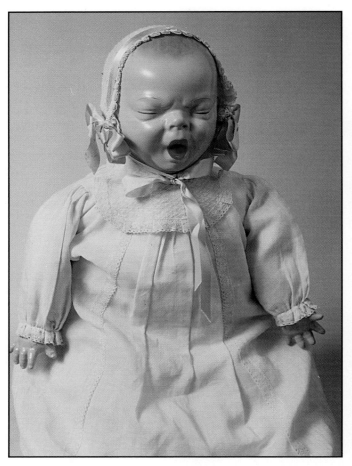

19" Baby Yawn. Marks: illegible.
5th Blue Book, pg. 143, pictured original paper hang tag: Georgene's Baby Yawn.
Composition flange head and hands to wrist. Cloth body and straight legs, soft stuffed. Molded painted blond hair, closed eyes, open/closed mouth. All original. $400.00.

20". Marks: none.
Ink stamp on body: Genuine//Madame Hendren// Doll//1720//Made in U.S.A.
Cloth tag on dress: Madame Hendren//Dolls//Every- body Loves Them. (Pictured in 1929 J. C. Penny cata- log "Head with felt finish," and named Val Encia.).
Composition shoulder head with felt finish, regular finish arms and legs to above the knee. Cloth body and upper legs. Jointed at shoulders, stitched hip joints. Mohair wig, painted blue eyes, with blue eye shadow, four highlights on iris. Open/closed mouth with four upper painted teeth. All original. $400.00.
Note: Besides the felt finish on head and Val Encia name, eye shadow and felt trimmed clothes are another indication that this doll was intentionally made to resemble Lenci creations. "Felt finish" in this case means a rough paint surface.

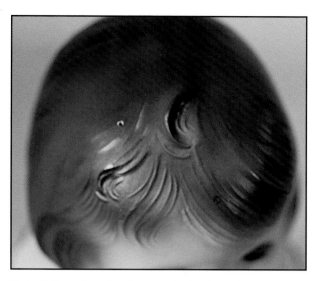

Not all Peaches had a pin hole for a hair ribbon, but all had the two small curls on top. Since some dolls were not marked, this is a good identification clue.

19". Marks: none (some came marked A.M. Co. Averill Manufacturing Co.).
Paper tag front: Peaches.
Paper tag back: A//Madame Hendren//Doll//Everybody//Loves Her//I Say Mama.
Composition head, shoulder-plate and limbs, cloth body, fully jointed. Molded painted brown hair with two small curls on top near pin hole for hair ribbon. Metal sleep eyes, closed mouth. All original including hair bow. $350.00.
Note: Also came in 14" (Bud), 17" (Polly Peaches). A painted eye version was available called Blossom Peaches. These smaller sizes were made of all composition.

16", Peaches.
Marks on head: not legible.
Dress tag: Madame Hendren//Dolls//Everybody Loves Them.
Composition head, shoulder plate and limbs. Cloth body, fully jointed. Molded painted brown hair with pin hole into head to accommodate hair ribbon. Gray tin sleep eyes, closed mouth. All original. Bernice Foster collection. $300.00.

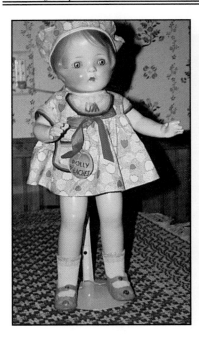

17". Marks: none (See Playthings ads March/April 1931).
Front paper tag: Polly//Peaches.
Back of paper tag: I am a Madame Hendren Doll with a genuine Flexo Body. (I don't know what is meant by Flexo Body.)
All composition, fully jointed. Molded painted brown hair and gray tin sleep eyes, closed mouth. All original. Collection of Mary Ellen Johnson. $300.00.

Little Cherub Created by Harriet Flanders

These dolls (below and on top of page 118) were sold as a set. Each came in her own box accompanied by a picture book entitled Little Cherub. Illustrations and verses were also by Harriet Flanders.

17". Marks: Harriet © Flanders. 1937.
All composition, fully jointed. Molded painted, black hair (note that hair has a hard edge not an airbrushed soft hairline, as is usual with other composition dolls). Painted brown eyes, closed mouth. All original. $250.00.

12". Marks: Harriet © Flanders. 1937.
Paper tag: Copyright by//Harriet Flanders//Little//Cherub//a Georgene//Doll.
All composition, fully jointed. Molded painted yellow hair (yarn sections are attached to cap), painted blue eyes, closed mouth. All original (felt daisies on side of bonnet). $250.00.

17". Marks: Harriet © Flanders.
All composition fully jointed. Molded
painted yellow hair, painted blue eyes,
closed mouth. All original. (This size was
also sold with sleep eyes.) $300.00.

27". Marks: none. Mid – late 30s.
Paper tag front: Mi-Own//Baby//Takes It's First
Step//And Says//Ma Ma.
Paper tag back: Georgine//Dolls//Made In U.S.A.
Composition flange head, molded painted blond hair
and sleep eyes. Open mouth with two upper and two
lower teeth, metal tongue. Cloth body and limbs,
inserted cardboard foot sole. All original. $200.00
(some repair on chin).

BED DOLLS (BOUDOIR DOLLS)
1920S – 1930S

Bed dolls were not made for children but were decorative objects used by adults in the home. All had very slim cloth bodies and extremely long, thin limbs. They could be bought dressed or undressed. Their heads, lower arms, and legs were made of cloth or composition. They had wigs and painted features. A rare few had sleep eyes. Most of them were ladies and featured the latest in make-up such as heavy eyelashes, eyeshadow, deep red lips, and beauty marks. They were dressed in the latest flapper styles or in fantasy costumes of the past. Most of these dolls have no identification marks. For this reason they are shown as a group in this section. (Also see "Cigarette Doll," Mutual Novelty Co.)

28", bed doll in all original orange outfit. I don't know if it's marked. Clothes are nailed on. Composition shoulder head, arms to above elbow, and short legs to above ankles with molded on black, high heeled pumps. Inserted, real upper lashes, painted lower lashes, blue painted eyes, brown eye shadow, black one-stroke brows. Red fingernails. Black beauty mark on left cheek. Original blond mohair wig. Cloth body stuffed with cotton. Cloth legs stuffed with excelsior. $350.00.

28". Marks: none.
Composition flange head, cloth body and limbs, mitten hands. Black cotton floss wig with braids coiled over ears. Painted eyes, hole in mouth to accommodate cigarette. Note unusual treatment of eye painting. Original blouse. $250.00.

30", boudoir doll with unusual, molded upper composition torso to below upper arm joints and to waist level. Long neck and swivel head. Short composition arms, very long cloth legs and body. Original white mohair wig, painted blue eyes and blue eye shadow, painted upper lashes. Eyes are outlined with black, black brows. Open/closed mouth with white space between lips. Old hat. $150.00.

BERWICK DOLL COMPANY
478 BROADWAY
NEW YORK, NEW YORK

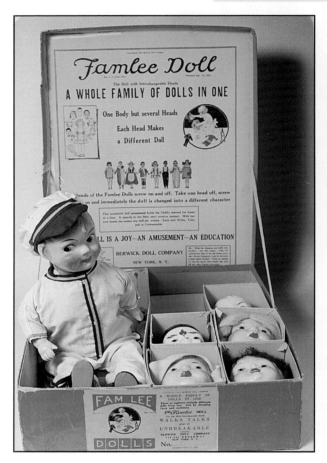

17", Famlee Doll. Marks: none (on metal socket: Pat. Apr. 12, 21).

Composition shoulder head, tied on lower arms and legs to above the knee. Stitched hip joints, cloth body. Heads are interchangeable and can be screwed onto the shoulder plate like a light bulb into its socket. All heads have painted eyes and closed mouths or open/closed mouths, molded hair, or mohair wigs over molded hair. Each extra head was accompanied by a set of clothes. Various size sets were available. They were sold with one body and three, five, seven, or twelve heads. It is not clear how many heads originally came with the set pictured. These sets were still advertised in 1931 (Playthings April 1931). $600.00.

Package insert to Famlee Doll Set.

My! what fun changing one dollie into another— Change from French dollie into Tim, the clown, then Simple Sue and all the others.

The Right Costume

When you are changing the characters I suppose you will give each doll her own costume. For example: Little Miss Sweet Face owns the nice white party dress. The Dutch Girl owns the Dutch Dress, and so on. Each doll has her own costume, as you can easily see.

Of course, they can borrow from each other if you will allow that. And maybe borrowing would be good fun too. Can you imagine Black Face Sam wearing the white party dress instead of his colored trousers? Wouldn't that look funny? Or Susie Bumps dressed up in pants? Oh, my! Yes, when you just feel in the mood to mix things up it would be lots of fun having the dollies loan their costumes to each other.

BERWICK DOLL COMPANY
Makers of
Famlee Doll Sets
A whole family of dolls in one
478-482 Broadway,
New York, N. Y.

BLUE BIRD DOLL CO.
111 SOUTH 6TH STREET
BROOKLYN, NEW YORK
1920

13", standing figure on pedestal. Marks: none.
Sticker on underside of base: The Vamp//Manufactured by the//Blue
Bird Doll Co.//Patents on Design and Earrings. See Toys And Novelties,
February, April, and July 1920.
She was made in various color bathing suits, with molded hair or wigged
with hair net covering the face as well as the hair do. All composition,
molded painted blond hair and painted black eyes. Open/closed mouth
with white line between lips for teeth. Real earrings are fastened with a
nail into the head. $125.00.

GEO. BORGFELDT
NEW YORK CITY
EST. 1881

According to the Coleman's, the Geo. Borgfeldt Co. was probably the largest producer of dolls in the United States as well as importers and exporters of dolls and toys with offices in most major cities as well as Paris, London, and Sonneberg, Germany. Before World War I, the company had exclusive distribution rights for German firms such as Kestner, Kammer & Reinhardt, Kaethe Kruse, Handwerk, Steiff, and many others.

Apparently, during World War I, it distributed dolls made in Japan. It seems that Borgfeldt did not get involved with the production of American-made composition dolls copied from German bisque dolls (like Horsman and Amberg).

K & K Toy Co., Inc. was a wholly owned subsidiary. Though many composition dolls were made there over the years, apparently not many were marked. In 1924, for example, Borgfeldt acquired exclusive rights to the Wonder Dolls of Paul Averill Inc. The Wonder Dolls were produced in the K & K factory.

Right from the start, it was the distributor for many American companies. Boregfeldt undertook the production and distribution of many artists' designs, such as the Kewpies by Rose O'Neill. It also handled the Bye-Lo baby created by Grace Storey Putnam and Georgene Averill's Bonnie Babe, both very successful bisque headed babies during the 20s. A composition Bye-Lo was also produced. It was reported in 1924, that Georgine Averill, of Averill Manufacturing Co., had been hired as superintendent of their toy department.

Without a firm the size of Borgfeldt, a legendary success story like Rose O'Neill's might not have been possible. Its active participation in the making and distribution contributed to the success of composition dolls. (Also see K & K Toy Co., Inc.)

11". Marks: none (Playthings, Jan. 1917).
Cloth tag: Happifat//U.S. Pat. Off. (Designed by Kate Jordan).
Composition flange head and short arms. Cloth body and limbs. Molded patented whisp of hair, brown eyes, closed mouth. All original. $400.00.
Note: Pappyfats were also made of bisque in smaller sizes.

Display ad, Playthings, April 1925, advertising eight different, 15" storybook dolls.
They seem to be economy model mama dolls with tied-on, short arms and all cloth legs. Note the open box in the left-hand corner. Packed with their accessories, they make attractive play sets. $150.00.

17", Mammy. Marks: none. Designed by famous puppeteer Tony Sarg.
Composition flange head, arms to above elbow, and molded shoes. Cloth body, upper arms, and legs, not jointed. Painted brown eyes, open/closed mouth with six molded, painted teeth. Black mohair wig, metal hoop earrings attached to wig cap. All original.
8" baby. Marks: R & B//Doll Co.
All composition, fully jointed. $900.00 set.

The Bye-Lo Baby

The bisque Bye-Lo baby was designed by Grace Storey Putman and introduced in 1922. It is not quite clear when the composition version of this famous doll became available. Montgomery Ward carried one in their line of 1927. An April 1934 ad in *Playthings* announced the "comeback" in composition of "this world famous doll." Another ad, dated 1943 (*Playthings*), was still advertising Bye-Lo babies wrapped in blankets or with fine fancy dresses.

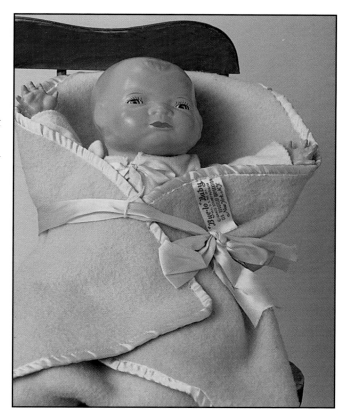

13". Marks on head: © Grace Storey//Putnam.
Tag on blanket: Bye-lo Baby//Reg. U. S. Pat.
Off.//© Grace Storey Putnam//Geo. Borgfeldt
Corporation//New York N.Y.
Composition flange head and hands, cloth
body, original flannel shirt, diaper, and blanket. Slightly molded, painted light brown hair,
blue sleep eyes, closed mouth. $400.00.

7½" (with cart), Stroller Doll (See Toys and Novelties, July 1945). Marks: none.
Box label: My Playmate//Reg. U. S. Pat. Off.//Stroller Doll //No. 7247.43//Geo. Borgfeldt Corporation, New York, N.Y.
All composition jointed at shoulders only. Blond mohair wig, painted blue eyes, closed mouth, mounted on wooden platform with four wheels (pull toy). All original. $100.00.

BRIDAL PARTY

Bridal Party.
Six dolls: bride, maid of honor, four bridesmaids.
6¾". Marks: none.
All composition jointed at shoulders only. Molded painted hair and eyes, closed mouth. Dressed in crepe paper outfits, trimmed with satin ribbon, holding bouquets. $150.00.

H. D. BUDDY LEE MERCHANTILE CO.

The Buddy Lee dolls were manufactured from 1922 on to advertise the various types of overalls the company made, and the dolls can be found dressed in miniature versions of these work uniforms. Later on, the dolls were produced in hard plastic.

13", Buddy Lee. All original. 1920s.
Marks: none on doll.
Cap marked: Union Made//Lee//Fade Proof//Sanforized.
Pants label: Union Made//Lee//Sanforized.
All composition, jointed only at shoulders with steel spring, molded painted black boots. Molded painted brown hair and black eyes (no iris). Closed mouth. $350.00.

BUTLER BROS.
NEW YORK CITY (AND SONNEBERG, GERMANY)
EST. 1877

This wholesale house had been started as a mail order business by three brothers. They were factory agents, importers, and jobbers with offices in most major American cities. They offered an extensive line of products for sale besides dolls and toys (similar to Sears Roebuck and Co.).

Unlike importers such as E. I. Horsman & Co., Inc., Louis Amberg & Son, or George Borgfeldt & Co., they apparently never were involved with the production of dolls. By 1914, they too were offering various American-made composition dolls for sale. By 1918, this offering was extensive. They listed dolls by Amberg, Averill, Effanbee, Ideal, and Jessie M. Raleigh. Butler Bros. claimed to be sole agents for the Raleigh dolls. Their 1918 catalog carried four pages of Raleigh dolls and in 1919 carried two pages. Their mama dolls were made by Effanbee and Gem Toy Co. (Coleman I and II, *Price Guide to Am. Coll. Dolls*, Westbrook/Ehrhardt).

In 1928, their catalog still carried an extensive line of composition dolls such as boudoir dolls, Bubbles, Flossie Flirt (Ideal), Grumpykins, Kiddie Pal, mama dolls, Patsy Ruth, and Sunny Girl (Coleman II). By 1935, they had virtually eliminated dolls from their wholesale catalog.

There is no doubt that large wholesale houses like Butler Brothers were important contributors to the success of American-made composition dolls. The effectiveness of their established nationwide distribution systems could not have been duplicated by newly established small American toy companies.

23". Marks: none.
Offered in Butler Bros. catalog, 1910. (A Collector's History of Teddy Bears, Schoonmaker, pg. 93.)
Composition head, painted blond hair, painted blue eyes, open/closed mouth. Straw stuffed, plush covered body and limbs, jointed at shoulders and hips, felt mitten hands. Fake lamb's skin cap and collar, leather belt tacked in place. $250.00.
Note: Head is a copy of Kammer & Reinhardt's #100 baby.

BROWNIES

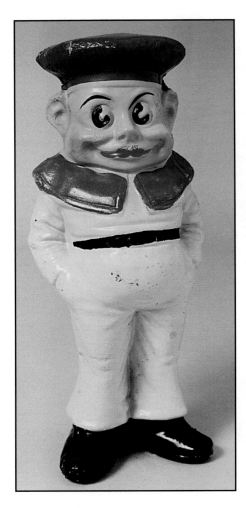

9", Brownie. Marks: none.
The Brownies were famous storybook characters created by Palmer Cox in 1892. All composition molded figure in white sailor suit with blue cap and collar, black shoes. Painted black eyes and closed mouth. $125.00.

13", Brownie. Marks: none. All original. 1920s.
Composition flange head, cloth body and limbs. No molded or painted hair. Irises are painted white and are raised in an exaggerated fashion. Closed mouth. $60.00 (fair condition).

CAMEO DOLL CO.
NEW YORK CITY AND PORT ALLEGANY, PENNSYLVANIA

The Cameo Doll Company was started in 1922 by Joseph L. Kallus. Mr. Kallus had previously founded the Rex Doll Co. in 1916, and when he returned from military service, he was involved with the Mutual Doll Company from 1919 to 1921. Prior to these activities, Mr. Kallus had worked for George Borgfelt & Co. and had helped with the development of Rose O'Neill's Kewpies. The association with Rose O'Neill and Borgfelt would last a lifetime.

Mr. Kallus's companies were largely responsible for the production of the composition Kewpies. He also produced the composition Bye-Lo for Borgfelt. Mama dolls were made by this company as well. According to Mr. Kallus, for many years Cameo was one of the three large companies that actually produced their own composition components. The other two were Effanbee and Ideal (Coleman II). Mr. Kallus did design some dolls for Ideal: Fanny Brice as Baby Snooks and Mortimer Snerd, Sunny Sue and Sunny Sam, King Little and Gabby (*Collector's Guide to Ideal Dolls*, Judith Izen).

In 1932, the company moved to Port Allegany and was sold to Strombecker Corporation in 1970. At that point Mr. Kallus founded Cameo Exclusive Products, which dealt with licensing agreements for dolls on which he owned copyrights. Kewpies and Scootles became available in vinyl.

Mr. Kallus, obviously, was the driving force at the Cameo Doll Company. At the same time, his professional career was overshadowed by the legendary success of Rose O'Neill's creations right from the start. When one looks at his first creation, the Bundie doll, it is a variation on the basic design and concept of the Kewpies. Though his comic characters were artistic achievements in their own right, all of them are hard to fine items. This fact lets one assume that they were available only for the expected life span of a doll (ca. four years).

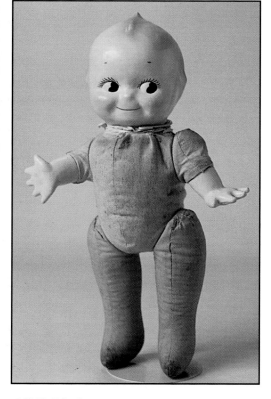

12". Marks: none.
Composition flange head and hands with spread out, pointed fingers. Cloth body and legs are one piece. Upper cloth arms are not stuffed and sewn to shoulders, i.e., no shoulder or hip joints. Molded painted light brown hair and painted black eyes. Closed mouth. Original dress. $250.00.

11½". Marks: none.
Composition flange head and short arms. Cloth body, legs and upper arms are cloth stuffed with cork, jointed with inside disks. ca. 1913 – 1921. $250.00.
Note: Heart-shaped, black eyes.

Left to right:
(1) 7" powder container.
Marks paper heart: Kewpie//Reg. U. S.//Pat. Off.
Paper label on back: Rose O'Nell 1913
Paper label on foot: La Compagnie Vendome//Paris//New York.
All composition, arms jointed only. Metal insert with holes at back of head. Molded painted top knot, black eyes, dots for eye brows. Molded painted blue wings on back. $150.00.
(2) 12". Marks red heart: Kewpie//Design Pat.//No. 43680//Reg. U. S.//Pat. Off. $150.00.
(3) 9", Marks: none. $80.00.

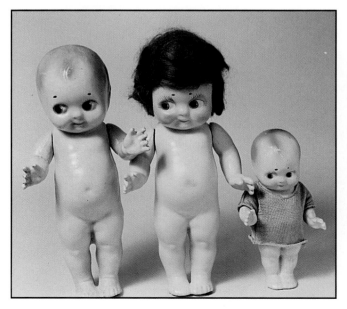

Three Bundie Dolls. See various Toys And Novelties and Playthings ads 1919 – 1921 by Mutual Doll Co., Inc, New York.
11", 11½", and 7".
All three have paper label on sole of feet: Des. Reg. XXc57518//By J.L. Kallus//BUN©DIE.
All composition, jointed at shoulders only with steel spring. Molded painted light brown hair (middle doll brown mohair wig). Painted blue eyes, closed mouth. Small doll has original shirt. Doll was also available with jointed legs. 7", $35.00; 11", $60.00; 11½", $75.00 (wigged).

17". Marks: none.
Sleeve tag: Little//Annie Rooney//Trademark//Copyright 1925 by Jack Collins//Pat. Applied For.
From newspaper cartoon by Jack Collins. Designed by Josef L. Kallus. (Distributed by Geo. Borgfelt & Co.)
All composition, jointed at shoulders and hips, no neck joint. Blond cotton yarn wig, painted black eyes, closed mouth. Molded, painted shoes. All original. (5" all bisque Little Annie Rooney, arms, wig, and tam not original.) $700.00.

Display ad, Playthings, April 1934, advertising the New Marcia Dolls. These dolls have never been seen. It is hoped that inclusion of this ad might bring the dolls to light.

LITTLE ANNIE ROONEY
The famous character appearing daily before millions of newspaper readers. Many styles, fully jointed composition. $1.00 and $2.00 retail.

Illustration from Cameo ad in Playthings, May 1938, showing Little Annie Rooney. While the cartoon version of this doll is familiar and pictured in this section, the doll introduced in this picture has never been seen. It is hoped that inclusion of this illustration might bring the actual doll to light.

5½", 10", and 15", Margie.
Marks on two smaller dolls (red label): Margie//Des. & Copyright//By Jos. Kallus. No marks on large doll. (See Playthings, June 30, 1930.)
All have composition heads and wood segmented bodies and limbs, except for large doll whose body and hands are also composition. All have molded painted light brown hair and painted blue eyes. Small doll has closed mouth, two larger dolls have open/closed with four painted teeth. 5½", $250.00; 10", $350.00 (with original box); 15", $350.00.

Pair 11" Kewpies. Marks: none.
Red heart on chest reads: Kewpie//Des. & Copyright//by//Rose O'Neill.
Arms jointed only, late 30s and 40s. $200.00 each.

11" pair of Kewpies, arms jointed only. Side view showing blue and red wings.

12", Giggles. Marks: none on doll.
Paper hang tag: Giggles//by//Rose O'Neill A//
Cameo Doll.
All composition, fully jointed (identical body and
limbs to Kewpie), molded painted light brown
hair with molded bangs and two holes in back
of hairdo to accommodate a hair ribbon. Painted
blue eyes, closed mouth. All original Nancy &
David Carlson collection. $650.00+ (rare origi-
nality and condition).

11" and 12". Both marked, front: Betty Boop//Des. &
Copyright//By Fleischer//Studios. (Both designed by
J. L. Kallus, Playthings, April 1932.)
Left: Composition head, legs, and hands. Wood body
and segmented arms.
Right: Composition head, body, and hands. Segmented
limbs and shoes of wood. Produced in green, red, and
black outfits. $650.00 each.

18". Marks: Letter "C" on hat and chest. On foot: Art Quality//MFRS//Cameo Products//Port Allegany, Pa.//DES & © BY J.L.K. (J.L. Kallus). Ca. 1930. Composition head and jacket. Hat and segmented limbs are made of wood. Waist joint under jacket. Jointed with steel springs, arms with elastic. Cording on chest is real yarn. Buttons are also separate, glued-on additions. $800.00.

Note: Doll was also used to advertise GE radios, and came inscribed: GE//General Electric//Radio on hat.

11". Label on chest: Pete//Des. & Copyright by J. L. Kallus (Playthings, July 1937). Composition head, wood segmented body with waist joint. Available in two sizes. $350.00.

13". Marks: none. Paper tag: Kewpie//Design and//Copyright by//Rose O'Neill//Cameo Doll. (Playthings May 1938 – Ad stated that dolls were available with soft as well as composition bodies with composition heads.) All composition, fully jointed. Molded painted blond tufts of hair, painted black eyes (no pupils), closed mouth. All original. $350.00.

7½", 12", 16", and 20" (Playthings, July 1937).
Marks: none.

Cloth tag on 12" and 20" doll's suit: Scootles//Reg. U.S. Pat. Off.//Copyright by Rose O'Neill//M'f'd. By Cameo Doll Co.// Port Allegany, PA.

All composition, fully jointed. Molded painted light brown hair, painted blue eyes, closed mouth. Came in six sizes. 7½", $350.00; 12", $450.00; 16", $500.00; 20", $800.00.

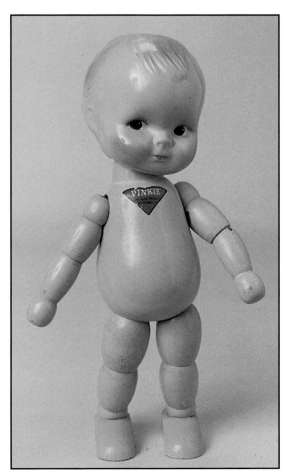

10". Marked in red triangle: Pinkie//Des. & Copyright// by Jos. Kallus.
Composition head, wooden body and segmented limbs. Molded painted blond hair and painted blue eyes, closed mouth. This same size doll has also been seen with differently formed hip joints and composition hands. $300.00.

Marks: *Joy//Des. & Copyr.//J. L. Kallus (Playthings, October 1933).*
15", composition heads with molded hair loop, body and hands. Wooden segmented limbs (composition lower legs with molded, bare feet for doll on right). Molded painted tufts of curls, painted blue eyes, closed mouth. Original costume. $300.00.
11", composition head and hands, wooden body, wooden segmented limbs. $250.00.
Note: 1933 ad also shows a Joy with cloth body and limbs.

13". Marks: Jeep// ©1935//King Features Syn. (Playthings, July 1937/May 1938).
All composition except for wooden segmented tail, fully jointed. $500.00.
Note: Just like Popeye, the Jeep belongs to the cast of characters of the famous cartoon Thimble Theatre by E. C. Segar (1894 – 1938).

14". Marks: Pop//Eye©1935// King//Features//Syn (Playthings, October/November 1936).
Composition head and body, fully jointed, including waist. Wooden segmented limbs. Oilcloth visor on cap, wooden pipe on metal stem, painted features. $450.00.
Note: Popeye was the most famous character of the cartoon strip Thimble Theatre created by E. C. Segar (1894 – 1938).

4½". Marks: POP EYE//© BY K.F.S. Ca. 1936. Wooden segmented doll, strung with elastic. $50.00. Though made of wood, included here for completeness.

17". Marks: none (Champ). All composition, fully jointed. Molded painted brown hair and painted blue eyes, painted freckles across bridge of nose. Original shirt.

Note: Johana Gast Anderton in her book Twentieth Century Dolls shows a well illustrated ad for this doll, wearing an identical shirt. The doll pictured here is on a Patsy-type body assembly and must be a replacement. The ad illustration shows a much stockier body type with specially modeled hands. The left hand is molded into a fist and the thumb of the right hand is very close to the palm. $150.00.

CAMPBELL KID TYPE

12", Campbell Kid type. Marks: none.

Composition flange head. Cloth body and limbs, jointed with outside disks. Sewn on black cloth boots and striped stockings. Molded painted brown hair and painted all black eyes. Closed mouth. Original dress. $125.00.

CARNIVAL DOLLS

In their 1918 Christmas catalog, Butler Brothers called them character dolls. To collectors today, this type is commonly known as carnival dolls, as they were available at carnivals and fairs. Examples with identification marks have been listed under their company headings. Those having no marks have been grouped together here, including the ones that the 1918 Butler Brother Christmas catalog identified as New Era Novelty Co. They too bear no markings.

Most carnival dolls were about 30" tall and came on crude, excelsior stuffed cloth bodies and were pin jointed with outside cardboard or metal disks. In spite of this crude construction, they are a most interesting lot, as all had character heads. Some were dressed in soldier, sailor, and baseball uniforms. (Also see American Doll Co., Effanbee, Elektra Novelty and Toy Co.).

24". Marks: none.
Composition flange head and short arms. Cloth body and limbs, stuffed with excelsior, jointed with outside disks. Molded hair is painted white. Black eyes without pupils, closed mouth, face markings. All original, except shoes. $200.00.

32". Marks: none (Butler Bros. 1918 catalog, New Era Novelty).
Composition flange head and short arms. Cloth body, and limbs stuffed with excelsior and jointed with outside disks. Molded painted brown hair and painted blue eyes, closed mouth. All original except cap and ruff. $200.00.
Note: This clown has no face markings.

28". Marks: none (Butler Bros. 1918 catalog, New Era Novelty Co.).
Composition flange head and short arms, cloth body, upper arms, and bent legs, stuffed with excelsior, jointed with outside disks. Molded painted brown hair and painted blue eyes. Open/closed mouth with two painted upper teeth. Original long slip, old baby coat. $150.00.

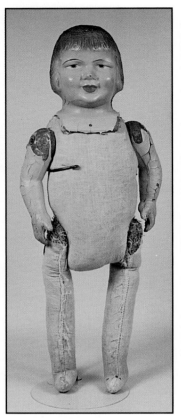

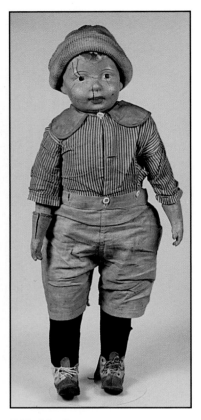

30". Marks: none (Butler Bros. 1918 catalog, New Era Novelty Co.).
Composition flange head, hands, and molded shoes. Cloth body and limbs stuffed with excelsior, jointed with outside disks. Molded painted black hair and mustache, painted brown eyes, closed mouth. All original except for tie. $500.00.
Note: This doll was listed as Comic. Since Louis Amberg and Son had exclusive license to make a Charlie Chaplin doll, other firms could not use that name.

29". Marks: none.
Composition shoulder head and full arms, cloth body and legs, stuffed with excelsior, pin jointed with outside disks. Molded, painted brown hair with bangs and painted blue eyes. Open/closed mouth with four painted teeth. $80.00 (fair).
Note: 1918 Butler Bros. catalog shows this doll dressed in old fashioned bathing suit with cap, bloomers and long sleeve top, slippers. (Also sold by Central Doll Mfg. Co. Inc., N.Y.C., dressed as nurse (January 1921).

29". Marks: none.
Composition flange head and short arms. Cloth body and limbs, stuffed with excelsior, jointed with outside disks. Molded painted brown hair and painted blue eyes. Open closed mouth with four painted teeth. All original except for shoes and stockings. $80.00 (poor).

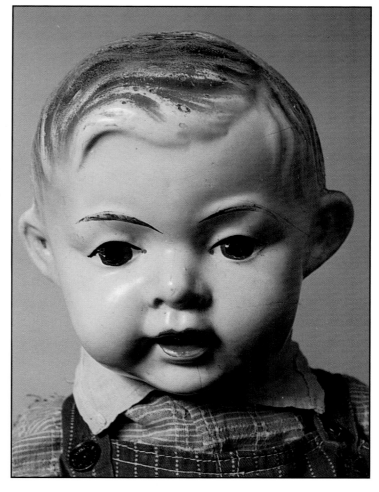

30". Marks: none.
Composition flange head and short arms, cloth body and limbs, stuffed with excelsior, jointed with outside disks. Molded painted brown hair and painted blue eyes. Open/closed mouth with two painted upper teeth. Re-dressed. $150.00.

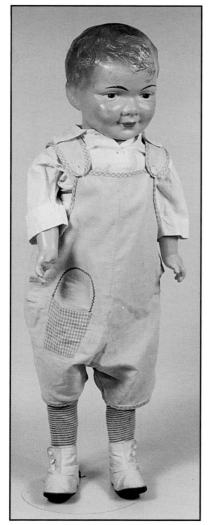

30". Marks: none.
Composition flange head and short arms. Cloth body and limbs, stuffed with excelsior, jointed with outside disks. Molded painted brown hair, painted blue eyes, closed mouth. Re-dressed in old children's clothes. $150.00.

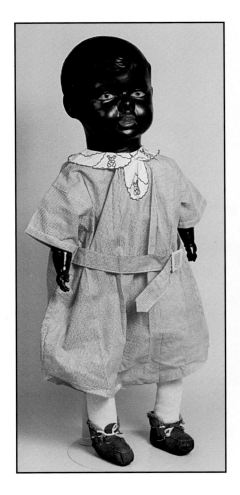 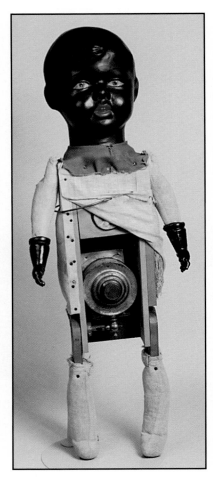 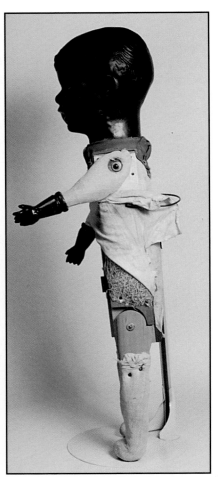

27". Marks: none. Doll with wetting mechanism. (Identical doll without mechanism pictured in Butler Bros. 1918 catalog. See white doll with original long slip.)

Composition flange head on specially constructed body of wood, upholstered with excelsior and covered with cloth. Whetting mechanism is constructed of shallow tin container with screw top and brass fittings, connected to right leg. Lifting leg would release the water from tin container. Also has mama voice set into chest. Short composition arms and head have been painted a deep brown. Black painted hair and olive color eyes. Open/closed mouth with molded tongue and two upper molded, painted teeth. Some paint and eyes original, mostly restored, re-dressed. $300.00.

30". Marks: none. Composition flange head and hands. Cloth body and limbs, stuffed with excelsior, jointed with outside disks. Molded painted hair and painted blue eyes, closed mouth. All original. $250.00.

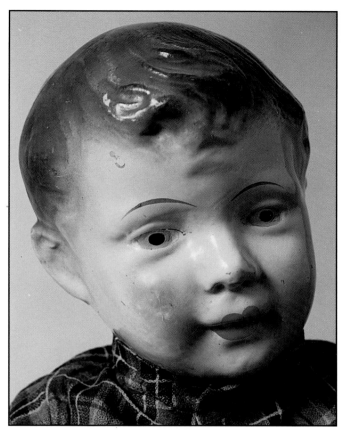

30". Marks: none. Composition flange head and short arms, excelsior stuffed body and limbs, jointed with outside disks. Molded, painted brown hair and painted blue eyes, closed mouth. All original (paper hat came with doll). $150.00 (fair).

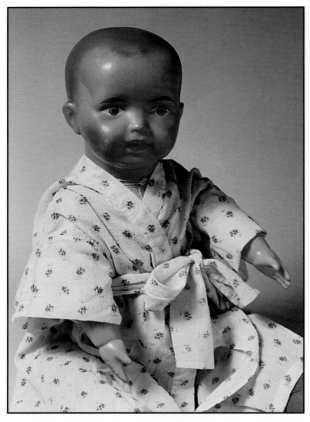

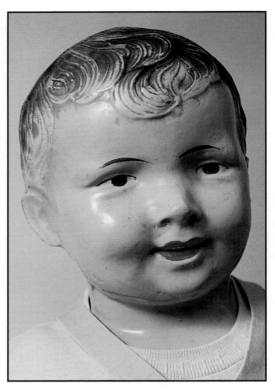

26". Marks: none.
Composition shoulder head on home-made cloth body. Molded painted brown hair and painted blue eyes, open/closed mouth with four molded painted teeth. Re-dressed. $100.00.

24". Marks: none.
Composition flange head and short arms. Cloth body, upper arms and bent legs, jointed with outside disks. Very slightly molded, painted hair and two-tone, painted blue eyes. Open/closed mouth with molded tongue and two painted upper teeth. $150.00.
Note: This is an early glue base, poured head (no seams inside). Walls of head rather thin.

9" (head only), Pinocchio. Marks: none (this would prob-ably make a 30" doll).
Composition flange head, molded painted gray hair and painted blue eyes, closed mouth. For body con-struction see 14" Pinocchio with identical face but shoulder head. $50.00 (head only).

14", Pinocchio. Marks: none.
Composition shoulder head, cloth body and limbs. Fabric of limbs is pink and body covering white. Limbs stuffed with cotton, body with excelsior, stitched joints. Yellow mitten hands are made of the same flannel as the short pants. Blue boots are part of leg casing. Molded painted hair and blue eyes, closed mouth. All original. $80.00.

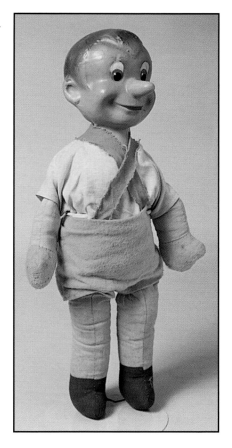

So called Carnival Kewpies were made in many sizes and sold by many companies. Those shown here are 9," 13," 18," and 24" tall, and have original wigs and clothes. Most of them are not marked. All of them are jointed at the shoulders only, with metal springs, have painted black eyes and closed mouths. The 13" one is actually a mechanical doll, who can shake her hips (also see The Zaiden Toy Works). 9", $40.00 (fair); 13", $150.00; 18", $100.00; 24", $150.00.

10". Marks: none.
Molded, painted hair, painted black eyes, closed smiling mouth. Molded union suit and high button boots, painted black. $40.00 (no paint).

16½" Lamp. Marks: none.
All composition on molded base, with molded socket on top of head for light bulb. Drill hole in middle of back to accommodate electric wire. Jointed arms, replaced mohair wig, painted black eyes, closed mouth, refurbished. $150.00.

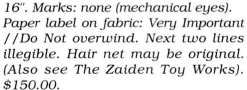

16". Marks: none (mechanical eyes).
Paper label on fabric: Very Important //Do Not overwind. Next two lines illegible. Hair net may be original. (Also see The Zaiden Toy Works). $150.00.
Original dark brown mohair wig. Blue tin eyes move from side to side when mechanism is wound (eyes do not close). Closed mouth. Wind-up mechanism was inserted into body through cut-out in back. Opening was covered with a piece of fabric.

11". Marks, paper label on bottom of molded pedestal: O-U-Kid. Original light blond mohair wig with hair net down to neck. Big black eyes, closed smiling mouth. Original dark blue crepe paper skirt. $80.00.
Note: Doll has molded, bare feet. Made by GEM Toy Co. (Coleman II, pg. 459).

CENTURY DOLL CO.
NEW YORK, NEW YORK
1909 – 1930+

The company was founded by Max Scheuer, a pioneer in the toy business, and his sons Bert and Harold. Max Scheuer retired in 1926 and died in 1933. Century used Kestner bisque heads on many of their later dolls. In 1928 – 1929, they merged with Domec to become the Doll Corporation of America, located in Lancaster, Pennsylvania (Coleman II, pg. 227). Besides bisque headed and cloth dolls, Century did carry a line of composition mama and baby dolls.

21". Marks: Century//Dolls. (WWI period.)
Paper label on body: Sunshine//Copyright 1910 by Sears Roebuck & Co.// Germany.
Composition shoulder head, pin-jointed leather body with cloth lower legs, bisque lower arms. Molded painted brown hair and blue eyes, closed mouth. $150.00 each.

13½". Marks: none.
(May have been sold by Century Doll Co. In 1917, they advertised special "grooves for sewing head to body.")
Composition flange head sewn to body, but not in the Horsman way. Four holes had been drilled for this: two each, front and back, and one on each side. Composition lower arms. Cloth body and limbs, jointed with inside disks. Molded painted blond hair, painted blue eyes, closed mouth. Re-dressed. $125.00.

28". Marks head: Doll Corp.//Of//America.
Shoulder plate: Century Doll Co.//Pat. Appl'd. 1924.
Composition socket head, shoulder plate, full arms and legs to above the knee. Cloth body. Original blond human hair wig, gray sleep eyes, open mouth with four upper teeth. All original. $350.00.
Note: This doll has a reverse neck joint; i.e., the shoulder plate has a depression which receives the socket head. On American composition dolls, the rounded joint part is usually molded onto the shoulder plate.

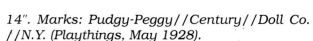

14". Marks: Pudgy-Peggy//Century//Doll Co.//N.Y. (Playthings, May 1928).
Composition shoulder head and limbs, cloth body, jointed at shoulders and hips. Molded painted reddish blond hair with molded hair loop. Green sleep eyes, open/closed mouth with molded tongue. Re-dressed. $150.00 (fair).

CINDERELLA

Top side of dress.

Reverse side of dress.

15". Marks: none. Cinderella with reversible dress.
All composition, fully jointed. Blond mohair wig, brown sleep eyes, closed mouth. All original except for flower wreath. $250.00.

COLEMAN WALKING DOLL

Harry H. Coleman, had invented a special toy and was issued patent No. 1,221,970, on April 10, 1917, for a nonmechanical walking doll. At that time, he was listed as a ventriloquist, living in New York City. He called his invention Dolly Walker, and registered the name as a trademark in the US. The patent was amply illustrated, and text and pictures described body and limbs of a doll, as seen in this section.

While the origin of the doll appears clear, the history of production and distribution is not. Between 1919 and 1920, three separate advertisements seem to picture the identical walking doll. The first ad appeared in the October 1919, issue of *Toys and Novelties*. The double page ad was placed by the Babs Manufacturing Corporation of Philadelphia. The left page showed " 'Babs,' The Walking Doll, height 28 inches." She had a short mohair wig and painted eyes. The right-hand page of the ad dealt with infringement: " 'Babs,' the walking doll, is manufactured and sold by the 'Babs' Manufacturing Corporation under United States Patent No. 1,221,970 granted on the tenth day of April, A. D. 1917, which patent it owns of record." The last paragraph read as follows: "The real Babs will always bear this company's trade mark: 'Babs', The Walking Doll. Refuse all others as infringements." No prices were given in this ad.

The most extensive advertisement was placed by the Wood Toy Company, Inc. of New York City for "Dolly Walker, The Only Natural Walking Doll. She is 28 inches tall...." Pictured is the same doll, but she has a real human hair wig with long curls and seems to have sleep eyes. Wholesale and retail prices were quoted in detail, as the doll was available in either gingham, organdy, or fancy net dresses, with painted or sleeping eyes, and with painted or real hair wig. "Ringlet Wigs, $3.00 per Dozen Extra." They also made the following statement in this ad: "One New York dealer sold over 1,000 last season in three months at a profit of $5,000. Any dealer can do proportionately as well by demonstration" (*Playthings*, August 1920).

The third ad was placed by the Manhattan Doll Co., Inc. of New York City (*Playthings*, June 1919) for "Walking Doll, Made in America, The Sensation of Fifth Avenue." They also quoted a height of 28", and the doll illustrated seems to have painted eyes and is wearing a similar long curl, human hair wig as seen in the Wood Toy Co. ad. They quoted retail prices for a "beautifully dressed doll as pictured, or (dressed) as soldier, sailor, or boy without wig." The ad also mentioned that their prices to dealers allowed a very wide margin of profit.

There is no doubt in this writer's mind that the dolls pictured in the three ads are identical versions of the doll, including the composition shoulder head, with squarish shape of face and an open/closed mouth with two painted teeth. The turned, wooden legs on this doll are very distinctive. They are not realistically shaped as on other dolls but look like wooden dowels and have peculiarly, shallow feet. All three ads present pictures large and clear enough to identify these features as being the Coleman walker.

Nothing further was found that would have explained what else, if anything, happened in the matter of legal rights, or would have further explained the relationship of the above three companies to Harry H. Coleman and his walking doll. However, the Colemans, in their *Encyclopedia*, Vol. I, pg. 156, do report that Emma Clear, well-known dollmaker and owner of the famous Humpty Dumpty Doll Hospital in Los Angeles, bought a half interest in the patent rights of Coleman's Dolly Walker in 1922.

Examples have been seen with a wire covering on the torso or a cardboard one as illustrated in this section, with painted hair or with mohair wig. A sleep eye version with a human hair wig, as advertised by the Wood Toy Co., Inc., has never been located.

28". Marks: none on shoulder head.
On underside of body platform: Patent In The USA//Other Patents Pending//Patents Applied For In Other Countries.
Numbers on right leg: 30336.
Composition shoulder head and lower arms, wooden body frame with cardboard cover, wooden upper arms, legs, and feet. Jointed at elbows and knees with metal hinges. Knee hinges are loaded with springs, so that knee joint will shut automatically when there is no pressure on the leg.* Light blond, original mohair wig, painted blue eyes and open/closed mouth with two painted teeth, multi-stroke brows. Original underwear, stockings, and shoes. Dress and hat are old but seem homemade. $350.00.
*(Pin jointed at hips).

Side view of wooden leg of Coleman Walker. Note the rather shallow foot and rounded sole. Metal hinge was installed in back of the knee.

Coleman Walker, undressed, showing body construction.

DOGS

16". Marks: none. 1930s.
Composition flange heads, painted features, open/closed mouths. Mama-type cloth bodies stuffed with cotton (no crier). $110.00 ea.

DOLL CRAFT NOVELTY CO. NEW YORK

16", Canadian Mounty. Marks: none (Made by Reliable, Canada, but probably sold by Doll Craft Novelty Co., New York). Composition flange head and lower arms. Cloth body, upper arms and legs stuffed with excelsior, stitched hip joints. Molded painted brown hair and painted eyes, closed mouth. All original. Epaulettes marked R.C.M.P. (Royal Canadian Mounted Police). $350.00.

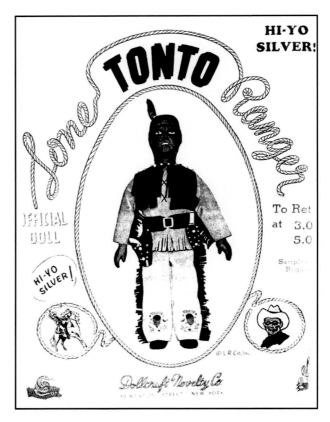

Display ad (Playthings or Toys and Novelties, 1937) advertising their Tonto doll. It seems that for this doll the same head was used as for the Canadian Mounty (produced by Reliable of Canada). $350.00+ depending on size/condition.

Display ad (Playthings or Toys and Novelties, 1937) advertising their Lone Ranger doll. It seems that for this doll the same head was used as for the Canadian Mounty (produced by Reliable of Canada). $350.00+.

In 1928, Domec merged with Century Doll Co., to form the Doll Corporation of America. The name Domec was kept after the merger as a trade name. They manufactured popular priced dolls for Carnivals, premiums and syndicated stores. (Coleman II, pg. 355).

13", Baby and Pillow. Marks: none but came with remnant of original box marked DOMEC DOLLS — (1920s). Composition flange head and short arms. Cloth body and limbs stuffed with cotton. (Similar construction to Dream Baby: squarish body and straight legs, with stitched hip joints.) Molded painted hair. Gray tin sleep eyes, closed mouth. Original slip and long gown, receiving pillow. $200.00.

VICTOR EKHARDT TOY CO. BROOKLYN, NEW YORK

We're In The Army Now!

Forward March!
with
VICTOR ECKARDT'S
MILITARY DOLLS
To Retail At $1.00

Feature these timely big value sellers now and right throughout the year for volume sales.

Write us today

VICTOR ECKARDT TOY CO.
132 Greenpoint Avenue   Brooklyn, New York

Display ad shown in June 1941 issue of Playthings. This ad has been included as dolls have been seen unmarked and can easily be identified by their large, cloth feet with cardboard insert sole. Doll on left in ad is all composition. 14", $100.00.

29", without hat. Marks: none, (See Playthings, June 1941 and October 1942).
Inscription on badge: Junior Police.
Composition flange head, cloth body and limbs (red, white, and blue plush), cardboard soles in feet, no joints. Plastic belt, handcuffs and wooden club, badge. Molded painted brown hair and painted blue eyes, closed mouth. $300.00.

ELEKTRA TOY & NOVELTY CO.
NEW YORK CITY
1912 – 1920

Collectors have been fascinated with the dolls sold by this company. Some were very large with distinctive heads on crude, excelsior stuffed bodies (so called carnival dolls). They were sold at fairs and carnivals. The firm also offered good quality all composition babies with unusual head sockets and jointed wrists.

All Elektra dolls are hard to find, and it has been frustrating that no additional information about products or the company has come to light. By chronologically examining and evaluating available data, it is hoped to at least establish some order.

In a June 1912 *Playthings* ad placed by the Elektra Company, they advertised themselves as "Manufacturers of Stuffed Animals and Unbreakable Dolls." Pictured were a Doggie Muff, a stuffed poodle, and a K & R 100 copy composition doll with cloth body and limbs. Their October 1912 ad again showed the muff and a pair of dolls called Amy and Laurie. The latter was a tie-in with the *Little Women* (Louisa M. Alcott) show just then playing in New York. The illustration in the ad shows that the Amy doll was a composition version of the German Heubach coquette with the molded, three-dimensional hair bow on the right side of her head. The Laurie doll has never been seen. It would be difficult to identify existing K&R 100 copies or coquettes as being Elektra, as these two molds were used by other American companies as well.

32", Dutch Girl. Marks: Elektra T. NC. NY.//Copyright. (See Playthings, February 1915, same doll in college girl costume.)
Composition flange head and short arms. Cloth body, upper arms, legs stuffed with excelsior and jointed with outside disks. Molded painted brown hair and painted blue eyes, open/closed mouth. All original clothes. $400.00.

The Colemans report in their *Encyclopedia*, volume I, that in 1914, Elektra "copyrighted three doll's heads, all designed by Ferdinand Pany." Most Elektra dolls bear a strong resemblance to German Kestner bisque babies, like the #211. One assumes that Mr. Pany made molds from German bisque heads and added on various hair styles, with a part for the boy and a big, flat bow and elaborate hairdo for the girl. The latter hair style is quite different from that of the Heubach coquette copy, whose hairbow is not flat but quite three dimensional. (This has to be kept in mind when trying to identify dolls from illustrations.) The Pany heads were obviously the ones used for the carnival dolls pictured in this section. (The third Pany head was for a black doll, according to the Colemans. See sitting black doll illustrated.)

The February 1915 ad shows a lineup of boy and girl dolls. Five sizes for the boys (same head as the jockey seen in this section) and two sizes for the girls (for the large one, same head as Dutch girl).

Finally, a September 1916 ad illustrated and advertised their 24" all-composition baby with jointed wrists, as seen here.

The Kewpie-type Rosy-Posy dolls seem to have been introduced last. A paper sticker on their base indicates a copyright date of 1917. The smaller one of these was also a copy of a German doll.

If one were to guess why Elektra Toy & Novelty did not survive the shake-out after the end of World War I, it was probably their lack of innovation. However fascinating Elektra's adaptations of German dolls are to collectors today, more was obviously needed at the time to meet renewed German and also domestic competition.

 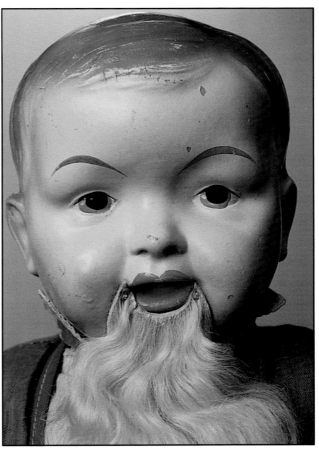

30", Uncle Sam. Marks: Elektra T.N.C. N.Y.//Copyright.
Composition flange head and short arms. Cloth body, upper arms and legs pin jointed with outside disks. Molded painted light brown hair and painted blue eyes. Deeply molded open/closed mouth. Nailed on goatee still attached to skin. (One assumes that when new, the nails were not visible.) All original. $500.00.
Note: Face has very much faded and is almost white.

29", Jockey. Marks: Elektra T.NC.NY.//Copyright (Playthings, February 1913).
Composition flange head and short arms. Cloth body and limbs stuffed with excelsior, jointed with outside disks. Molded painted brown hair and blue eyes, open/closed mouth with molded tongue. All original jockey uniform. $200.00.

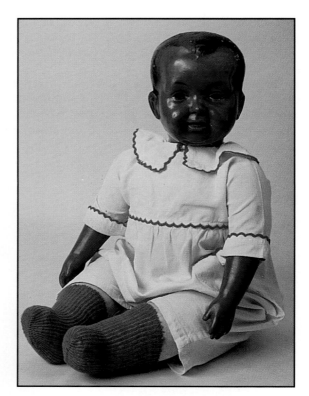

20". Marks: Elektra T. NC NY.//Copyright. Composition flange head and lower arms, appropriate old body with bent legs jointed with inside disks. Molded painted black hair and painted brown eyes, open/closed mouth. Re-dressed. $250.00.

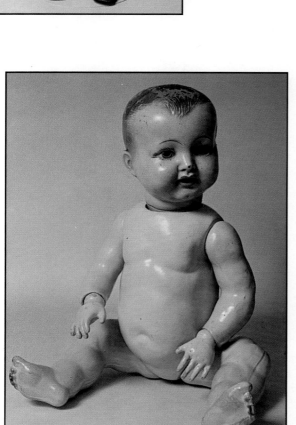

22". Marks: Elektra T.N.C. NY//Copyright (Playthings, April/ September 1916. Wigged version was called Chubbie and Tootsie Wootsie.)
All composition, fully jointed including wrists. Molded painted brown hair and painted blue eyes. Open/closed mouth. $350.00.
Note: This is a socket head with a hook screwed into underside of wooden section for stringing. Also note yellowing of composition parts. May have been varnished instead of oil painted.

16". Marks: ETAN Co. N.Y.
All composition, fully jointed with bent legs. Molded painted brown hair and painted blue eyes, open/closed mouth, re-dressed. Head all original body/limbs repainted. (Same socket head as 22" baby.) $200.00.

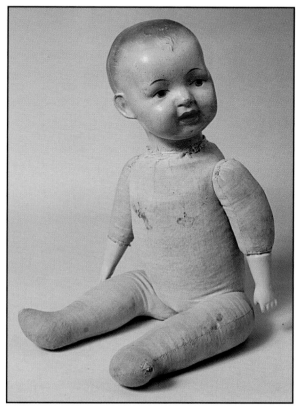

17". Marks: Elektra T. NC. NY.
Composition flange head and short arms. Cloth body, upper arms, and bent legs. Molded painted brown hair and painted blue eyes. Open/closed mouth. Body assembly is contemporary but not original to this head. $150.00.

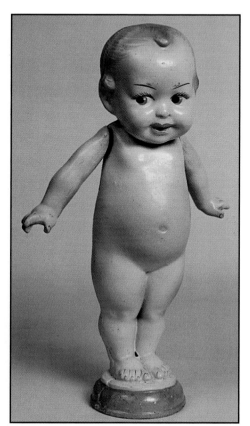

11", Rosy-Posy. Marks on bottom of base: Made by Elektra. Toy & Novelty Co//Rosy-Posy (picture of rose) Copyright 1917 (in small circle)//New York U.S.A.
All composition molded all in one piece, except for arms. Molded hair wisp in front/sides. Hair is not airbrushed but painted with light brush strokes. Blue eyes painted to side. Open/closed mouth with two upper, molded teeth. Note nicely outlined toes, fingers, and nails. (Copy of German doll.) $125.00.

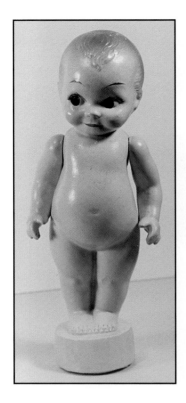

13". No marks on doll, but paper label on bottom reads *Made By Elektra Toy & Novelty Co.//Rosy-Posy//Copyright 1917//New York, U.S.A.* (in the middle of round paper sticker is a red rose).
All composition with molded-on base, jointed at shoulders only. Painted light brown hair and black eyes to right. Closed mouth. Red painted toenails and toe separations. $80.00 (replaced arms).

EMPIRE TOY MFG. CO.
17 BOWERY
NEW YORK, NEW YORK

19", Charlie. Marks: none (*Playthings*, August 1916).
Composition flange head and short arms. Cloth body and limbs, jointed with outside disks. Cloth black boots are part of leg casing. Molded painted black hair and painted brown eyes. Black mustache on upper lip, closed mouth. All original including cane. $350.00.
Note: Since Louis Amberg & Son had exclusive rights for a Charlie Chaplin doll, Empire could call theirs only Charlie.

EUGENIA DOLL CO.
NEW YORK, NEW YORK

Beginning in 1946, Eugenia Doll Co. vigorously advertised their products with well designed and illustrated full-page ads or even double page spreads in the trade magazines *Playthings* and *Toys and Novelties*. It is not clear how long before that date the company was in existence. As these ads indicate, they produced the usual variety of popular babies and children made of composition. One notice in *Playthings* dated April 1947, indicated that they were addressing the higher end market and that their dolls were available at such stores as Macy's, Bloomingdale's, and Arnold Constable. Even the 10" all composition toddlers seen in this section are of unusually high quality for such a small doll (smooth composition, well finished seams, excellent decoration).

When, in 1948, Montgomery Ward introduced their Personality Pla Mate dolls, which were produced for them by Eugenia, quality was again stressed. As we can see from the 1948 Montgomery Ward catalog page, some of the Pla Mate dolls were made of composition and some of hard plastic. While composition as a doll-making material was eventually phased out, Eugenia continued to offer high quality dolls made of hard plastic.

Page from 1948 Montgomery Ward Christmas catalog showing a set of five Personality Pla Mate dolls, made by Eugenia exclusively for them. The two large dolls are made of hard plastic and the three smaller ones of composition. Large dolls were 18" and 20" tall. Smaller dolls were 16". Doll in yellow dress was listed as 17" tall, but extra inch may have been accounted for by a higher wig. Smaller dolls were called Kathryn (Kathie), Sandra (Sandy), and Roberta (Bobbie). 18" Carolyn (Carol). 20" Barbara (Babs).

16". Marks: none. This is one of the Personality Pla Mate dolls made for Montgomery Ward by the Eugenia Doll Company (Playthings, December 1948).

All composition, fully jointed. Platinum blond synthetic wig (probably a replacement, as catalog specified "mohair"). It is also not clear if this is an original outfit. It has snap closures. Eugenia mentioned buttons and button holes for closures on garments. $250.00.

10", Twin dolls with sleeper carrying case (12x9x19"). Marks: none (Playthings, May 1947. Janie and Johnnie were sold in 10", 12", and 14", no mention of trunk).
All composition, fully jointed. Molded painted dark brown hair, blue sleep eyes, closed mouths. All original, including bedding and curtains (not sleepers). $400.00.

10". Marks: none.
Pants tag: Made in U.S.A.//Eugenia Doll Co., N.Y. 3, N.Y.//America's Finest.
All composition, fully jointed. Molded painted brown hair, blue sleep eyes, closed mouth. All original. $150.00.

FLEISCHAKER & BAUM
MANUFACTURERS OF EFFANBEE DOLLS

Bernard E. Fleischaker and Hugo Baum formed a partnership in 1910. Walter Fleischaker, brother of Bernard, was also involved. Compared with such established enterprises as E. I. Horsman & Co. or Louis Amberg & Son, they were the new kid on the block. Although many similar, small companies were created and disappeared during the first decade of composition dollmaking, Fleischaker & Baum were here to stay. By the mid-1920s, this company was on their way to being a leading manufacturer of composition dolls. Their early glue base composition parts (marked "Deco") were produced by Otto Ernst Denivelle (Coleman II, pg. 335 and 336).

Early in their career, Fleischaker & Baum understood the value of trademarks. Out of the initials of their last names they created the acronym Effanbee. EFF for Fleischaker and BEE for Baum. Effanbee was used as early 1913 as a name for their line of dolls and registered as a trademark in 1918 (Coleman I). In their 1915 catalog, every page was headed with the word "Effanbee" within a border. Soon, their dolls were simply known as Effanbee Dolls. The company strove for quality and advertised it well.

During the 1920s, Effanbee offered a broad line of mama doll babies and children, but also reacted to other important happenings in the doll business. One of the big events of the 1920s was the very successful introduction of the bisque head Bye-Lo Baby by Grace Story Putnam and sold by Geo. Borgfeldt & Co. in 1922. Like many other firms, Effanbee responded with a doll that looked very similar (Baby Effanbee and Pat-O-Pat). But they also came out with infants that were successful in their own right, such as Bubbles, which was introduced in 1924.

Of course, Effanbee's big break came with the introduction of the 14" all-composition Patsy in 1928. Soon Patsy had smaller and larger siblings. Clever promotion and advertising kept this line of dolls alive right through the 30s.

In 1933 (*Playthings*, September 1933), Effanbee presented a particularly clever promotional idea. A Patsy Fan Club was established with its own magazine, *The Patsytown News*, published by Fleischaker & Baum. An ad in the October 1933 issue of *Toys and Novelties* announced that "Over 200,000 Little Girls will see this Newspaper." In it, the Effanbee dolls were treated like real children. They had tea parties and other dolls dropped in for visits (always Effanbee dolls). *Patsytown News* also reported on the doings of real live people like Aunt Patsy. Aunt Patsy traveled throughout the country, visiting the toy departments of large department stores in big cities, demonstrating Effanbee dolls. Children could write to Aunt Patsy, and the letters were published in "Aunt Patsy's Corner" in the *Patsytown News*. New dolls were regularly introduced to the children. Extensive articles praised their wonderful, large wardrobes, and the children were invited to come to the local toy store to see them. One wonders how parents reacted to *The Patsytown News*. Similar to modern TV advertising, the children were reached directly, whereas toy ads in magazines were read by the parents only.

Mama dolls were still made in the 30s. During this decade, the all rubber, drink and wet Dy-Dee Baby certainly was Effanbee's most successful introduction. At the time, Ideal came out with their Shirley Temple Doll and the Alexander Doll Company with the Dionne Quintuplets. Effanbee created dolls in the image of W. C. Fields and Charlie McCarthy. The company held a unique position with the American Children created by Dewees Cochran and the Historical Series. The Anne Shirley/Little Lady doll was very popular throughout the 1940s.

Fleischaker & Baum was sold to Noma Electric Corporation in 1946 (*Toys and Novelties*, March 1946). Management was retained and assurances given that Effanbee policies would not change. Apparently things did not work out as well as expected. According to M. Kelly Ellenburg, author of *Effanbee, The Dolls with the Golden Hearts*, Noma had ownership until 1953, after which point Bernard Baum (son of Hugo), Perry Epstein, and Morris Lutz formed a partnership and bought back the company. To this day, Effanbee has remained a manufacturer of high quality dolls.

14". Marks: none.
Composition flange head and molded, painted laced boots. Brown plush body, arms, and upper legs. Separate piece of plush attached to waist. Brown leather belt and neck bank are replacements. Jointed at shoulders and hips. Painted green eyes, open/closed mouth with six painted teeth. (Face has been touched up.) $400.00.

Fleischaker & Baum ad, Playthings, February 1912.
Note: The similarity of Foxy Teddy Bear's molded head with that of the plush body cat seen above.

Baby Dainty, Johnny Tu Face, and Miss Coquette were some of the earliest dolls advertised by Effanbee after Foxy Teddy Bear (*Playthings*, June 1912).

14". Marks: none (Baby Dainty – Playthings, June 1912). Doll has identical hands with extremely narrow wrists seen on Johnny Tu Face, a doll also shown in the 1912 ad. Composition flange head and short arms. Cloth body and limbs jointed with inside disks. Light brown hair shows hardly any modeling. Painted blue eyes, closed mouth. Old clothes. $125.00.

15". Marks: none (Johnny Tu Face – Playthings, June 1912).
Composition flange head and short arms. Cloth body and limbs, curved legs with black boots that are part of the leg casing. Molded painted hair and blue eyes, open/closed mouth with eight molded/painted teeth. One molded painted tear on crying face. All original. $350.00.

*12". Marks: DECO. See their 1915 catalog.
Composition flange head, cloth body and limbs
jointed with outside disks. Black cloth boots.
Molded painted brown hair with molded hair
ribbon and bow, painted blue. Painted brown
eyes, open/closed mouth with white line
between lips. Original dress. $150.00.
Note: Copy of German bisque head Heubach
Coquette.*

*15", Coquette. Marks: DECO. See their 1915
catalog.
Composition flange head and short arms.
Appropriate old cloth body and limbs, jointed
with outside disks. Molded painted brown hair
with molded hair ribbon that is same color as
hair. Molded bow has been partly cut off and a
hole drilled through the remaining protrusion to
accommodate a hair ribbon (identical hair modeling as smaller Coquette). Painted blue eyes to
side, open/closed mouth with white painted
line between lips. Old dress. $200.00.
Note: Copy of German bisque head Heubach
Coquette.*

Early Infants (ca. 1912) with Cloth Bodies

If anyone has ever wondered why so few of Effanbee's early infant dolls are known, it may be that
they were not recognized as such by collectors because of their slightly curved legs and black cloth
boots. This realization dawned when the following dolls were examined. They came in an original short
infant dress and a long christening gown. Yet, both had only very slightly curved legs and black cloth
boots (boots actually part of the leg casing).

14". Marks: 124N.

Flared composition head and lower arms. Cloth body, upper arms, and legs, jointed at shoulders and hips with inside disks. Painted brown hair, some modeling in front, painted blue eyes. Mouth with drill hole. All original. $150.00.

Note: Mouth area has been modeled with a slight pucker.

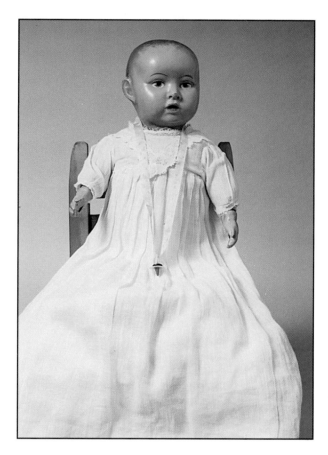

14". Marks: F.+ B. – N.Y.//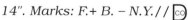

Flared compositon head and short arms. Cloth body, upper arms, and legs, jointed with inside disks. Very slightly molded, painted hair and painted blue eyes, open mouth. All original. $150.00.

Note: This may be an open mouth Baby Dainty.

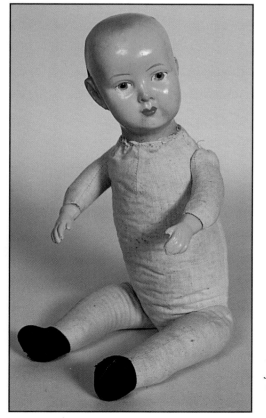

15". Marks: F. + B. – N.Y.// ⓒⓞ

Flared composition head and hands, cloth body and limbs, jointed with inside disks. Painted light brown hair with almost no modeling, painted blue eyes, closed mouth. $80.00. (No original clothing but constructed in the same manner as the previous two dolls.)

11". Marks: F. + B. – N. Y. (has so-called Horsman hands). Composition flange head and hands. Cloth body and limbs jointed with inside disks. Sewn in striped stockings and black cloth boots. Molded painted black hair with short bangs and molded loop on top of head. Painted black eyes, closed mouth. Re-dressed. $250.00.

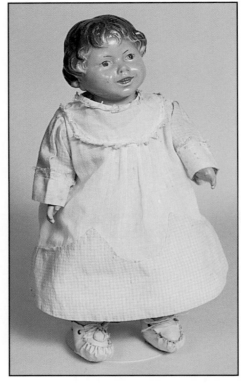

14". Marks: none (resembles Johnny Tu Face – very slim wrists).
Flared composition head and short arms. Cloth body, upper arms, and legs, jointed with outside disks. Elaborately molded, painted hair and painted blue eyes. Open/closed mouth with four upper and four lower molded, painted teeth. Old clothes. $250.00.

15". Marks: 364.
Flared composition head and short arms. Cloth body, upper arms, and legs, sewn-in black boot, jointed with inside disks. Molded painted hair and painted blue eyes. Puckered mouth with hole that does not go through. Squeeker in body in front. When pushed in, it still emits a faint whistle. All original. $150.00.
Note: This head is a copy of K*R #115 – German bisque head (Fiammingo head). With non-puckered mouth, this doll, named Billy Boy, is shown in Effanbee 1915 catalog.

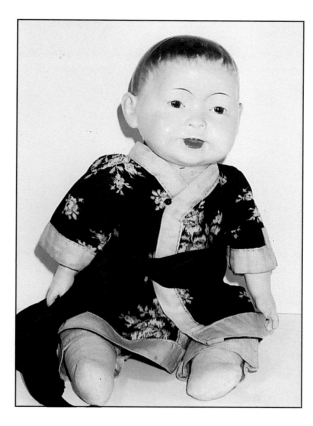

14", Oriental Baby. Marks: none. Label on kimono sleeve: Effanbee//Trade Mark (copy of bisque headed Kestner #243) ca. 1914..
Composition flange head and short arms. Cloth body, upper arms, and bent legs, jointed with inside disks. Molded painted black hair and painted brown eyes. Open/closed mouth with two upper molded, painted teeth. All original. $350.00.
Kathie Hill collection.
Note: Doll was also offered in 17" size with human wig.

Creative Use of German Bisque Heads in Domestic Mold Making

During the first decade of American composition dollmaking from 1910 to 1920, most companies copied some German doll heads. The trade magazines *Playthings* and *Toys and Novelties*, for example, featured countless advertisements by various firms showing dolls looking similar to the German Kestner doll No. 211. Most of the early composition dolls were not marked, and one would not be able to tell one Kestner No. 211 copy from another, were one to trace them back to a specific manufacturer.

Additional popular German bisque doll heads were used in mold making. Usually, little or nothing was changed. Fleischacker & Baum (Effanbee) sometimes departed from this practice and considerably altered some features. Effanbee marked their heads with numbers and the dolls produced from these molds can be found illustrated in old Effanbee catalogs. This helps in the study of their dolls.

The most easily traced head used by Effanbee in their mold making was that of the ever-popular Grumpy doll. This German bisque headed doll was manufactured by Gebrueder Heubach. Grumpy had a molded hairdo with very distinctively modeled curls. This makes verification from one doll head to another rather easy. Besides making an identical copy of the bisque Grumpy, Effanbee designed two variations that only borrowed some basic features. For one of these babies, Grumpy's scowl was smoothed out and the lips changed to a smile, while the squarish shape of the face and very distinctive hair modeling were left in place. Three dimples were added. The 1916 Butler Brothers catalog listed a 20" version of this smiling baby.

For another model, Grumpy's scowl had again been smoothed but this time the lips didn't smile. The corners of the mouth were raised only slightly, producing a rather serious looking face.

The other bisque doll head that was used by Effanbee in their mold making was Kammer & Reinhard's No. 114. When dressed as a boy, Kammer & Reinhardt called this doll Hans and when dressed as a girl it was identified as Gretchen. Unlike Grumpy, Hans and Gretchen had real hair. While the E. I. Horsman firm produced a wigged composition copy of the No. 114 model, Effanbee went another route. The pouty facial features of this famous head were retained, but molded hair was developed for a composition boy named Johnny Jones and a girl called Pouting Bess. Both dolls were pictured in the

1915 Effanbee catalog which was reproduced in Patricia N. Schoonmaker's book *Effanbee Dolls: The Formative Years 1910 – 1929*.

While the German dolls were sold with five-piece composition baby bodies for Grumpy and ball-jointed ones for No. 114, the corresponding American composition dolls were offered on cloth bodies stuffed with cork. They featured curved or straight legs.

14". Marks: DECO//174 (Baby Grumpy, 1915 Effanbee catalog).
Flared composition head and short arms, cloth body, upper arms, and bent legs, jointed with inside disks. Molded painted hair and painted blue eyes. Closed mouth. Re-dressed. $300.00.

15". Marks: 106 backwards (Aunt Dinah, 1915 Effanbee catalog).
Flared composition head and short arms, cloth body, upper arms, and legs, sewn-in striped stockings and black boots, jointed with inside disks. Molded painted black hair and painted brown eyes, open/closed mouth with two painted upper teeth. Re-dressed. Smiling Grumpy face. $600.00.

Left: 20". Marked 108 (1915 Effanbee catalog).
Right: 14". Marked 104.
Flared composition head and short composition arms. Cloth body, upper arms, and bent legs, jointed with inside disks. Molded painted hair and painted blue eyes. Open/closed mouth with two upper painted teeth. Large baby: old romper. Small baby: original clothes. Smiling Grumpy face. 14", $250.00; 20", $400.00.

14". Marks: 34.
Flared composition head and short arms. Appropriate old cloth body, upper arms, and legs, jointed with inside disks. Re-dressed. Serious looking Grumpy face. $150.00.

Three Johnny Jones (1915 Effanbee catalog).
22". Marks: 158.
15½". Marks: 156.
13". Marks: 152.
Flared composition heads with identical hairdos, short composition arms. Cloth body and limbs joined at shoulders and hips. Two larger dolls with inside disks, smaller with outside disks. Large soldier all original. K*R #114 copy with molded hair. 22", $350.00; 15½", $250.00; 13", $150.00.

15". Marks: 166 (Pouting Bess, School Girl, 1915 catalog). Flared composition head and short arms, contemporary cloth body, upper arms, and legs, jointed with inside disks. Molded painted hair and painted blue eyes, closed mouth. Re-dressed. K*R #114 copy with molded hair. $350.00.

Close-up of 15" Pouting Bess.

12". Marks: 162 (Pouting Bess, 1915 Effanbee catalog).
Flared composition head, cloth body and limbs, jointed with inside disks. Sewn-in black boots. Molded painted brown hair and blue eyes. Closed mouth. Re-dressed. $250.00.
Note: Compare with 15" Pouting Bess Marks: 166. While hair modeling is identical, the face seems to be of a different mold.

Three Betty Bounce dolls (1915 catalog).
12". Marks: 70. Re-dressed.
14". Marks: DECO. Dress tagged: Effanbee (all original).
11". Marks: 70. All original (Tiny Tad).
Composition flange heads and short arms, cloth body, upper arms, and legs, jointed at shoulders and hips, large doll with inside disks. Molded painted dark hair and painted eyes, closed mouth. Large doll: staple for fastening bow. Small doll: molded loop. Two small: black boots. 12", $100.00; 14", $250.00; 11", $200.00.

30". Marks: 802 (Effanbee?). Before 1920. Composition flange head and short arms. Cloth body and limbs are stuffed with excelsior and jointed with large, outside cardboard disks. Elaborately molded light brown hair. Grayish blue eyes with inwardly curved iris/pupil area, two-tone irises, open/closed mouth. Re-dressed. Also see Carnival Dolls. $250.00.

171

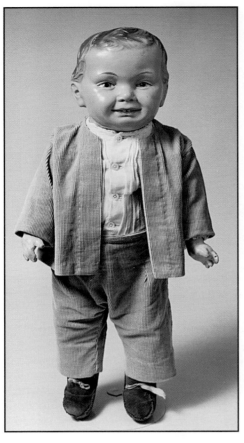

13". Marks: 303.
Flared composition head, cloth body and limbs with stump hands, black cloth boots. Jointed with outside disks. Molded painted hair and painted eyes, closed mouth. All original. $150.00.

20". Marks: 27c (Effanbee?). 1910 – 1915.
Composition flange head. Old, appropriate body. Molded painted brown hair and painted blue eyes. Open/closed mouth with two molded painted teeth. Re-dressed. $250.00.

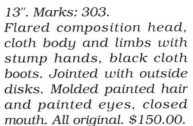

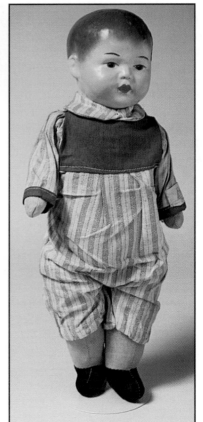

14". Marks: none on doll, sleeve tag: Effanbee//Trade Mark.
Before 1920 (head is made of glue base composition).
Composition flange head, cloth body and limbs jointed with outside disks. Black cloth boots are part of leg casing. Original romper. Head has been restored, left eyebrow original, some of hair. $100.00.

14". Marks: 455.
Composition flange head and short arms, cloth body, upper arms, and curved legs, jointed with inside disks. Molded painted hair and painted blue eyes, closed mouth. Re-dressed. $80.00.

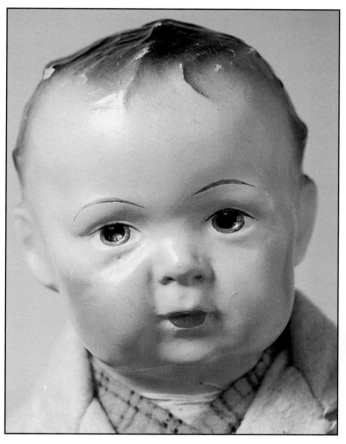

14". Marks: 24 (Baby Huggims as pictured in 1915 Effanbee catalog).
Composition flange head and short arms, cloth body and limbs jointed with outside disks. Sewn on black cloth boots. Molded painted hair and blue eyes, closed mouth. Re-dressed. $250.00.

24", Baby Catherine. Marks: Effanbee. Sleeve tag: Effanbee.
Composition shoulder head and arms to below elbow. Cloth body, upper arms, and full bent legs stuffed with cork, jointed with inside disks. Original dark brown mohair wig. Gray celluloid sleep eyes. Closed mouth, replaced bonnet. $250.00.

"When buying a doll or any stuffed toy, look for the Effanbee label."
Playthings February/March, 1918.

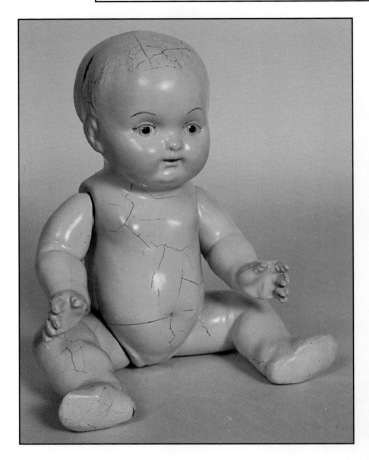

12". Marks on back: Effanbee (in script). Body and head one piece, jointed at shoulders and hips. Faintly molded, painted hair and blue eyes, closed mouth. Bunches of hair come to a point all around the head. $100.00.

7". Marks: Effanbee (in script).
All composition, jointed only at shoulder. Original mohair wig over molded hair, head band. Painted brown eyes and brown skin color, closed, smiling mouth. Molded, painted necklace. See Playthings, June 1918. – "Mid Season Effanbee Novelty Dolls. A winsome toy. Suitable also for ornamental and decorative purposes." A full page ad was illustrated with a picture of this doll. $150.00.
Note: This is a copy of the German bisque Baby Bud.

Babies from Effanbee's 1915 Catalog

Even though they vary in size from 12" to 19", don't have identical markings, and their mouths are treated in different ways, the following five dolls seem to have come from identical head molds, and the face is recognizable in the 1915 Effanbee catalog. To be those of infants, their facial features are quite distinctive. The rather square face has a pointed chin and a well formed, narrow nose. There is very little hair modeling. One can faintly see a pointed shape in front. This doll is illustrated in the 1915 Effanee catalog on several pages. On pages 12 and 13, the models with bent or straight legs with black boots are called yet again Baby Dainty. (The doll shown in the 1912 ads mentioned before and also called Baby Dainty is of a different mold. In the 1920s, yet another popular Effanbee doll would be called Baby Dainty.)

In the 1915 catalog, a doll with white socks and ankle strap shoes (still same head) is called Baby Blanche, and the boy Kutie. On page 19 of the same catalog, the doll is shown in three sizes with painted hair and wigs. All have bent legs. No name is mentioned here. The dolls are advertised as "Semi dressed baby dolls." Only the smallest does not have a pacifier in her mouth. On pages 14 and 15, these babies are shown in long christening dresses, similar to the 11" baby included here. All versions mentioned before wore the shorter type baby dress and caps.

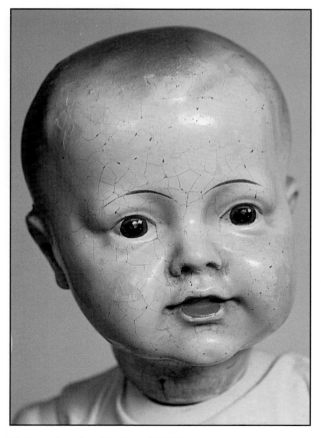 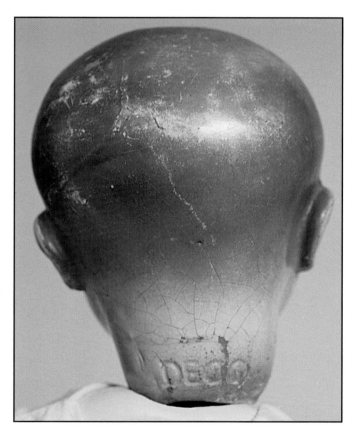

5", head only. Marks: DECO.
May have come on five-piece baby body.
Molded, painted brown hair and eyes. Open/closed mouth. $40.00 (head only).

19". Marks: 7 c.
Composition flange head and hands. Cloth body, upper arms, and curved legs, outside joints. Molded painted brown hair and brown eyes, open/closed mouth with two upper molded painted dark teeth and molded tongue. $80.00.
Note: Disproportionately small composition hands are original.

15". Marks: 54.
Flared composition head and short arms. Cloth body, upper arms, and legs, jointed with inside disks. Brown mohair wig. Painted brown eyes, open mouth with two upper molded teeth. Redressed. $125.00.

14". Marks: Patent Pending. Ca. 1915.
Composition flange head and short hands (right hand modeled into a fist). Cloth body, upper arms, and bent legs, jointed with inside disks at shoulders and hips. Faintly molded, painted light brown hair. Individually rocking gray tin sleep eyes (mounting rod from eye mechanism has poked through at temples on both sides). Open mouth with two molded painted upper teeth, old romper. $125.00.
Note: According to Coleman II, Otto Denivelle was granted a U.S. patent for sleeping eyes, the rods of which were imbedded in the walls of the heads. Because of this description and the flaw visible at the temples (the rods have poked through), it is assumed that this is one of the dolls with the Denivelle sleep eyes. Because of this design flaw, probably not many dolls were sold with this mechanism. For description of the early sleep eyes that did work, see chapter on sleep eyes. (The head was taken off and examined. The doll does not have Ideal sleep eyes.)

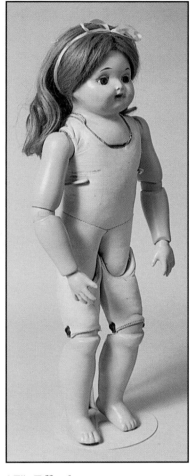

11". Marks: 52.
Flared composition head and short arms. Cloth body, upper arms and bent legs, jointed with outside disks. Molded, painted hair and painted blue eyes. Open/closed mouth with two upper painted teeth. All original. $125.00.

20". Marks: Effanbee (head and back). This is Mary Jane (See Coleman II). Composition socket head on ball-jointed body. Blond human hair wig. Gray celluloid sleep eyes, open mouth. Re-dressed. $250.00.

17". Effanbee.
Composition shoulder head on pin-jointed leather body, ball-jointed limbs, human hair wig, gray tin sleep eyes, open mouth with two upper molded painted teeth. $250.00.

The following three dolls resemble the German bisque head doll Hilda by J. D. Kestner.

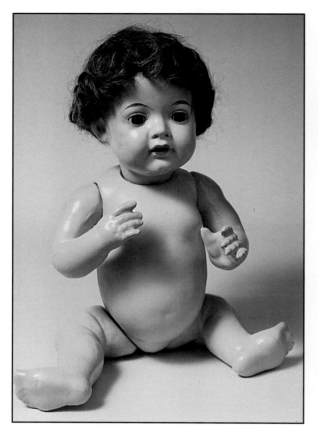

16", Hilda look-alike. Marks: Effanbee (high on crown in back of head).
Composition socket head and five-piece body and limbs, jointed at shoulders and hips. Human hair wig, celluloid sleep eyes, open mouth with two molded, painted upper teeth. Multi-stroke eyebrows and lashes all around the eye opening. Body and wig are contemporary but not original to this head. Wig and body assembly are of Horsman manufacture. $150.00.

14". Marks on back: DECO (Playthings, July 1916).
All composition fully jointed with steel springs, bent legs. Original blond mohair wig. Gray sleep eyes, open mouth with two upper molded painted teeth, doll is very faded. $80.00.

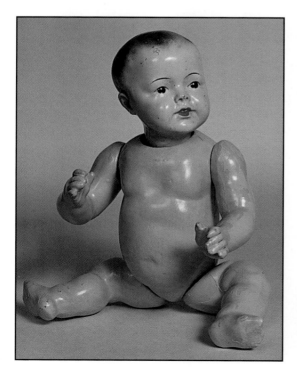

13". Marks head and body: DECO (Playthings, September 1916).
All composition, fully jointed. Faintly molded brown hair, painted blue eyes. Open/closed mouth with two painted upper teeth. $150.00.
Note: Even though much reduced in size and having painted eyes, the resemblance to Hilda is still noticeable.

Fleischaker & Baum produced quality dolls. The quality idea was promoted with slogans such as "Effanbee Durable Dolls," "The Dolls With The Golden Hearts," and "Effanbee Dolls, They Walk, Talk, Sleep."

From 1923 on, every Effanbee doll was accompanied by a metal heart (various inscriptions) on a necklace or bracelet, a round metal pin or, later, by a heart-shaped golden paper hang tag.

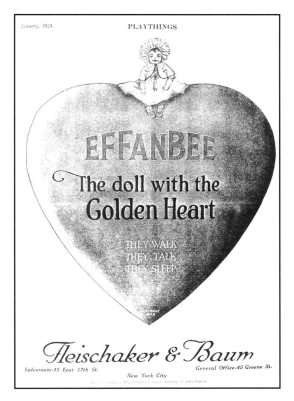

30". Marks: Mae//Starr//Doll.
Composition shoulder plate, arms, and legs to above the knee. Cloth body. Jointed at shoulders, stitched hip joints. Dark brown human hair wig, blue sleep eyes, open mouth with four upper teeth. A phonograph mechanism was inserted in the cloth body, with crank on the side, and the undergarment has appropriate openings for it and slit for access to record mechanism. Mae Starr comes with six nursery rhyme disks. All original with necklace and Effanbee heart pendant. Nancy Carlson collection. $850.00.

20", Betty Lee. Marks: Effanbee (Playthings, August 1924).
Dress Tag: Effanbee//Dolls//Finest and Best.
Blue Bird Pin: Effanbee//Dolls//Finest and Best.
Composition shoulder head and arms, composition legs to above the knee. Jointed at shoulders, stitched hip joints, cloth body. Reddish blond mohair wig over molded hair. Gray celluloid over tin sleep eyes. Open/closed mouth. All original. $350.00.

19". Marks: *Effanbee//Rosemary//Walk Talk Sleep (within oval)//Made In U.S.A. (Playthings, January 1926).*
Composition shoulder head, arms, and legs to above the knee. Cloth body and upper legs, stitched hip joints. Jointed at shoulders. Red mohair wig, gray sleep eyes, open mouth with four upper teeth. All original. $400.00.

25". Marks: *Effanbee//Rosemarie//Walk Talk Sleep//Made in USA.*
Dress Tag: *Effanbee//Dolls//Finest And Best//Made In USA.*
Composition shoulder head, arms and legs to above the knee, cloth body. Jointed at shoulders, stitched hip joints. Blue tin sleep eyes, open mouth with six upper teeth. Original brown human hair wig. All original. Original metal necklace with heart-shaped pendant inscribed "Effanbee." $550.00.

13". Marks: *Effanbee.* Dress Tag: *EFFanBEE.* 1920s.
Composition shoulder head and arms. Cloth body and legs. Jointed at shoulders, stitched hip joints. Dark brown mohair wig. Painted blue eyes, closed mouth. All original, old shoes and socks. $200.00.

16". Marks: Effanbee//Dolls//Walk Talk Sleep. Ca. 1929. Composition shoulder head, arms, and composition legs to above the knee. Cloth body and upper legs. Jointed at shoulders, stitched hip joints. Blond mohair wig over molded hair, Baby Dainty mold. Blue/gray celluloid over tin sleep eyes that can also move from side to side. Open mouth with four upper teeth. All original. $400.00.

14". Marks: Effanbee//Baby Dainty. Ca. 1929. Composition shoulder head and limbs, jointed at shoulders and hips. Cloth body. Molded painted blond hair and blue eyes, closed mouth. All original. $350.00.

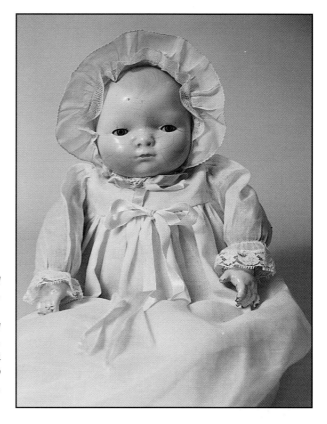

14". Marks: Effanbee (Baby Dainty, Playthings, July 1925; also called Baby Effanbee, Toys and Novelties, February 1925). Composition flange head and arms to wrist. Cloth body and limbs with stitched joints at shoulders and hips, straight legs. Molded painted blond hair and gray tin sleep eyes, re-dressed. Came with painted or sleep eyes and was Effanbee's version of the Bye-Lo Baby. $250.00.

12", light blue outfit, all original.
Marks: Effanbee//Dolls//Walk Talk Sleep.
Tag: Effanbee//Doll//Finest & Best//Made in USA (This is Grumpykins, Playthings, March 1927).
13½", pink romper, black molded shoes repainted.
Marks: same. Romper tag: same.
11", black Grumpykins.
Marks: same. Re-dressed.
18". Marks: Effanbee//Baby Grumpy//Copyright 1923. Bent legs.
26". Marks: Effanbee//Dolls//Walk Talk Sleep. Top of arms also marked Effanbee. Re-dressed.
All have composition shoulder heads, arms, and legs, jointed at shoulders and hips except black doll has cloth legs, stitched hip joints. Pink romper. Molded painted socks and shoes, legs to above the knee, also stitched hip joints.
11", black, $350.00; 12", $300.00; 13½", molded shoes, $350.00; 18", $400.00; 26", $800.00. This is Effanbee's redesigned Grumpy introduced in 1923.

11½", pair of Effanbee Grumpy dolls dressed as Pennsylvania Dutch dolls by Marie Polack. Copyright 1936. (See Effanbee Dolls, The Formative Years, 1910 – 1920, P. N. Schoonmaker.) Composition shoulder heads to below the arms, composition arms and black molded boots. Jointed at shoulders, no hip joints. Painted blue eyes, closed mouth. Mohair wigs and a beard. All original. $500.00 pair.

22". Marks: *Effanbee//Bubbles//Copyright 1924//Made in USA.*
Dress label: *Effanbee//Bubbles//Reg. U. S. Pat. Off.*
Composition head and body to under arms, all composition bent legs and arms, jointed at shoulders and hips, cloth body. Molded painted blond hair, green celluloid sleep eyes, open mouth with molded tongue and two upper teeth. All original. $500.00.

Pat-O-Pat Puppet using Bubbles head. Measurements of pillow 10x14".
Marks on head: *Effanbee Bubbles.*
Marks, round metal pin: *Pat-O-Pat//Trademark //Clap Hands, Clap Hands, 'Til Daddy Comes Home//Effanbee//Dolls.*
Composition flange head and hands, cloth body (no legs). Molded painted blond hair and painted blue eyes, open/closed mouth, all original. $250.00.
Note: Pillow has a slit in back for hand to be inserted to support head and activate hand clapping mechanism in body. Arms move forward and hands clap together. Nancy and David Carlson collection. $250.00.

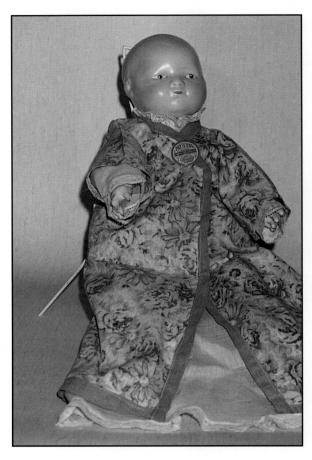

14". Marks: Effanbee/ made in USA. 1920s.
Pin: Pat-O-Pat//Trademark//Clap Hands, Clap Hands, 'Til Daddy Comes Home//Effanbee//Dolls. Composition flange head and hands, cloth body and legs. Molded painted blond hair and painted blue eyes, closed mouth. When mechanism in body is activated by pressing on the doll's stomach, the hands come forward. All original. Arlene and Don Jensen collection. $500.00.

15". Marks: Effanbee//Lovums.
Dress tag: Effanbee//Durable//Dolls//Made In USA. (Was called Baby Evelyn, Patsy Newsletter, March/April 1993, P. N. Schoonmaker.)
Composition flange head and arms, painted cloth body and swinging legs. Molded painted hair and painted blue eyes, open/closed mouth with two upper painted teeth. All original. $350.00.

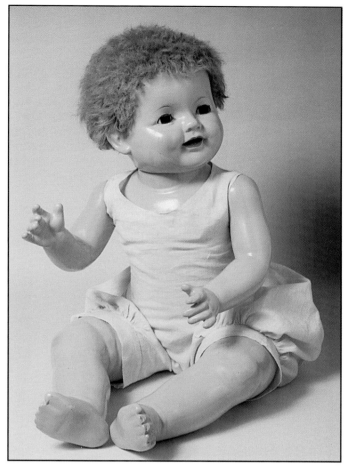

26". Marks: *Effanbee//Lovums//©//Pat. No. 1,283,558. Late 1930s.*
Composition head, shoulder plate, full arms, and bent legs to above the knee, fully jointed, cloth body. Original lamb's skin wig over molded hair, sleep eyes, open mouth with celluloid tongue, two upper and two lower teeth. Original underwear. $400.00.

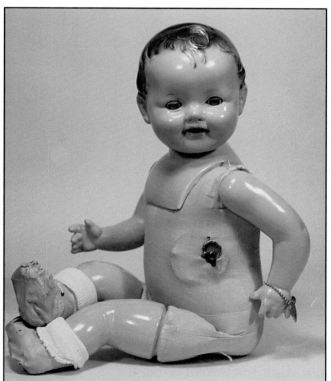

20". Marks: *Effanbee//Lovums//© Pat. 1,283,558.* Heartbeat Doll *(Effanbee, The Dolls With The Golden Heart, M.K. Ellenburg).*
Composition head, shoulder plate, and limbs. Cloth body with inserted heartbeat mechanism. When wound, a ticking sound can be heard. Molded painted hair and brown sleep eyes. Open mouth with metal tongue and two upper and two lower teeth. Original metal heart bracelet. $350.00.
Note: Came gift boxed with stethoscope.

Text on inside cover of Lambkins oval box reads

"A Note to the Proud Owner of This New EFFanBEE Doll: Dolly will surely love her new home and you will have lots of fun caring for her. And you will find her such a wonderful playmate, with her nice pink cheeks, pretty eyes, little tilted nose, and her dainty clothes. Perhaps you will want to name her after someone you love. It will be great fun to pick out a name that will be just right.

Remember Dolly has feelings like yourself, so play with her as you would with your little friends. Treat her gently and be sure to put her to bed on time. Of course, we hope your Dolly never gets sick. But no matter how strong dolls and children are, accidents will happen and they get hurt. If anything like this occurs, our Service Department will be glad to repair the doll, charging only for the new parts required. The address is EFFanBEE Doll Company, 42 Wooster Street, New York City.

Lambkin//Trademark//An//EFFanBEE Durable Doll."

Note: In their October 1931 ads in *Playthings*, Lambkins is also spelled without a "b" and with no "s" at the end.

Also note the reference to their Service Department for doll repair.

16". Marks: Lambkins (Playthings, October 1931).
Composition flange head and limbs wired onto cloth body, loosely stuffed with cotton. Limbs can rotate. No molded hair, painted only. Green glassene sleep eyes, open mouth. Note molded painted, golden baby ring on left middle finger. All original. Came with extra slip and dress and in blue or pink oval box and pillow tied with pink or blue satin bow, matching pink or blue shirt. All original. $600.00 each.

16", Lambkins on original pillow.
Note: Special limbs were designed and made for Lambkins that were not used on any other doll. For most dolls, generic limbs were used. Sometimes, the same arms and legs were used by several companies at the same time. Nancy and David Carlson collection.

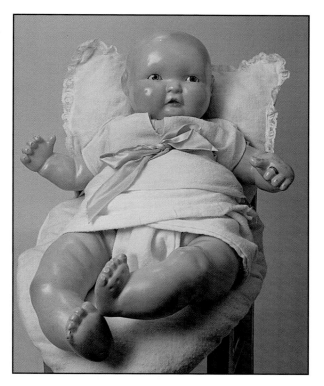

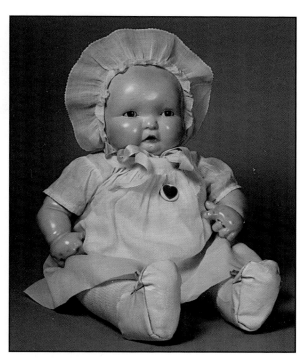

15". Marks: © Lambkins.
Composition flange head and arms are wired to body. Painted golden baby ring on left middle finger. Soft cloth body and legs. Painted blond hair (no modeling), sleep eyes, open mouth. All original including pin. Nancy and David Carlson collection. $375.00.
Note: This version of Lambkins has all cloth legs.

19". Marks: Sugar Baby (Patsytown News, 1936, Vol III, No. 2).
Composition flange head and limbs, cloth body, stitched hip joints. Molded painted blond hair, blue sleep eyes, closed mouth. Bib embroidered "Sugar Baby." All original, except bonnet. $400.00.

17" and 20". Marks: Edgar Bergen's//Charlie McCarthy//an//Effanbee Product. Same information on round metal pin, plus on rim: Reg. No. 396708. Came in three sizes: 15", 17", and 20" (Playthings, March 1938). Composition shoulder head and hands, molded shoes and socks. Cloth body, arms, and legs, stitched joints at shoulders and hips. Molded painted brown hair and painted brown eyes. Cut out, movable jaw, painted lips and row of painted lower teeth. Monocle (on string) has been inserted into hole by right eye. All original. $750.00 each. (For further information on famous ventrilloquist, Edgar Bergen and his puppet, see Doll Reader October 1990, Don Jensen.)

18" (without hat), W. C. Fields, Effanbee, 1938. Marks: none. Composition flange head, hands, and black shoes. Cloth body and limbs. Molded painted brown hair and painted blue eyes. Hinged jaw with painted tongue and lower teeth. Stitched shoulder and hip joints. All original. $950.00. (W.C. Fields, famous comic of stage and screen, 1879 – 1946.)

The Patsy Family

Effanbee's most successful line of dolls were the Patsy dolls. Introduced as Mimi in 1927, this 14" all-composition charmer with painted hair and eyes was named Patsy the next year. Larger and smaller versions of this doll followed in short succession as did numerous variants. A 14" Patsy and 16" Patsy Joan were re-issued in 1946.

Anyone interested in the in-depth study of these famous dolls should consult Patricia N. Schoonmaker's *Patsy Doll Family Encyclopedia*, Vol. I and II.

14". Marks: Effanbee//Mi-Mi//Pat. Pend. Doll.
All composition, fully jointed, molded painted
brown hair with molded hair band, painted blue
eyes, closed mouth, swim suit. Nancy and David
Carlson collection. $400.00 – 500.00.
Note: Mi-mi was advertised only briefly in the
Playthings issue of December 1927. In Playthings,
January 1928, the identical illustrated ad now
featured the doll's name as Patsy.

30", cloth-body Patsy using Marilee mold and
Marilee.
Patsy marks: Effanbee//Patsy//Copyr//Doll.
Marilee marks: Effanbee//Marilee//Copr//Doll.
Composition shoulder heads and full arms, legs
to above the knee, cloth bodies and upper legs.
Jointed at shoulders, stitched hip joints. Blond
and dark brown human hair wigs, blue sleep
eyes, open mouths with four upper teeth. All
original. Nancy and David Carlson collection.
$1,500.00 each.
Note: Both dolls wearing identical style dresses.
Also note that Marilee has small bag attached to
her dress containing her Effanbee heart necklace. Bag marks: "Genuine Human Hair Wig."

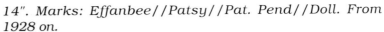

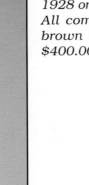

14". Marks: Effanbee//Patsy//Pat. Pend//Doll. From 1928 on.
All composition, fully jointed. Molded painted reddish brown hair and brown eyes, closed mouth. All original. $400.00 – 500.00.

14". Marks: Effanbee//Patsy//Pat. Pend.//Doll.
All composition, fully jointed. Molded painted reddish brown hair and brown eyes. Closed mouth. All original. Hair ribbon has elastic in back so that it will stay on. $400.00 – 500.00.

14". Marks: Effanbee//Patsy//Pat. Pend//Doll.
All composition, fully jointed, medium blond human hair wig, brown sleep eyes, closed mouth all original. Joanne Schaefer collection. $650.00.
Note: This is a factory original variation using a Patricia head and Patsy body.

*14". Marks on head: Effanbee//Patsy Baby.
Marks on body: Effanbee//Patsy.
All composition, fully jointed. Brown, curly wig over molded hair, brown sleep eyes, closed mouth. All original. This is a factory original variation, using a Patsy Baby head. $450.00.*

*11". Marks: Effanbee//Patsy Jr.//Doll. 1930.
All composition, fully jointed. Molded painted brown hair and painted light brown eyes, closed mouth. All original including extra bonnet with rabbit ears. $500.00.*

*11", pair. Marks: Effanbee//Patsy Jr.//Doll.
Pin marks: White Horse Inn//An//Effanbee//Doll.
Front of box marked Patsykins (See Patsytown News, Vol 4, No. 1, 1937).
All composition, fully jointed. Molded painted brown hair and painted brown eyes, closed mouth. All original. $500.00 each.
Note: Costumes inspired by Broadway musical "White Horse Inn," which opened on Broadway, New York City, in 1936.*

9½", George and Martha Washington, 1932.
Marks: Effanbee//Patsyette.
All composition, fully jointed. White mohair
wigs over molded hair. Painted brown (George)
and blue (Martha) eyes, closed mouth. All
original.. Issued on the occasion of George
Washinton's 200th birthday. $600.00 pair.

9". Marks: Effanbee//Patsyette (Toys and
Novelties, August 1931).
All composition, fully jointed. Molded painted
hair and painted brown eyes, closed mouth.
All original. $600.00 pair.

Three Patsyette dolls dressed in versions of "White Horse Inn"
costumes. Nancy and David Carlson collection. $350.00 each.

16". Marks: *Effanbee//Patsy Joan.1931.*
All composition, fully jointed. Molded painted brown hair, green sleep eyes, closed mouth. Original outfit, old shoes and socks. $600.00.

A full-page ad in *Playthings* in their September, 1933, issue announced:
"Now Patsys Have Hair
Striking Improvement In The Famous Patsy Family.
Stylish Personality wigs now grace the heads of Patsy dolls, accenting the beauty of this quick selling family.
This added sales feature is a new exclusive Effanbee Creation warmly welcomed by Merchants — doubly appealing to Little Mothers."

20". Marks: *Effanbee//Patsy-Ann//©
//Pat. #1283558.*
All composition, fully jointed. Blond mohair wig over molded hair, sleep eyes, closed mouth. All original. Nancy and David Carlson collection. $1,000.00.

19". Marks: *Effanbee//Patsy-Ann//©//Pat. #1283558.*
All composition, fully jointed. Molded painted black hair, brown sleep eyes, closed mouth. All original. Robin Tickner collection. $2,000.00+.

22". Marks: *Effanbee//Patsy Lou. 1930.*
All composition, fully jointed. Molded painted brown hair, green sleep eyes, closed mouth. All original clothes marked Effanbee//Durable//Dolls. $600.00.

27". Marks: *Effanbee//Patsy-Ruth. 1936.*
Composition head, swivel shoulder plate and limbs, cloth body jointed at neck and shoulders, stitched hip joints. Brown human hair wig over molded hair, sleep eyes, closed mouth, all original. Victoria Applegate collection. $1,500.00.

27". Marks on head: *Effanbee//Patsy Ruth. Ca. 1935.*
Original box marked Patricia Ruth//Genuine Human Hair Wig// Trademark - Reg.//An//Effanbee//Durable//Doll.
All composition, fully jointed, reddish blond human hair wig, green sleep eyes, closed mouth. All original. Nancy and David Carlson collection. $2,000.00.

30". Marks: Effanbee//Patsy-Mae. 1935.
Composition head, swivel shoulder plate and limbs.
Cloth body. Jointed at neck and shoulders, stitched
hip joints. Blond human hair wig, sleep eyes,
closed mouth. Tagged original clothes (NRA tag).
Nancy and David Carlson collection. $2,000.00.

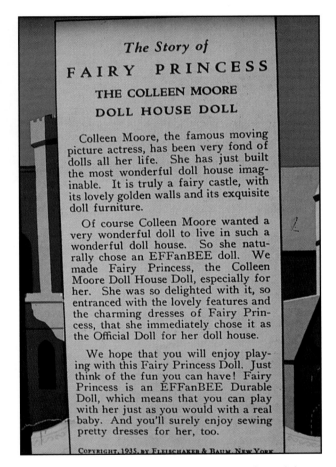

The Story of
FAIRY PRINCESS
THE COLLEEN MOORE
DOLL HOUSE DOLL

Colleen Moore, the famous moving picture actress, has been very fond of dolls all her life. She has just built the most wonderful doll house imaginable. It is truly a fairy castle, with its lovely golden walls and its exquisite doll furniture.

Of course Colleen Moore wanted a very wonderful doll to live in such a wonderful doll house. So she naturally chose an EFFanBEE doll. We made Fairy Princess, the Colleen Moore Doll House Doll, especially for her. She was so delighted with it, so entranced with the lovely features and the charming dresses of Fairy Princess, that she immediately chose it as the Official Doll for her doll house.

We hope that you will enjoy playing with this Fairy Princess Doll. Just think of the fun you can have! Fairy Princess is an EFFanBEE Durable Doll, which means that you can play with her just as you would with a real baby. And you'll surely enjoy sewing pretty dresses for her, too.

COPYRIGHT, 1935, BY FLEISCHAKER & BAUM, NEW YORK

Partial close-up of suitcase cover (inside).

5½". Marks: Effanbee//Wee Patsy. Copyright by F
& B. 1935.
Yellow heart on red pin: Colleen Moore//Fairy
Princess//An EFFanBEE//Doll.
All composition, jointed at shoulders and hips
only. Molded painted light brown hair and painted
blue eyes, closed mouth. Molded painted black
shoes and white socks. Three extra outfits in original
suitcase. $600.00.
Note: This doll was also used for other play sets,
such as a sewing kit of similar arrangement and
size (no reference to Fairy Princess).

*5½". Marks: Effanbee//Wee Patsy.
Two Wee Patsy dolls from doll house set, in their original outfits dressed as maid and cook. Nancy and David Carlson collection. Black, $850.00; maid, $550.00.*

10". Marks: Effanbee//Patsy Baby. Ca. 1932. All composition, fully jointed with bent legs. Molded painted blond hair and green celluloid sleep eyes, closed mouth. All original. $750.00.

8". Marks: Effanbee//Baby Tinyette (on back). 1933.
All composition, fully jointed. Molded painted brown hair and painted blue eyes, closed mouth. All original with original box. $400.00.

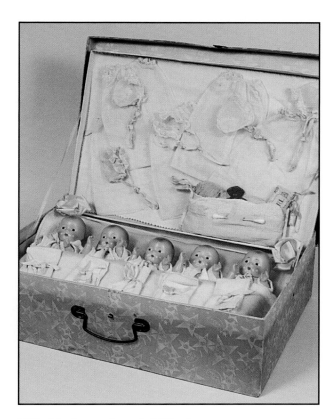

6½". Marks on head: Effanbee.
Marks on body: Effanbee//Baby Tinyette.
All composition, fully jointed, bent legs. Molded painted light brown hair and painted brown eyes, closed mouths. Babies are wearing diapers, simple long cotton gowns, and flannel sacques. They are tucked into a pink blanket trimmed with two satin bows. Pinned on top are five extra diapers. The carrying case has an insert tray. Fastened to it are five long, lace trimmed organdy gowns and bonnets. A cloth bag with a sponge, hot water bottle, bar of soap, and wash cloth is also trimmed with bows. The bag has two punched holes in front and may have held an implement such as a cotton swab. $1,600.00.
Note: This set was obviously sold to compete with Madame Alexander's quintuplets.

9" Patsy Babyette twins in original box.
Marks on head: Effanbee.
Marks on body: Effanbee//Patsy Babyette.
All composition, fully jointed, molded painted brown hair, gray sleep eyes, closed mouths. $600.00 set.

Boxed set of Effanbee Twins, Babyette mold, ca. 1946.
10½". Marks: Effanbee (only).
Composition heads turn and swivel on wooden neck piece. Cloth bodies are tied onto these pieces. Cloth arms and full straight cloth legs have stitched joints. Tied on celluloid hands. Molded painted brown hair, brown tin sleep eyes, closed mouths. Walking harness made of pink cotton tape with brass clips. $1,200.00.
Heart tag front:
I am an//Effanbee//Durable Doll//The Doll//with//Satin /Smooth//Skin.
Inside of double sided tag:
A note to the proud owner of this NEW EFFANBEE DOLL. You will find your Dolly a wonderful playmate, with her dainty clothes, her satin/smooth skin and pretty eyes. You will have lots of fun caring for her.
EFFANBEE Dolls are like real healthy, happy children. They are strong and beautifully finished. That is why they are called EFFANBEE Durable dolls. Their clothes are always stylish and well tailored and can be washed time after time, as they are made of the finest color-fast fabrics.
Back of tag:
A New//Effanbee//Playmate//For ...//From ...//May you and your//dolly have many//happy times together.//Trade Mark Reg.//Made In//U.S.A.

14". Marks on head: Skippy//©//O. L. Crosby.
Body: Patsy//Pat. Pend//Doll.
Pin: Effanbee//Dolls//I Am//Skippy//
Trade Mark//The Real American Boy.
Playthings, January 1929. Toys and Novelties, September
1940, advertising Skippy with magic hands.
All composition, fully jointed. Molded painted blond hair
and painted blue eyes, closed mouth. All original. $600.00.

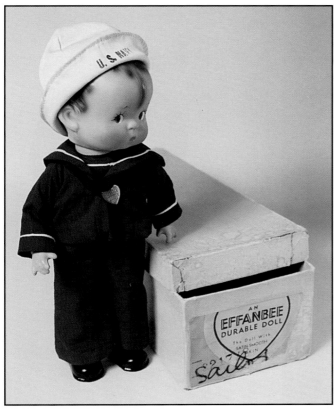

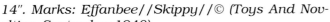

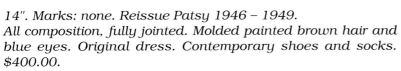

14". Marks: Effanbee//Skippy//© (Toys And Nov-
elties, September 1940).
Metal heart: Effanbee Durable Doll.
Composition head, arms, and legs to above the
knee. Molded boots, ribbed socks and knee are all
painted black. Jointed at shoulders, no hip joints.
Head swivels on wooden neck piece. Cloth body.
All original. $800.00.

14". Marks: none. Reissue Patsy 1946 – 1949.
All composition, fully jointed. Molded painted brown hair and
blue eyes. Original dress. Contemporary shoes and socks.
$400.00.

The Anne Shirley Dolls

Effanbee had two types of Anne Shirley dolls, and this has caused a lot of confusion with collectors.

The movie, *Anne of Green Gables*, had been released in 1934. The main character in this story was named Anne Shirley and played by Dawn O'Day. Effanbee was licensed to sell an Anne Shirley doll, and they used existing members of the Patsy family, including Patricia, for this purpose. *The Patsy-town News* of 1937 (Vol. 4, No. 1) reported that Anne Shirley was available in 9½", 11", 13½", 16", and 19", showing a Patricia and Patsyette dressed as Anne Shirley. A wig with bangs and braids, soft felt hat with upturned brim, and a dress with pleated skirt were the common denominators. Their paper wrist tag read "I am Anne Shirley, inspired by Anne Shirley in RKO-Radio's Anne of Green Gables." Following are three examples of the movie Anne Shirley.

14". Marks: Effanbee//Patricia.
Paper tag: I am//Anne Shirley//Inspired by RKO-Radio's//Anne of//"Green Gables" an//Effanbee//Doll.
All composition, fully jointed, blond or red human hair wig, brown celluloid sleep eyes, closed mouths. All original. Nancy and David Carlson collection. $800.00 each.

11½". Marks on head: Effanbee//Patricia Kin.
Body: Effanbee//Patsy Jr.//Doll (Anne Shirley).
All composition, fully jointed. Human hair wig, gray tin sleep eyes, closed mouth. All original. $400.00.

The following illustrations show Effanbee's other Anne Shirley doll, so identified on the back of her body. By 1939, Effanbee promoted the Anne Shirley dolls as Little Lady. Most were now marked only Effanbee and Made In USA, and their paper hang tags read I Am Little Lady an Effanbee Durable Doll. The Little Lady dolls came attired in short, little girl dresses, but also in elaborate gowns, or even black negligees. In the early 40s, Montgomery Ward carried a large line of Little Lady dolls dressed in the aforementioned styles. They were advertised only as Effanbee Dolls. Little Lady was very popular and was sold throughout the 1940s.

The Anne Shirley marked body limb assemblies were also used for various other Effanbee dolls, such as the American Children designed by Dewees Cochran and the Historical Series.

17". Marks on head and body: Effanbee// USA.
Tag: I Am//Little Lady//An//Effanbee// Durable//Doll.
All composition, fully jointed. Brown cotton yarn hair, brown celluloid sleep eyes, closed mouth. All original including bridal bouquet. $400.00.
Note: Accompanied by booklet "How to make your own glamorous Hairstyles" and styling comb (missing).

20". Marks: Effanbee//Anne Shirley (on back) (see similar outfits pictured in 1940 and 1941 Montgomery Ward catalogs, also see Playthings, March 1943).
All composition, fully jointed. Blond human hair wig, blue sleep eyes, closed mouth. All original. $500.00.

18". Marks on head: Effanbee//USA.

Marks on body: Anne Shirley (as advertised in 1943 Montgomery Ward catalog).

All composition, fully jointed. Blond mohair wig, blue sleep eyes, closed mouth. Original clothes consisting of black bra, panties, and robe. $400.00.

Right: 18", Little Lady. Marks: Effanbee//USA, head and body.

Tag front: I Am//Little Lady//an//Effanbee//Durable Doll.

Tag back: A New//Effanbee//Playmate//For _____//From _____. May you and Little Lady have many happy times//together//Trade Mark Reg.// Made in//U.S.A.

All composition fully jointed, blonde human hair wig. Blue sleep eyes, closed mouth. All original.

Left: 15". Identical doll in red plaid dress with brown mohair wig and braids. Identical tag. Peggy Millhouse collection. $500.00 each.

27". Marks: none. Ca. 1948.

All composition fully jointed, blond human hair wig, blue sleep eyes, closed mouth, painted fingernails. All original. $500.00.

Note: Original advertising for identically dressed doll in Effanbee, The Dolls with the Golden Heart, Ellenburg, pg. 118, Ill. 179. Also see Effanbee ad in Playthings, April 1948, for same doll in different style, fancy outfit with umbrella.

Little Lady jigsaw puzzle, 15¾" x 8¾". The cover picture of this puzzle shows a munber of wonderful fashions that were created for the Little Lady doll by Effanbee. $50.00.

The American Children Dolls Designed by Dewees Cochran

Famous designer and sculptor, Dewees Cochran, had created and executed portrait dolls of individual children, ordered by well to do parents. Most of these dolls were made of latex composition (not illustrated).

Based on this experience, Ms. Cochran was commissioned by Effanbee to design four basic types, representative of American children. These American Children dolls were introduced in 1937, and in 1939, *Life* magazine carried a well illustrated report on the subject. The article claimed that while the individually crafted dolls had been sold for $85.00, the Effanbee composition American Children had been introduced at Saks Fifth Avenue in New York, and were selling at $25.00. All of the dolls illustrated with the *Life* magazine article were shown with sleep eyes and closed mouth.

A 1938 issue of *The Patsytown News* (Vol. 5 No. 1), pictured a group of these portrait children and mentioned that they were available in 14", 16", and 20". All of them seem to have painted eyes and closed mouths. This article further stated that there were three different types available, named Gloria Anne, Peggy Lou, and Betty Jane.

The dolls came with painted or sleep eyes and closed mouths. One of them had an open mouth. All were produced with body assemblies marked Anne-Shirley on their backs. The heads were marked Effanbee American Children. Some heads were not identified at all (the open mouth one). The arms of the American Children were made of hard rubber and have separated fingers so that gloves can be worn.

The open mouth American Child was also used for an ice skater named Ice Queen, in competition with the Sonja Henie doll by Madame Alexander. An all original example of this doll is illustrated in *Effanbee The Dolls with the Golden Hearts*, by M. K. Ellenburg. John Axe, in *The Encyclopedia of Celebrity Dolls*, shows an illustration of this doll dressed as Snow White From *Grimm's Fairy Tales*, with original paper hang tag.

For additional information and pictures see *Focusing on Effanbee Composition Dolls #1*, by Jan Foulke.

Three all original American Children. 14"
and 18", sleep eyes and open mouth.
21", painted eyes and closed mouth.
14", $550.00; 18", $650.00; 21", $1,500.00.

21". Marks on head: Effanbee//American//Children.
Back: Effanbee//Anne-Shirley.
All composition, fully jointed, dark human hair wig, painted eyes, closed mouth. All original. Nancy and David Carlson collection. $1,500.00.

Additional original clothes for American Children dolls and front panel of box.

Original box, American Children.

*21". Marks on head: Effanbee//American//
Children.
Back: Effanbee//Anne-Shirley.
All composition, fully jointed, blond human hair
wig, painted eyes, closed mouth. All original.
Nancy and David Carlson collection. $1,250.00.*

*17". Marks: none.
All composition, fully jointed, brown
human hair wig, painted eyes, closed
mouth. All original. Nancy and David
Carlson collection. $1,850.00.*

Effanbee Historical Dolls

In 1939, Effanbee introduced a group of dolls that were dressed in authentic historical costumes. An ad placed in the November 1939 issue of *Playthings* read as follows: "You are invited to view "The Fashion History of America" depicted by thirty rare dolls. A $10,000 exhibit of unusual interest. An amazing collection of dolls! Thirty of them, dressed in American fashions dating from the buck skinned Indian squaw of 1492 to the gay sophisticate of 1939 ... a group conceived by a twenty-year-old designer who found American history hard to learn! So these thirty dolls were costumed to make American history vividly alive to children! They are exquisitely done ... probably among the most expensively gowned dolls in the world! Bring your own youngsters — your little friends — for an interesting lesson in history. Mrs. Bea Orland, founder of the Patsy Doll Club, is in charge of the exhibit." This display traveled throughout the country, showing at large department stores.

The 20" exhibition dolls' heads were marked Effanbee American Children and are identical to the ones used for the American Children Portrait series designed by Dewees Cochran. While some of the American Children had sleep eyes and open mouths, the heads used for the exhibition dolls had painted eyes and closed mouths only. They were dressed in silks and satins. The 15" so-called replica dolls were intended for sale to the public, and the Little Lady heads were used for them. Instead of silk and satin, the authentic costumes for these dolls were made of cotton. They too had painted eyes and closed mouths. The large as well as the small sets featured Anne-Shirley marked body assemblies.

All were accompanied by a booklet entitled "Romance of American Fashions" told by Effanbee Historical Dolls. Each doll was pictured in this book, followed by the name of the period represented and the date.

20". Marks on head: Effanbee//American //Children Body Marks: Effanbee//Anne-Shirley.
All composition, fully jointed. Arms are made of hard rubber and have separated fingers. Medium blond human hair wig, painted blue eyes, closed mouth. All original outfit made of satin is hand embroidered. original metal heart bracelet. Represents: 1804 Louisiana Purchase. $2,000.00.
Note: This is one of the original, large exhibition dolls.

15". Marks on back: Anne Shirley.
All composition, fully jointed. Blond human hair wig and painted blue eyes, closed mouth. All original costume representing 1711 Colonial Prosperity. Original metal heart bracelet, booklet, and original box, decorated with stars and stripes. $600.00.
Note: This is one of the replica dolls.

Dy-Dee Baby

While this is a book about American-made composition dolls, an example of this all-rubber baby is included here. Introduced in 1934, it became a tremendously popular doll during the 30s, 40s, and into 50s. *Fortune* magazine carried an article in their December 1936 issue stating "Dolls made in America once meant Billiken and Bye-Lo and Patsy, now means chiefly Shirley and Dy-Dee and the Dionnes."

Using a hard rubber head for these dolls was a brilliant idea. During the 30s, a few babies with composition heads were outfitted with drink/wet mechanisms. But the risks were great. Composition dolls would be severely damaged if their insides came in contact with water.

Dy-Dee came in many sizes, and all kinds of equipment was available, such as bathinettes and lavish layettes. The doll pictured below is one of the original Dy-Dees. Later, another model was introduced that had separately applied soft rubber ears. In 1948 Dy-Dee could even blow bubbles.

For further, extensive information on Dy-Dee see *Patsy and Friends Newsletter* May/June 1993 and July/August 1993 (Patsy Moyer).

14". Marks on body (ink stamp): Effanbee (subsequent lines illegible, 1934 until late 40s; see Playthings, April 1934).
Box lid: Dy-Dee Baby//The Almost Human Doll.
Hard rubber head, rubber body and limbs with bent legs. Molded painted blond hair and brown celluloid eyes. Open mouth with rubber tongue that has hole in it connected to wetting mechanism. All original clothes. $300.00.

Mickey was a very popular doll and was sold with the following names, depending on changes in construction, hair style, and clothes: Tommy Tucker, Bright Eyes, Baby Bright Eyes, Twins Mickey and Janie.

14". Marks: EFFandBEE (Toys and Novelties, September 1947).
Paper heart tag front: I Am//Mickey//With Moving Eyes //An//Effanbee//Durable Doll.
Back of tag: A New//Playmate//For ...//From ...//May you and Mickey//have many happy//times together// made in//USA.
Box front: An//Effanbee//Durable Doll//The Doll With //Satin Smooth//Skin.
Composition flange head and hands. Soft stuffed cloth body and limbs. Molded painted brown hair and gray plastic sleep eyes, closed mouth. All original. $350.00.

19", Mickey. Marks: Effanbee//Made in U.S.A.
Composition flange head, arms, and bent legs to above the knee. Blond human hair wig over molded hair, blue sleep eyes that also move from side to side, closed mouth. All original clothes. $400.00.

16", Baby Bright Eyes. Marks: Effanbee//Made In U.S.A.

Heart-shaped paper tag: See separate illustration. Composition flange head, full arms, and bent legs to above the knee. Cloth body, jointed at shoulders, stitched hip joints. Blond human hair wig over molded hair. Sleep eyes that also move from side to side. Closed mouth. All original, with extra set of clothes and carriage blanket in trunk measuring 18 x 13½ x 8½". $500.00.

Front and back of paper tag.

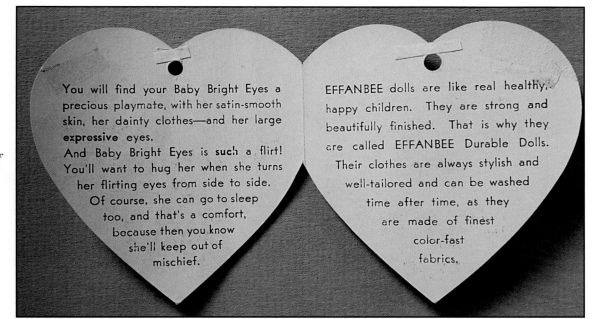

Inside of paper tag.

You will find your Baby Bright Eyes a precious playmate, with her satin-smooth skin, her dainty clothes—and her large **expressive** eyes.
And Baby Bright Eyes is **such** a flirt! You'll want to hug her when she turns her flirting eyes from side to side. Of course, she can go to sleep too, and that's a comfort, because then you know she'll keep out of mischief.

EFFANBEE dolls are like real healthy, happy children. They are strong and beautifully finished. That is why they are called EFFANBEE Durable Dolls. Their clothes are always stylish and well-tailored and can be washed time after time, as they are made of finest color-fast fabrics.

14". Marks: FanB//Made In USA (Mickey & Janie; see Toys and Novelties October 1946).
Composition head, arms, and bent legs. Cloth body, jointed at shoulders, stitched hip joints. Head swivels on special wooden neck piece. Blond mohair wigs, sleep eyes, closed mouths. All original outfits. Original carrying case came with two extra outfits pinned to inside cover of case. Francis Sackett collection. $800.00.

14". Marks on head: Effanbee//Suzanne. Ca. 1940.
Marks on body: Suzanne//Effanbee//made in//USA
Paper tag in shape of bell: Doll//with//Magnetic//
hands//Pat. No. 2,213,901//Manufactured//By//
F.A.O. Schwarz//745 Fifth Ave.//New York, N.Y.
All composition, fully jointed, blond human hair wig,
blue sleep eyes, closed mouth. Original nurse's uniform. Extra set of clothes consisting of dress,
panties, and cape. Cap for this outfit is missing.
Around the inside of the box all kinds of implements
are attached with blue ribbon bows, such as
swabs, a play thermometer, bandage. All have tiny
pieces of metal attached. A magnet is imbedded in
the doll's palm, and those metal pieces will attach
themselves to the magnet when pressed against the
palm. Original heart bracelet. $500.00.

11½" pair. Marks: Effanbee//Suzette.
All composition, fully jointed. Mohair wigs
(blond and auburn) over molded hair, painted
eyes (blue and brown), closed mouths. All original
including heart bracelets. Nancy and David
Carlsen collection. $375.00 each.

11". Marks: Suzette//Effanbee.
Made in U.S.A. Three Suzettes, all
composition, fully jointed, molded
painted black hair and eyes. All original, dressed in authentic Hawaiian
costumes. Middle doll representing
King Kamehameha, wearing red
feather cape. Nancy and David Carlson
collection. $400.00 each.

12". Marks: F & B//Babyette (Playthings, June 1945).
Paper tag: Sh - Sh//Quiet//Babyette//is Sleeping//Effanbee Doll Co.
Back side: Babyette's Luaby Rock a-bye baby.
Composition flange head and hands. Soft stuffed cloth body and limbs. Molded painted hair. Eyes are modeled closed. Closed mouth. Basket lining, skirt and pink ribbon were copied from the torn originals. Tag is a copy. $250.00.

12", group of three Portrait Dolls, ca. 1942.
Marks: None (see original catalog illustration, Ellenburg, Effanbee: The Dolls with the Golden Hearts).
All composition, fully jointed, blond or auburn hair, brown or blue sleep eyes, closed mouths. All original. Nancy and David Carlson collection. Gibson Girl, $275.00; right, $225.00; left, $200.00.

Material shortages during World War II and shortly thereafter necessitated substitute wigs. When found in the original settings, the cotton yarn wigs are surprisingly attractive, even on debutantes in long, fancy gowns (not pictured). One cannot help but admire the dollmakers' resourcefulness.

20", Patricia (Toys and Novelties, March 1942. Patricia — A Doll With Glamour).
16" and 12" Brother and Sister.
Composition swivel heads mounted on wooden neck piece, composition hands. Cloth body, arms, and legs, stitched shoulder and hip joints. Cotton yarn wigs, painted eyes, and closed mouths. All original. 20", $350.00; 16", $300.00; 12", $250.00.
Note: Brother and Sister have also been seen with paper tag: I Am Sugar Pie An Effanbee Durable Doll (Patsy and Friends, Issue 32, November/December 1992, illustration).

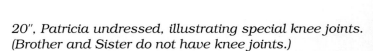

20", Patricia undressed, illustrating special knee joints. (Brother and Sister do not have knee joints.)

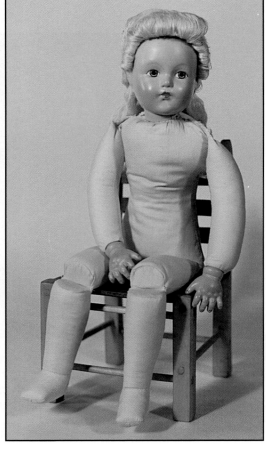

19". Marks: Effanbee (on head and body). Late 1940s. This is Honey.
All composition, fully jointed. Blond human hair wig. Blue plastic sleep eyes that also move from side to side, closed mouth. All original. $500.00.
Note: This doll is definitely made of composition. Most Honey dolls were made of hard plastic.

Unrelated front end of Betty Butin-Nose box reveals the correct spelling for this name.

8". Marks: Effanbee (Betty Butin-Nose).
All composition with arms of hard rubber, fully jointed. Molded painted hair and painted brown eyes, closed mouths. All original. $225.00 each.

8". Marks: Effanbee (Betty Butin-Nose). Double sided paper heart: I Am//An//Effanbee//Trade Mark //Durable//Doll//Made In// U.S.A.
All composition, fully jointed. Molded painted black hair and painted eyes, closed mouth. All original Oriental outfit. $400.00.
Note: No mention of Butin-Nose on the tag.

8". Marks: Effanbee (Betty Butin-Nose). All composition with arms of hard rubber, fully jointed. Molded painted hair and painted eyes, closed mouths. All original. $225.00 each.

8". Marks: Effanbee (on back). (This is Butin-Nose.) Cloth tag sewn into skirt seam (heart-shaped outline): Effanbee//Durable//Dolls//Made In U.S.A. Paper wrist tag: I am//An//Effanbee//Trade Mark//Durable Doll//Made In//U.S.A. All composition, fully jointed, hard rubber arms. Molded painted brown hair and painted brown eyes (boy blue), closed mouths. All original. $225.00 each.

8". Marks: Effanbee (Betty Butin-Nose). All composition, fully jointed. Molded painted brown hair and painted blue eyes, closed mouth. All original. Nancy and David Carlsen collection. $275.00.

14". Marks: none (Candy Kids, Toys and Novelties, September 1947).
All composition, fully jointed. Molded painted hair and brown and blue sleep eyes, closed mouths. All original including real leather boxing gloves. Trunks and robes marked Champ. Black, $600.00; white, $400.00.

Pull Toy — Walking Mammy and Carriage
Doll: 9½" tall; carriage: 8" tall and 7" long, including handle bar. Marks: none. See Toys and Novelties, March 1947, full page illustrated ad placed by Noma. Effanbee was a subsidiary of Noma at the time. The ad also showed Flippo the Seal, Elephant and Barrel, Panda and Walking Horse with Farm Wagon; all of them pull toys with rounded off feet and mechanism like the doll.
Doll: All composition, jointed only at shoulders and hips. Lower arms attached to coil springs. Molded painted black hair, painted brown eyes, open/closed mouth with white line between lips. Molded high boots with three white molded painted buttons. Original dress and head scarf. Doll has been restored.
Carriage: Body and hood made of composition, mounted on metal frame. Metal handle bar and wheels. When toy is pulled, Mammy wobbles from side to side and feet move back and forth, giving the impression of walking. Carriage had partial restoration. $700.00.

Right: Close-up of Walking Mammy.
Below: Walking Mammy without clothes.
Note: Upper arms are coiled springs. Hooks attached to palms to be inserted into holes in handle of carriage. Boots are rounded off to facilitate walking. Hook on front lower torso to be attached to rod located at front of carriage.

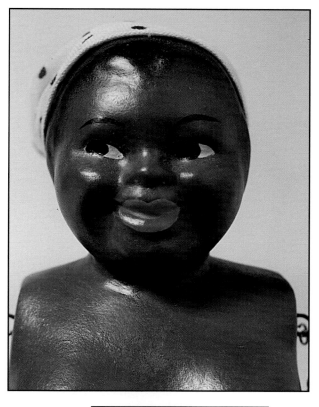

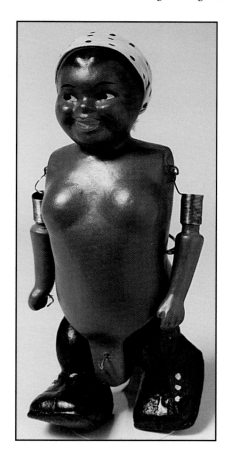

19″. Marks: none (Howdy Doody. *Toys and Novelties*, October 1948/March 1949).
Composition flange head and hands, cloth body and limbs. Molded painted brown hair and sleep eyes, freckles across nose and cheeks. Open/closed mouth with four upper molded/painted teeth. Jaw has separation indication, but jaw is not separate and movable. All original except for boots and hat. $350.00.

**FAIR AMUSEMENT CO.
142 FIFTH AVE.
NEW YORK**

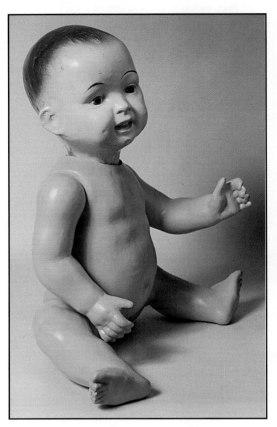

23". Marks: none (Playthings, April 1914 and August 1915). All composition, fully jointed. German-type socket head, molded painted hair, painted blue eyes, open/closed mouth with molded upper gums and tongue, two painted teeth. $100.00.

FAM DOLL COMPANY

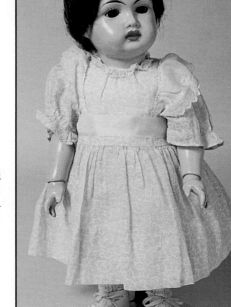

*14". Marks: FAM Doll//14".
Composition socket head, ball-jointed body. Brown human hair wig, gray celluloid sleep eyes. Open/closed mouth with five painted teeth. Redressed. $200.00.*

FAMOUS DOLL STUDIO, INC.
NEW YORK CITY

14", Sani Doll. Marks: none (Playthings, March 1917).
Composition shoulder head and arms to above the elbow, cloth body, upper arms, and bent legs, jointed with inside disks. Molded painted brown hair and painted blue eyes. Molded, continuous row of upper teeth and molded tongue, double chin. Re-dressed. $150.00.

16", Sani Doll.
Marks: none.
Same as above, except straight legs. $125.00.

RALPH A. FREUNDLICH

Ralph A. Freundlich had worked for the Jeanette Doll Co. in New York City and started his own business in 1929. In 1923 – 24, he also owned the Silver Doll and Toy Manufacturing Co. The June 1934 *Playthings* issue announced the relocation of manufacturing operations to Clinton, Massachusetts. The accompanying picture showed a large four story building. The article also mentioned that a railroad siding would be built for this factory. A February 1930 *Playthings* ad showed a very cheap looking mama doll that they were offering as a "$1.00 Retailer." In other words, the wholesaler probably bought it for 50¢. Apparently, they were manufacturers of an economy line of dolls. According to an article in *Doll Reader*, February 1994, by Marian H. Schmuhl, the company assets were liquidated in bankruptcy proceedings in 1945. This article also showed pictures of the actual manufacture of composition parts, confirming that such production took place there.

12". Marks: none (see Playthings ad January 1932, placed by Ralph A. Freundlich, Inc. Identical set sold by Bloomingdale's).
All composition, fully jointed, molded painted light brown hair and eyes. Set also includes two extra dresses with bonnets, flannel coat and beret, pajamas, extra pair shoes and socks. Cardboard trunk measures 8 x 6½ x 13". $150.00.

Display ad Playthings, February 1932.
Text reads as follows: "Each set contains a 12" bunny doll with moving head, arms and feet. Dressed in underslip, dress, apron, cap and real shoes and stockings that are removable. Then there's a highly amusing cardboard cut-out of a cat, dog and bear, mounted on one rocking base, and one fluffy yellow chick. All packed in a strong trunk box with metal catch for the lid, and a metal handle. Each trunk is covered with a colorful eye-catching Easter design."

9½", Puss in Boots. Marks: none.
All composition, fully jointed, painted white. Cat's head is on Patsyette-type body with bent right arm. Clothes are made of felt and black oil cloth boots (feet bare), painted green eyes. All original. $150.00.

12", Rabbit. Marks: none. All composition, fully jointed, Patsy type body assembly. Head is painted pink with painted brown eyes, other body parts are painted flesh color. All original. $100.00.

9½", Red Ridinghood, Grandma, and Wolf. Marks: none. They are pictured in the 1934 Sears Roebuck catalog, shown barefoot also advertised as being sold in a "fancy, lithographed schoolhouse box." The set sold for $1.00.
All three dolls are made with Patsyette type body assemblies including bent right arms. All original. $700.00 set.

10", *Three Little Pigs and the Wolf. Marks: none. All composition, fully jointed, painted brown eyes, closed mouth. All original. Came as a set in a carrying case. Sherryl Shirran collection. $700.00 set.*

10", *Little Orphan Annie and 7", Sandy. Marks: none (Playthings, April 1936). Both items were sold boxed as a set with booklet and cost $1.00 retail.*

All composition, fully jointed. Annie has molded painted yellow hair with black high-lights. Big, round eyes painted blue, closed mouth. Sandy is molded all in one piece. All original. (Little Orphan Annie, cartoon by Harold Gray, 1894 – 1968, appeared in the Tribune.) $350.00 set.

19" *(also came in 27" size). Marks: none (Playthings September 1937). Dolls were advertised as Goo-Goo Eye Dolls. Each doll had a paper tag pinned to it's chest in the shape of a doll head with big eyes, inscribed on the forehead: Goo-Goo//Doll. Composition flange head, cloth body and limbs softly stuffed with cotton, stitched hip joints. Same fabric jacket. Molded painted blond hair and stationary plastic eyes with floating pupils, closed mouth. Metal staple in top of head for attachment of hair ribbon. $80.00.*

14". Marks: none (see similar dolls in Playthings, September 1937).
Composition flange head, molded painted blond hair, stationary eyes with floating pupils, closed mouth. Cloth body and limbs, detachable collar, sailor hat is stapled on. $80.00.

14", Dummy Clown. Marks: none.
Composition head and arms to above elbow, straw stuffed body and limbs, swinging legs, jaw is activated with string at back of head. (Freundlich had patent #403.407, issued February 25, 1938 for Dummy Dan.) Original suit. $65.00.

10". Marks: none. Paper tag: Dummy//Don//Made in USA. (Same face as Dummy Dan, the Ventriloquist Man. See Doll Reader, June/July 1979, pg. 37, Jan Foulke.)
All composition, jointed only at shoulders and hips. Molded painted brown hair and painted brown eyes, closed mouth. All original. $45.00.

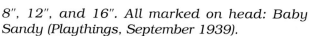

18", *Davy Crockett Dummy.*
Pin: Davy Crockett//Indian Fighter.
Tag: Side 1: Talk with/Davy Crockett/The/Leda/Company.
Side 2: Davy Crocket/Hero of/The Alamo.
Hard plastic head and hands, moving eyes (also of hard plastic) and jaw. Cloth body and limbs. All original with pin and tag. $150.00.
Note: Though of hard plastic, included here for completeness sake.

8", 12", and 16". *All marked on head: Baby Sandy (Playthings, September 1939).*
All composition, fully jointed, molded painted hair.
8", *painted eyes, closed mouth, re-dressed. $120.00.*
12", *painted eyes, open mouth with two upper teeth, all original with pin. $300.00.*
16", *sleep eyes, open mouth with two upper teeth, all original with pin. $500.00.*
Note: This is a portrait of baby Sandra Henville, who starred in such pictures as East Side of Heaven and Unexpected Father (Universal).

8" and 11", Baby Sandy. Marks: Baby Sandy.
All composition, fully jointed. Molded painted hair
and painted blue eyes, open mouth with two upper
teeth (8", closed mouth). All original. 8", $150.00;
11", $250.00.
Note: It is not clear why the dolls are dressed in
Tyrolean costumes.

15" and 18", WAVES, soldier, General
McArthur, sailor, and WAAC of WW II, ca.
1942. Marks: none.
All composition, jointed at shoulders and
hips only, with molded hats, molded
painted brown hair and painted blue
eyes, open/closed or closed mouths. All
original, except for sailor. Military,
$250.00 each; General, $350.00.

GEM TOY COMPANY
NEW YORK
1913 – 1930+

In their early years, the Gem Toy Company produced dolls whose molds were obviously developed from German examples. Gem continued this copying process. In 1926, they were advertising their New Gem Baby Doll, which was a copy of Horsman's Tynie Baby. Horsman took them to court and lost, as their dolls were marked with initials only. Besides mama dolls, they later had a baby doll that looked very similar to Horsman's Dimples and then Effanbee's Lovums. In 1931, they were advertising a Patsy look-alike. They produced the Five-In-One Doll in about 1924. (See *Doll Reader* September 1993; Multi-head.)

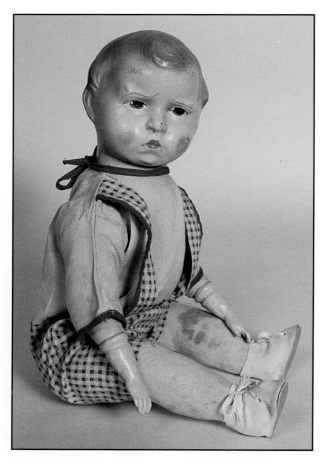

16". Marks: none (Playthings, January 1915). Composition flange head and hands, cloth body, upper arms, and bent legs. Molded, painted hair and painted blue eyes, closed mouth, re-dressed. $150.00.

17". Marks: GEM//401 (Gem Toy Co. NY).
Composition head, plush body and limbs, jointed with inside disks. White felt mitten hands and sewn on boots. Detachable white collar is made of fleece. Black oilcloth belt and detachable lower half of jacket tacked to waist. Molded painted brown hair and painted blue eyes. Closed mouth. All original. $500.00 (mint).

19", Clicquot Club Kid. Marks: none, (Playthings, January 1924).
Composition shoulder head, cloth body and limbs, jointed at shoulders, swinging legs. Molded painted black hair, painted blue eyes, wide, smiling closed mouth. Head has been repainted. Tan felt mittens are sewn in. Original white plush suit and cap as well as brown felt boots can be removed. $150.00 (fair).
Note: The ad stated that Gem Toy Co. was offering this doll with special permission from the Clicquot Club Company.

THE GERLING TOY CO. NEW YORK, NEW YORK

13". Marks: none.
May have been sold by the Gerling Toy Co., New York or S. & H. Novelty Co., of Atlantic City. Both were listed in Playthings in 1929 and 1930, advertising dancing dolls.
Composition shoulder head with molded blond, curly hair. Painted blue eyes, closed mouth. Cloth bodies and limbs, with loose, stitched joints, buttoned together at fingertips and on shoulders, heads also. Identical heads were used for both dolls. All original. $200.00.

14". Marks: none (Playthings, February 1929).
Paper hang tag: Gerling's Dancing Dollies//Trade Mark//Patent Pending//Makers//Gerling Toy Co., N.Y.
Hang tag on back: Instructions//Hold the end of string so that doll's feet touch the floor. Move up and down slightly — Watch Them Dance.
Composition shoulder heads, cloth bodies and limbs. Mohair wigs, blue painted eyes, closed mouths. They are buttoned together at hands, each other's backs and heads. Lead string attached at head juncture. Identical heads used for both. All original. $400.00.

GERMAN NOVELTY CO.
NEW YORK CITY
1914 – 1915

16". Marks: none.
Tag on clothes: G.N. Co//Tipperary Tommy//Reg. U.S., Pat. Off. No. 82999.
Composition flange head and hands, cloth body and limbs, jointed with inside disks. Molded painted hair and blue eyes, open/closed mouth. All original (oil cloth boots). $175.00.

EUGENE GOLDBERGER
BROOKLYN, NEW YORK
1917 – 1930+

E. Goldberger produced a general line of dolls. From 1923 on, they used the trademark "EEGEE." Apparently, they did not mark many of their dolls, as few have survived that can be attributed to E. Goldberger.

14". Marks on shoulder head: GOLD DOLL.
Identical copy of Effanbee Patsy head with molded hair ribbon in front over bangs. Hair is painted light orange. Blue painted eyes and closed tiny mouth. Full composition arms. Crude, straw stuffed cloth body and straight, swinging legs. Re-dressed. $100.00 (fair).

17". Marks: none on doll.
Oval metal pin: Miss Charming// Everybody Loves Me (Playthings, July 1936).
All composition, fully jointed. Legs feature a walker mechanism. When legs are moved back and forth, head turns from side to side. Green sleep eyes, open mouth with six upper teeth. Original, blond mohair wig and clothes. The doll also came in a 14" size. $400.00, head restored.
Note: The same ad also showed a picture of Baby Charming (an all composition toddler), "a companion line — consists of a complete assortment of baby dolls with and without wigs."

GUND MANUFACTURING COMPANY NEW YORK CITY

HERBY

8" tall, 9" long, Mechanical Crawling Baby. Marks: none (Playthings, January 1915).
Composition flange head and hands. Cloth body and legs. Metal windup mechanism inside body. Molded painted brown hair, painted blue eyes. Closed mouth with tip of molded tongue showing. All original with key. $150.00 (fair).

12", Herby. Marks: none (see More 20th Century Dolls, Anderton, COM-S6ab, 1935). Herby, little brother of main character, Smitty, from the cartoon strip "Smitty" by Walter Berndt, Chicago Tribune-New York News Syndicate from 1922 on. It's companion strip, Herby, was created in 1930 (ran until 1973).
All composition, jointed at neck and jaw. Molded painted clothes and cap. Pupilless black eyes. $200.00.

HOLLYWOOD DOLL MANUFACTURING CO. GLENDALE, CALIFORNIA

A September 1945 ad in *Playthings* proclaimed that the firm were "manufacturers of 5" to 20" Dolls." The ad further listed the 5" dolls in the following series: Little Friends Series, Playmaters Series, Nursery Rhymes Series, Hollywood Book Series, Lucky Star Series and Princess Series. They came individually boxed.

HOO CHOY

13½", HOO CHOY, The Little Godess of Good Luck. Marks: none (information copied from paper tag on all original doll when seen at doll show).
All composition jointed at shoulders only with coil spring. Molded painted black hair, and black eyes (no pupils), closed mouth. Middle doll has her original black mohair wig over molded hair. Molded painted black slippers. All original clothes.
Middle doll: original mohair wig. $200.00 each.

5". Marks: Hollywood//Doll (Playthings February 1945).
Original box label: Hollywood Doll// Playmates//Wee Bonnie Lassie//Hollywood Doll Mfg. Co., Glendale, Calif.
All composition, jointed at shoulders and hips only. Dark brown mohair wig, blue painted eyes, closed mouth. Molded painted white slippers, original outfit. $50.00.
Note: This is a high quality doll: smooth composition, well finished mold seams, well painted features and eyelashes. Hems on garments are finished.

13½". Same data as previous three dolls, but with original cap. Collection of Ray and Betsy Baker. $350.00 (rare, complete condition).

MARY HOYER DOLLS
READING, PENNSYLVANIA

Mary Hoyer started her career as a designer of knitted and crocheted garments for children. The home instruction booklets for these fashions were published by yarn companies and the Hoyers themselves. Soon, Mrs. Hoyer decided to add matching garments for dolls and was looking for a suitable doll that might serve as a model. She located a slim bodied one at the Ideal Novelty & Toy Company. Ideal liked the idea of marketing a doll with accompanying instructions for knitting and crocheting clothes but later decided that the item did not fit into their sales program. Ideal offered to sell undressed dolls to Mrs. Hoyer. The Ideal doll was 13" tall, had painted or sleep eyes, a mohair wig, and a double jointed waist. When this style doll was discontinued by the Ideal Novelty and Toy Company, Mrs. Hoyer had her own model designed by Mr. Bernard Lipfert in 1937. The doll was 14" tall. It was produced by the Fiberoid Company in New York and had painted eyes and a mohair wig. Apparently, the first 1,500 dolls were not marked. On the next order the mark "The//Mary Hoyer//Doll" was used. Later composition dolls of the same model had sleep eyes.

Mary Hoyer dolls were sold by mail and came undressed. The instruction booklets "Mary's Dollies" were sold separately and later included patterns for sewing doll clothes. Also available were kits containing enough yarn and required trims to make a specific outfit. Eventually, a wide range of accessories was offered as well. Ready made, tagged doll clothes could also be bought from the Mary Hoyer firm.

The composition Mary Hoyer dolls were discontinued in 1946 and hard plastic was used for their production. (*Mary Hoyer and Her Dolls*, Hobby House Press, Inc.)

Note: While the literature reports that Bernard Lipfert designed the 14" doll for Mrs. Hoyer, it is almost impossible to distinguish the Mary Hoyer doll from a 14" example sold by Arranbee and other companies.

14". Marks: The//Mary Hoyer//Doll. 1940s.
Dress Tag: Mary Hoyer//Reading//Pa.//Ocean City//NJ.
All original. All composition, fully jointed, dark brown mohair wig, blue sleep eyes, closed mouth.
$400.00.

E. I. HORSMAN & COMPANY
NEW YORK CITY

E. I. Horsman & Company of New York City had been importers, assemblers, wholesalers, and distributors of dolls since about 1878. Billiken, introduced in 1909, was their first big success with a composition doll. The Billiken image had been famous before the Billiken doll. Patent No. 39.603, dated October 6, 1908, was granted to Florence Pretz. In various forms, Billiken was promoted as a good luck charm. Horsman seized on this fame and the popularity of the teddy bears and created the Billiken doll with a plush body.

Billiken was followed by Baby Bumps (based on the German Kammer & Reinhardt firm's #100 baby) and the Campbell Kids, designed by Grace Drayton. Variety was created by dressing one style of doll in different outfits and wigs, thus producing new identities. Yet, the period from 1910 to 1920 was the most productive ever in terms of different doll types. This was true for the numbers created from German character doll heads as well as for new designs. Most of the models for Horsman's Can't Break 'Em lines were created by Helen Trowbridge. If survival rate is any indication, Horsman had early on the largest and most varied line of American-made composition dolls during this first decade of production.

Horsman's composition parts were produced by the Aetna Doll & Toy Co. In 1909, Aetna had bought out Solomon D. Hoffman including the Can't Break 'Em composition formula. Horsman distributed the whole Aetna output. In 1912, they produced over 4,000 doll heads a day for Horsman. Aetna merged with Horsman in 1919. Along with everybody else in the industry, Horsman produced a great many dolly face mama dolls during the 1920s. Baby Dimples was probably their greatest sales success with a composition character doll during the 1920s.

In 1930, Horsman bought the composition doll line of Louis Amberg and Son. Drink and wet baby dolls made of all rubber were a new innovation during the thirties, and Horsman had their own version, plus several other new creations. The Campbell Kids of 1947 were their last sales leader in composition dolls. Composition as a material for producing dolls was phased out and replaced by plastics.

Special Finish for Horsman Dolls
from 1910 – 1920

The Horsman firm was very productive during this period, creating and producing numerous dolls of new design. Yet, in their surface treatment of the composition parts, the makers were apparently trying to imitate the appearance of the ever-popular European bisque dolls. It is not clear how the bisque like finish was achieved. It is not quite as smooth as that of contemporary American-made composition dolls. When examined today, the surface of most examples is obscured by dirt. In protected areas (under wig, chin, on shoulder plates) the bisque like finish can be observed in its original state. Apparently, this special surface treatment was used only by Horsman on all their composition dolls during this early decade. Being aware of this fact provides an additional identification tool. Also, a sewn-on head (thread going through the composition, even on flared heads) is another indicator that the doll was sold by Horsman.

Note: With cleaning, this surface treatment changes character, and features including cheek blush rub off quite easily. Therefore, these early Horsman dolls should be left undisturbed whenever possible.

Can't Break 'Em: trademark for Horsman's glue base composition. Adtocolite: trademark for Horsman's wood pulp composition (see *T & N*, July 1918).

15", Billiken. Marks: none (Playthings 1910, "Trademark, Copyright No. 28790, March 20, 1909, by the Billiken Company"). Billiken was available in 12", 15", and 25" sizes. The 12" size was also available dressed in Japanese kimono. A Sister Billiken was advertised in 12" and 15" sizes. She had a wig and was also dressed in a kimono.

Composition head sewn to plush body, felt paw pads, jointed at shoulders and hips. Molded painted features and hair. $500.00.

12". Marks: none (E. I. Horsman).
Label sewn to chest: The//Billiken//Company//
Chicago.
Ink hand printing on soles of feet: The Lucky Billiken N. Y. 7/12/09.
Composition head sewn to plush body. Jointed at
shoulders and hips. Molded top knot, painted hair,
closed eyes and closed mouth. Toe demarcations
stitched with embroidery yarn, felt paw pads.
$350.00.
Note: Apparently, hair on the early Billiken was
hand painted and has a hard edge. Compare with
15" Billiken, whose hair was airbrushed and has a
soft hair line. (Tip of top knot repaired.)

This illustration shows various other Billiken items available at the time, attesting to the tremendous popularity of the Billiken image. Bookends were made of plaster as well as bisque, small figures of celluloid. Even gold stick pins were available (shown on the Billiken doll). The dark metal still bank on the left is marked "Patent//NO 39603" and "Billiken" on the opposite side. This design patent was issued to Florence Pretz on October 6, 1908. The same size plaster paperweight on the far right has a metal coin impressed into its bottom that is Marked "Billiken"//Trademark// Copyright 1908 by//The Craftsman's Guild Pat. Oct. 6, 1908. The //Billiken//Company//Chicago// The.God.Of.Things.As.They.Ought. To.Be.

18". Marks: none (Horsman finish, K*R look-alike).
Flared composition head sewn to body. Cloth body, arms (stump hands), and bent legs, jointed with outside disks. Molded, painted brown hair and painted blue eyes, open/closed mouth. Re-dressed. $150.00.

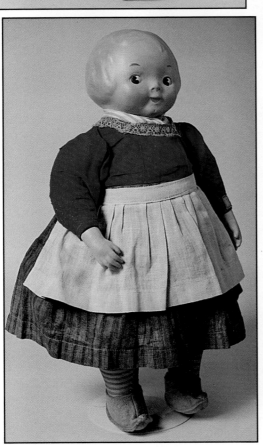

9". Marks: none.
Suit tagged: Bumps Junior//Trademark//Manufactured by//E. I. Horsman Co.//New York. (note box markings). Flared composition head sewn onto body. Cloth body, arms with stump hands and curved legs, jointed at shoulders and hips. Slightly molded painted hair, painted blue eyes, open/closed mouth. All original. $150.00.
Note: This doll seems to resemble German Kestner #211.

16", Dutch Campbell Kid. Marks: E.I.H. ©1910.
Label on sleeve not legible. All original, but restored face/hands. Composition flange head stitched onto body, composition hands to above the wrist. Cloth body and limbs jointed with inside disks. Blue and white striped stockings are the casing for the legs. Molded painted blond hair and black eyes (a heart shape on its side), open/closed mouth. $350.00.

15". Marks: E.I.H. ©1910.
Composition head sewn to cloth body, composition hands. Cloth body and limbs, jointed at shoulders and hips with inside disks. Molded painted blond hair and black eyes, open/closed mouth. All original. Nancy and David Carlsen collection. $350.00.

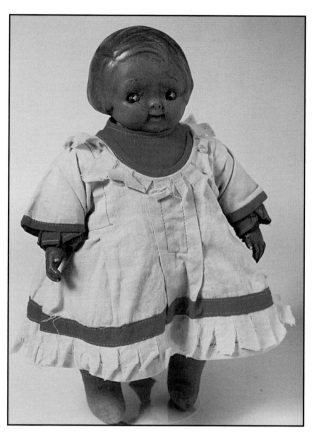

11", Campbell Kid (this is Pocahontas, Playthings, May 1911). Marks: E.I.H. ©1910. Composition flange head and arms to above the wrists. Cloth body and limbs jointed at shoulders and hips with inside disks. Painted brown complexion, molded painted black hair and eyes (heart shape on its side), open/closed smiling mouth. All original. $350.00.

10". Marks: none.
Sleeve tag: The Campbell Kid//Trademark//L'CD. By E.I. Horsman & Co.//Gesetzlich geschuetzt//Deutschland (translation last three words: Protected by patent in Germany).
Flared composition head sewn to body. Cloth body and limbs, jointed with inside disks at shoulders and hips. Straight legs. Black cloth boots are part of leg casing. All original. $350.00.

Left: 9", Campbell Kid. Marks: none.
Right: 8½", Campbell Kid. Marks: E.I.H.
©1910.
Note: Unusual small size and construction
(on right). $35.00 poor condition.

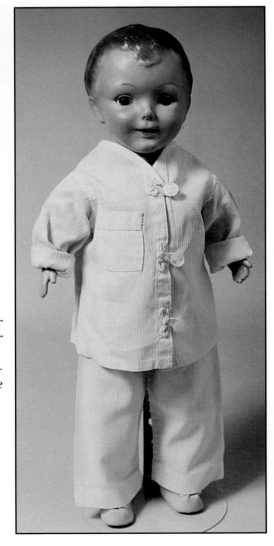

15". Marks: E.I.H. ©1910 (Playthings, May 1911, No. 14).
Flared composition head and short arms. Cloth body, upper
arms and legs jointed with inside disks. Molded painted hair
and painted brown eyes. Closed mouth. Re-dressed.
Note: This is Little Nemo from comic strip "Little Nemo in Slum-
berland," created by Windsor McCay. It first appeared in the
New York Herald, October 15, 1905. $250.00 fair condition.

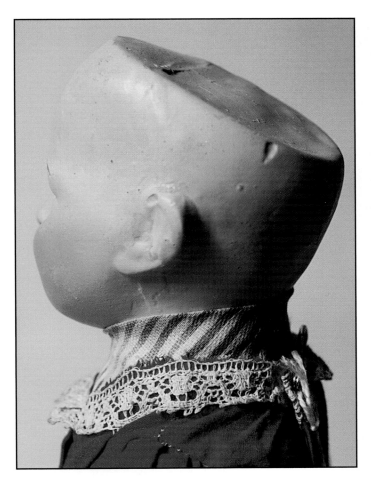

15". Marks: none (Dutch Gretchen, Playthings, 1911).
Flared composition head stitched to body. Composition hands to above the wrist. Cloth body and limbs jointed with inside disks. Horizontally striped stockings go all the way up to hips. Original blond mohair wig. Painted blue eyes, open/closed mouth with modeled upper teeth. All original. $250.00.
Note: Flat top of head. Mold was taken off German bisque head. (Mate of Dutch Boy in the Strong Museum Collection, Rochester, N.Y.)

241

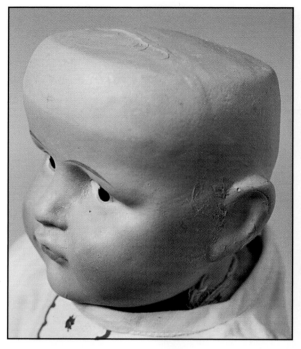

12". Marks: none (K*R #114 Look Alike, Play-things, May 1911, #13 "Miss Mischief Can't make her eyes behave").
Composition flange head stitched to body, short composition arms, cork stuffed body and straight legs, jointed with inside disks. Original, blond mohair wig. Painted blue eyes, closed mouth, original felt shoes. $250.00.
Note: Flat top of head same as Dutch girl.
Also see Effanbee's 15" Pouting Bess. She has identical face but molded hair.

11" (from tip of nose to tip of tail).
Cloth label on stomach: Puppie Pippin//Copyright 1911//by E.I. Horsman.
Composition head sewn to body, painted black eyes. Velour body and limbs, jointed at shoulders and hips. Sewn on tail. $400.00.

Display ad from September 1912 issue of Playthings. Similar to Pussie* and Puppie Pippin, this moose seems to have a composition head on a velour body and limbs. Picture indicates that limbs are jointed at shoulders and hips.

*Pussie Pippin not pictured.

The Craze

Horsman's

"TEDDY BULL MOOSE"

TRADE MARK REGISTERED

A READY-MADE DEMAND FOR IT THE COUNTRY OVER

SELLS AT SIGHT

NEW YORK HERALD
Sunday, Sept. 15th
SAYS:

"Teddy Bull Moose has routed Teddy Bear, ... he is monarch of all the toys."

"Can't-Break-Em" Composition Head from Plastic Model
Copyrighted 1912 by E. I. Horsman Co.

Price $8.50 Per Dozen

SEND IN YOUR ORDERS

Orders Filled in Rotation as Received

E. I. HORSMAN CO. 365 Broadway NEW YORK

13". Marks: E.I.H. ©1911 (Playthings, September 1912, called Polly Prue).

Flared composition head sewn to body. Composition hands, cloth body and limbs, jointed with inside disks. Molded painted blond hair, painted blue eyes, closed mouth. All original. $350.00.

Note: Dressed in frilly white dress and bonnet, she was called Fairy and was made under license from N. K. Fairbank Co., Chicago, makers of Fairy soap. The doll could then be obtained as a premium for buying Fairy soap.

4¼" tin advertising plate for Fairy soap. When comparing the face of the Polly Prue with that of the girl pictured on the plate, one realizes that an attempt at portraiture was made: square face with pointed chin, deep wave on forehead.

243

14". Both marked: E.I.H. ©1911.
Sleeve label: The Jap Rose Kid//Trade Mark//Process Pat. Nov. 1911//LIC'D by Jas. S. Kirk & Company// Copyright by E.I. Horsman Co.
Flared composition head sewn to body and short arms. Cloth body, upper arms, and legs jointed with inside disks. Molded painted black hair and painted brown eyes. Open/closed mouth, original clothes. Girl: same construction and knee joints, head restored, kimono copied from boy's. $350.00 ea.
Note: The Jas. S. Kirk Soap Company apparently used two Japanese kids as advertising emblem. A January 1912, Playthings editorial further stated that soap manufacturers were prominent advertisers, and they obviously thought it a smart move of Horsman to enter into this licensing arrangement. They further stated that Kirk was as well known in the west as Fairbank on the East Coast and that the Jap Rose Kids were as well known on the Pacific Slope as the Campbell Kids in the east.

14". Marks: E.I.H. ©1911.
Flared composition head and short arms. Cloth body, upper arms and legs, jointed with inside disks, pin jointed knees. Molded painted hair and painted blue eyes. Deep cheek dimples. Original sailor dress.
Note: This doll was also used for the girl of the Jap Rose Kids pair. She was also sold as Camp Fire Girl and was Gretel of a Hans and Gretel pair. Wigged with side-glancing eyes, she was called Sunbonnet Sal. (See various Playthings ads 1912 and 1913.) $150.00 head restored.

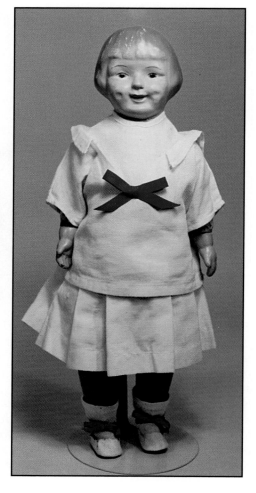

11". Marks: none (Playthings, September 1912).
Cloth tag on body: Copyright 1910//By E. I. Horsman.
Flared composition head sewn onto body, short arms, cloth body, upper arms, and straight legs, jointed with inside disks. Painted brown eyes, closed mouth, molded, red turban. All original. $380.00.

11". Marks: E.I.H. (rest illegible) (Playthings, July 1913, Carnival Baby).
Flared composition head sewn to body, short composition arms, both painted white. Cloth body, upper arms, and legs, jointed with inside disks. No hair paint. Painted black eyes, open/closed mouth. Three shapes painted onto face. All original (hat, pompons on shoes missing). $100.00.

14". Marks: none (Playthings, July 1913, Boy Scout).
Flared composition head sewn to body, short composition arms. Cloth body, upper arms, and legs, jointed with inside disks, pin-jointed knees. Molded painted hair and painted blue eyes, closed mouth. All original except boots, hat missing. $250.00.
Note: This doll also came dressed as Robby Reefer, a sailor and as Schoolboy, wearing a dress shirt and tie, dark knee pants (elastic at knees), white socks, and black slippers.

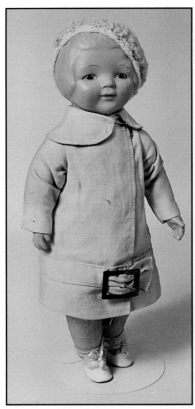

14". Marks: E.I.H. ©1913 (Playthings, July 1913, shown in identical outfit, called Little Sunshine).
Composition shoulder head sewn to body, short composition arms. Cloth body, upper arms, and legs, jointed with inside disks, pin joints at knees. Molded, painted blond hair and painted blue eyes, closed mouth. Original coat dress, old shoes and socks. $350.00.

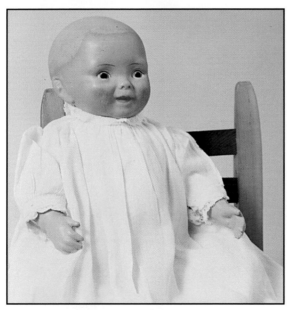

12". Marks: E.I.H. ©1910.
Composition flange head sewn right onto body. Short composition arms. Cloth body, upper arms, and bent legs, jointed with inside disks. No molded hair, remnants of hair color (may have had a wig), painted blue eyes, open/closed mouth, re-dressed. $100.00.

16". Marks: E.I.H. ©1910.
Cloth label on body: Copyright 1910 //E. I. Horsman.
Flared composition head sewn to body. Composition hands. Cloth body and limbs, jointed with inside disks. No molded hair, spray painted only. Re-dressed (felt slippers/socks seem original). $200.00.
Note: This is Baby Peterkin. His oddly striped hair can be recognized in several Playthings ads of 1912 and 1913.

12". Marks: E.I.H. ©1910.
Composition flange head sewn to body. Composition arms to above the wrist. Cloth body and limbs, bent legs, jointed with inside disks. Faintly molded painted light brown hair and painted blue eyes. Closed mouth. Original bloomers and matching short dress. $100.00.

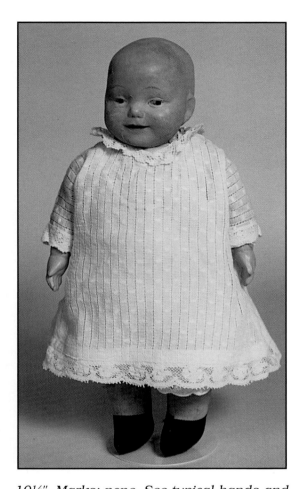

10½". Marks: none. See typical hands and finish, stitched-on head.
Composition head and hands, cloth body and limbs jointed with inside disks. Black sewn-on cloth boots. No hair modeling, blue eyes painted to one side. Open/closed mouth. Old clothes. $50.00 (discolored).

10". Marks: none (SFBJ #227 copy).
Composition head sewn onto body. Composition hands, cloth body and limbs, jointed with inside disks. Black boots are part of leg casing. Molded painted hair and eyes, open/closed mouth with two upper molded, painted teeth. Re-dressed. $100.00.

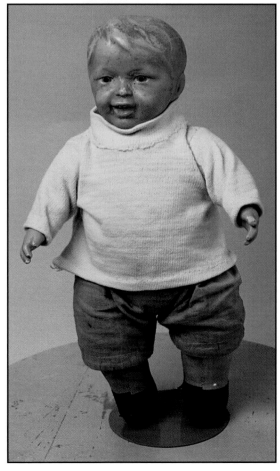

Early Horsman Babies

As early as 1913, Horsman had an impressive line of baby dolls. Their trademarks for them were Nature Babies and Gold Medal Babies and they were given names like Baby Darling, Baby Rosebud, Baby Blossom, Suck-a-Thumb, Baby Premier, Christening Baby. Since names changed with size or outfit of a given doll, they are of little relevance, unless a baby is found in original clothes that are tagged (paper hang tag).

There seems to have been three basic types:

1. A dolly faced baby with painted or glass eyes, an open/closed mouth, molded hair or wig.

2. A character baby with painted eyes, open/closed mouth (large size with molded teeth), and molded hair. All have dimples in their cheeks that are placed a little too high, and are more prominent on some examples than on others (see baby with composition legs in this group).

3. A wide eyed baby with painted eyes, open/closed mouth (smaller sizes open mouth), molded hair.

These dolls were very popular and sold over most of the decade. (*Playthings*, May 1920).

Dolly Faced Babies

18". Marks: E.I.H. ©1915.
Composition shoulder head and lower arms. Cloth body, upper arms, and bent legs, jointed with inside disks. Original blond mohair wig, stationary blue glass eyes, open/closed mouth. Available in long and short dresses in sizes, 16", 18", 21", 26", and 30." $250.00 fair condition.

21". Marks: none.
Flared composition head sewn to body. Short composition arms. Cloth body, upper arms, and curved legs, jointed with inside disks. Molded painted brown hair and painted blue eyes. Open/closed mouth. Re-dressed. $250.00.

248

18". Marks: none.
Composition shoulder head and lower arms. Cloth body, upper arms and bent legs, jointed with inside disks. Molded painted blond hair and painted blue eyes, open/closed mouth. All original, including typical Campbell Kid-type felt slippers with top strap. $250.00.

16". Marks: E.I.H. © A. D. Co.
Composition shoulder head and lower arms. Cloth body, upper arms and bent legs, jointed with inside disks. Molded painted blond hair and blue eyes. Open/closed mouth. All original. $250.00.

10". Marks: none.
Flared composition head sewn right to body. Composition hands to above wrists. Cloth body, arms, and bent legs, jointed with inside disks. Molded painted blond hair and blue eyes. Open/closed mouth. All original. $150.00.

Character Babies

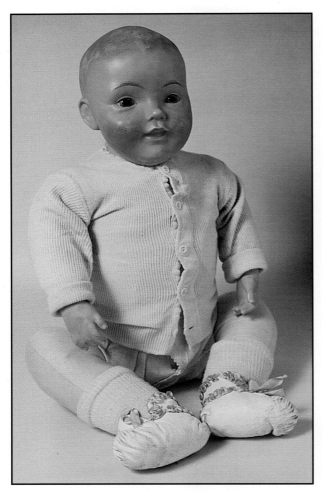

23". Marks: none.
Flared composition head stitched to body, short composition arms. Cloth body, upper arms, and curved legs stuffed with cork and jointed with inside disks. Molded painted blond hair, painted blue eyes, open closed mouth with four molded upper teeth and molded tongue. Re-dressed. $350.00.

17". Marks: E.I.H. © 1915.
Composition shoulder head and short arms. Cloth body, upper arms, curved legs stuffed with cork and jointed with inside disks. Molded painted blond hair and painted blue eyes. Open/closed mouth with molded tongue, redressed. Head has been repainted. $150.00.

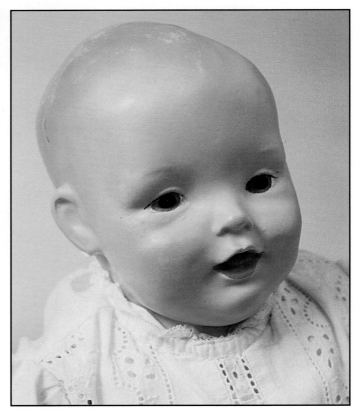

12". Marks: E.I.H. © 1911 (Playthings, February 1912).
Composition flange head, lower arms, and legs to above the knee. Molded painted blond hair and painted blue eyes, open/closed mouth, dimples in cheeks. Cloth body and upper limbs, jointed with inside disks. Re-dressed. $150.00.
Note: Unusual composition legs (all other babies have cloth legs).

9". Marks: none.
Composition head and hands, cloth body, arms, and bent legs jointed with inside disks. Molded painted brown hair and painted blue eyes. Open/closed mouth. Re-dressed. $80.00 fair conditon.

Wide Eyed Babies

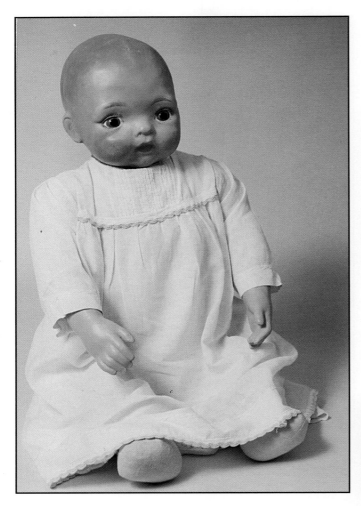

19". marks: none.
Flared composition head stitched to body.
Composition lower arms. Cloth body, upper
arms, and bent legs, jointed with inside
disks. Faintly molded painted blond hair and
painted blue eyes. Open/closed mouth with
molded tongue. $250.00.
Note: A similar size doll dressed in short
infant dress and hooded jacket was called
Babe Premier (Playthings, September, 1913).

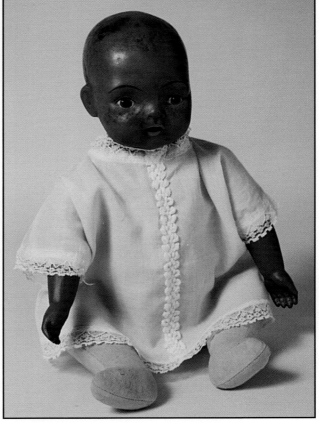

13". Marks: E.I.H. © 1913.
Composition shoulder head and lower arms, paint-
ed brown. Cloth body, upper arms, and bent legs
made of light colored fabric, jointed with inside
disks. Slightly molded, painted black hair, painted
brown eyes, open mouth. Re-dressed. $250.00.
Note: This open mouth baby in long infant dress
(size unknown) is called Baby Blossom in ads.
(Playthings, October 1913).

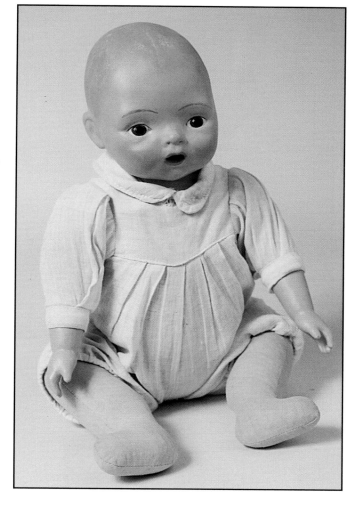

12". Marks: E.I.H. © 1913.
See description of identical brown doll. Re-dressed. $200.00.

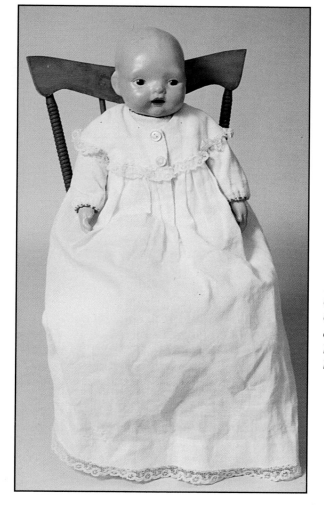

10". Marks: E.I.H. © 1910 (Baby Blossom, Playthings, October 1913).
Composition flange head sewn right onto body, short composition arms. Cloth body, upper arms, and full bent legs, jointed with inside disks. Head and hands have been repainted, re-dressed. $100.00.

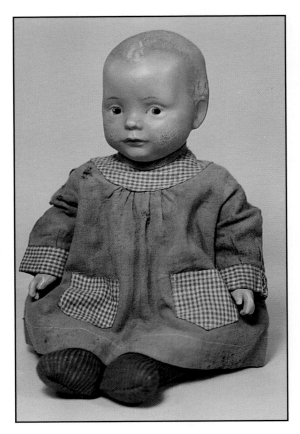

13". Marks: none (Our Baby, Playthings, October 1913). Flared composition head sewn to body, composition hands. Cloth body, upper arms, and bent legs, jointed with inside disks. Molded painted hair and blue eyes, closed mouth. Re-dressed. $250.00.

11½". Marks: none.
Composition head sewn onto body. Short composition arms. Cloth body, upper arms, and straight legs, jointed with inside disks. Very faintly molded hair. Painted blue eyes, closed mouth. Re-dressed. $150.00.
Note: Identical head to Our Baby.

Ca. 10", Scooter is 12½" long. Marks: none on doll. Scotter has paper label, the front of which is missing: (Irish) Mail Kid Trade Mark Reg.//... Patent applied for// ... Farm (?) Hill-Standard Mfg. Co.//... makers of the//... and car (Playthings, February 1915, ad shows similar pull toys).
Composition head is sewn to body. Cloth body and limbs, sewn-in black boots. Arms are jointed with outside disks. Loose hip joints. Molded painted light brown hair and painted blue eyes, closed mouth. Doll is attached to scooter at seat and hands. All original. $600.00.
Note: Head identical to Our Baby.

13". Marks: none (Baby Butterfly, Playthings, January 1914, Pat. November 28, 1911 and June 24, 1913, reg. trademark, three sizes).

Flared composition head sewn to body, short composition arms. Cloth body, upper arms, and curved legs. Molded painted black hair and painted brown eyes, closed mouth. Re-dressed. This head has been repainted, but copied from original example. $250.00.

14", Cotton Joe. Marks: none (See 1914 Marshall Field & Co. catalog, page 17, illustration and description).

Composition flange head sewn onto body, short composition hands. Cloth body and limbs jointed with inside disks, body and cloth arms light tan fabric, straight cloth legs made of olive color material. Black painted hair has hardly any modeling, brown painted eyes, open/closed mouth. Shirt probably original, replaced trousers and shoes. Also see other 14" Cotton Joe in this section with different head mold. $250.00.

14". Marks: none.
Tag sewn into body seam: Copyright 1910//By E.I. Horsman Co.
Tag on trousers: Trade Mark //Cotton Joe.
Flared composition head sewn to body, short composition arms, cloth body, upper arms, brown legs, jointed with inside disks. Slightly molded painted black hair, painted brown eyes, open/closed mouth with white line between lips. All original, except shoes. $250.00.
Note: This is a copy of SFBJ #227, French bisque head. Also see previous Cotton Joe with different head mold.

14". Marks: E.I.H. © 1914.
Composition shoulder head and short arms. Cloth body, upper arms, and legs, jointed at shoulders and hips with inside disks. White socks are actually part of leg casing. Molded painted light brown hair and painted blue eyes, closed mouth. Original jumper dress. Shoes replaced. $150.00.
Note: The 1915 Horsman catalog showed various numbers of this doll, with molded hair or wigs, dressed as boys and girls in a variety of costumes.

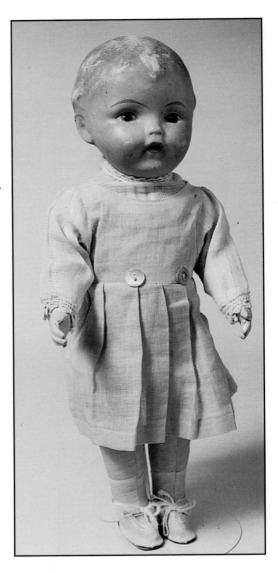

16". Marks: E.I.H. © 1915.
Composition shoulder head and full arms that are molded kind of flat. Cloth body and legs. Arms jointed with elastic, legs with inside disks. Blond mohair wig, blue painted eyes, open/closed mouth. Original clothes. $150.00.

*20". Marks: E.I.H. © 1914 (1915 Horsman catalog).
Composition shoulder head and short arms. Cloth body, upper
arms, and legs, jointed with inside disks (also pin jointed at
knees). Mohair wig, stationary glass eyes, open/closed mouth
with four upper molded painted teeth. Old clothes. $500.00.*

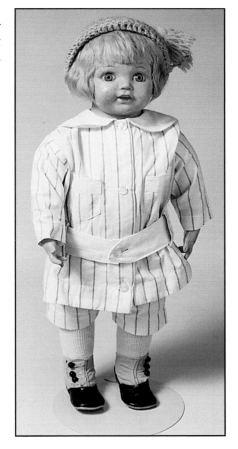

*16". Marks: E.I.H. © 1914.
Composition shoulder head sewn
onto body. Composition arms to
below the elbow, cloth body, upper
arms, and full legs, jointed with
inside disks. Molded painted
brown hair and painted blue eyes,
open/closed mouth with two molded painted upper teeth. All original
clothes. $200.00.
Note: Doll was shown on front
cover of April 1915 Playthings in
three sizes. Toys and Novelties full
page ad of April 1917 shows doll
in corduroy coat, hat, and muff. A
baby is also shown that has the
identical head.*

*16". Marks: E.I.H. ©
1914 (1915 catalog
she is called Topsy).
Composition shoulder
head sewn onto cloth
body. Short composi-
tion arms. Cloth body,
upper arms and legs
jointed with inside
disks, pin jointed
knees. Molded painted
black hair, wire staple
for holding hair ribbon.
Painted dark brown
eyes, open/closed
mouth. Re-dressed.
$350.00.*

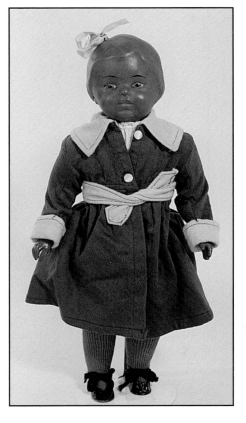

The Gene Carr Kids

These are characters from the cartoon strip *Lady Bountiful*, created by Gene Carr. E. I. Horsman obtained the rights to produce these characters in doll form. There were five Kids named Snowball, Mike, Jane, Skinney and Blink. The dolls were created by Bernard Lipfert (Coleman I) and were pictured in a *Playthings* ad of June 1915. Snowball was a black boy. All had big grins on their faces with two upper teeth. Three of them had big, round eyes. Skinney and Blink had theirs molded shut.

14", Gene Carr Kid. Marks: illegible. Composition flange head sewn to cloth body, composition hands. Cloth body and limbs, jointed with inside disks. Molded painted reddish hair and painted blue eyes. Open/closed mouth with two upper molded, painted teeth. All original. $350.00.

14". Marks: none. Flared composition head sewn to body, composition hands. Cloth body and limbs jointed at shoulders and hips. Painted, closed eyes, open/closed mouth, no teeth. Re-dressed. $250.00.

8". Marks: E.I.H. © (This is Peek-A-Boo, Playthings, June 1913).
All composition, jointed only at shoulders. Molded painted light brown hair and black eyes. Molded and painted, very short eyebrows. Closed mouth. $70.00.
Note: Also came with molded top knot and lock on forehead (Playthings, December 1913).

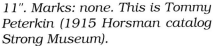

11". Marks: none. This is Tommy Peterkin (1915 Horsman catalog Strong Museum).
Identical construction to Drayton Dimples shown in this section, except for glass eyes. All original. The catalog page showed five Peterkins with glass eyes and mohair wigs (identical) as seen here. Five painted eye versions have molded hair. All had been given names and were dressed in various costumes. An entry in the March 1915 Playthings issue announced a Peterkin named The Panama Kid. The boy that dug the ditch, a charming little brown-skinned youngster from the land of the big canal. $200.00 fair conditon.

13", Baby Bubbles. Marks: E.I.H. © 1915. (1915 Horsman catalog, Strong Museum, pictured in identical sleeper and called "The jolliest, fattest elf of the year. Bursting with health and good humor. Dressed in his go-to-bed nightie.")
Flared composition head sewed to body. Composition hands to one inch above the wrist. Very round all cloth body stuffed with cork, cloth upper arms and legs, jointed with inside disks. Feet have cardboard sole insert. Molded painted blond hair and blue eyes, closed mouth. Original sleeper. $350.00.
Note: Peterkin head was used.

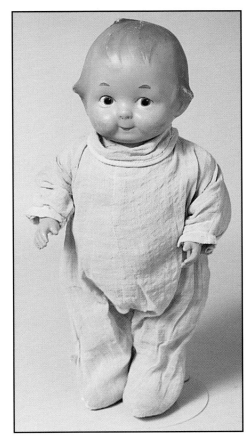

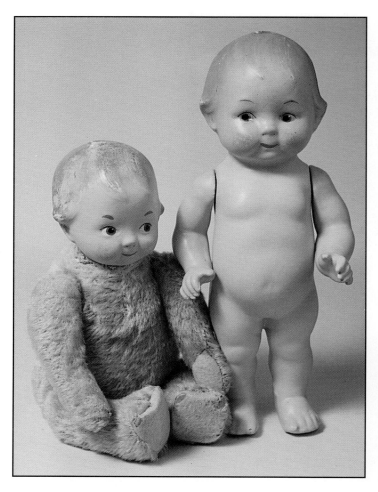

Left: 11", Peterkin. Marks: none.
Composition head, plush body and limbs, jointed at shoulders and hips. Molded painted brown hair and painted blue eyes, closed mouth. (No original advertising available for this version of Peterkin) $350.00.
Right: 12", Peterkin Marks: none (Toys And Novelties, July 1918 – This ad was advertising the all composition Peterkin as their new version of him and that the doll was in its third year of production ("Heads copyrighted 1914 by E. I. Horsman Co.")
All composition, jointed only at shoulders. Head mold and decoration same as above. $200.00.

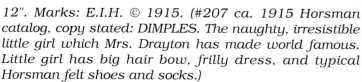

12". Marks: E.I.H. © 1915. (#207 ca. 1915 Horsman catalog, copy stated: DIMPLES. The naughty, irresistible little girl which Mrs. Drayton has made world famous. Little girl has big hair bow, frilly dress, and typical Horsman felt shoes and socks.)
Composition head, arms, and legs including lower torso. Cloth body stuffed with cork, jointed at shoulders only. Original blond mohair wig, painted blue eyes. Molded, painted, short eyebrows, closed mouth. $100.00 fair condition.
Note: Unusually flat arms on side next to body. (Same body construction as Tommy Peterkin.)

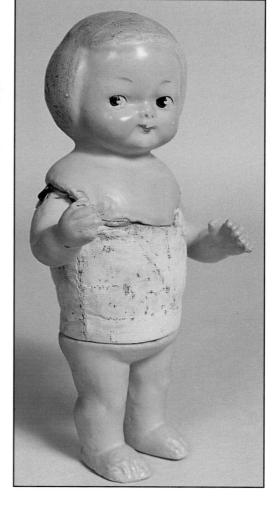

8½". Marks: none. German papier mache composition doll similar in construction to Drayton's Dimples (included for comparison purposes and may have been sold by Horsman).
Composition shoulder head, full arms, legs, and lower torso. Stuffed cloth body. Arms pin jointed to outside. Black eyes, closed mouth, molded painted brown hair. $50.00.

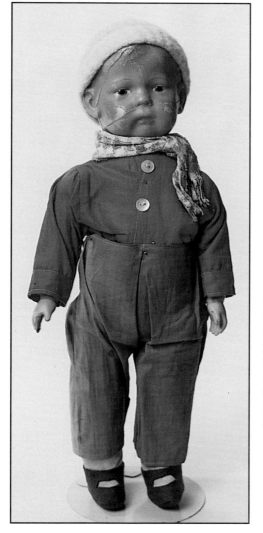

15". Marks: none (he is one of the Art Peasant Dolls seen in 1915 catalog at Strong Museum).
Flared composition head and short arms, cloth body, upper arms, and legs, jointed with inside disks. Molded painted hair and painted brown eyes, closed mouth. All original, except for cap. $150.00 (poor condition).
Note: The catalog illustration shows an identical outfit and a companion girl doll. This doll very much resembles the Kaethe Kruse No. 1 doll after the Fiammingo head.

12". Marks: E.I.H. © 1915.
Frisky Fido (see 1915 Horsman catalog at the Strong Museum, No. 129, "A new creation by Mrs. Drayton. Fido's clothes are by the best tailor in Dogville").
Composition flange head, cloth body and limbs jointed with inside disks. Painted brown eyes. Protruding, molded, painted tongue. Blouse is original. Pants should be striped knickers, also a bow tie. $100.00 fair condition.
Note: The catalog also shows No. 130, Pussy Precious, A companion pet for Fido. "This is the original innocent pussy that ate the canary." (Same construction and composition cat's head.)

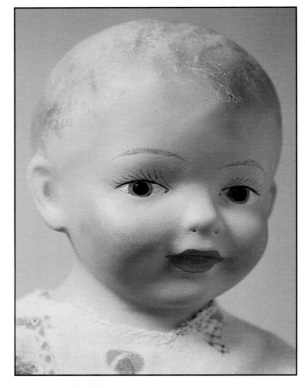

16". Marks: E.I.H. © 1916.
Composition shoulder head and short arms, cloth body, legs, and upper arms, jointed at shoulders and hips with inside disks. Faintly molded, painted light brown hair and painted blue eyes, open/closed mouth. Face has been restored. $150.00.

15½". Marks: T. T. Co. Cloth tag: Uncle Sam's Kids//Trade Mark//Design Patent Applied For//E. I. Horsman Co., New York (See Toys and Novelties, May 1917, Design Pat. April 1917, Miss Sam (not illustrated), Master Sam, All Names Trade Mark).
Composition shoulder head and short arms, cloth body, upper arms, and legs, jointed with inside disks. Molded painted light brown hair and painted blue eyes, closed mouth. All original. $350.00.

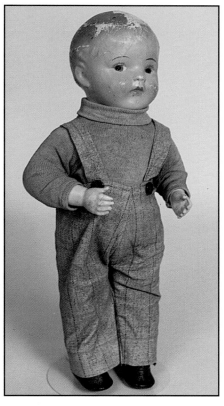

16". Marks: E.I.H. © 1917 (Rookie, Toys and Novelties, May, 1917).
Composition shoulder head and arms. Cloth body, upper arms, and full legs, jointed with inside disks. Molded painted light brown hair and blue eyes, open/closed mouth. All original. $250.00.

16". Marks: E.I.H. Co. on head and torso (Toys and Novelties, July 1918).
Composition socket head on slant hip, ball-jointed body. Original blond mohair wig, gray celluloid sleep eyes, closed mouth. Old clothes. $300.00.

14". Marks: E.I.H. © 1914.
Tag on pants: Jackie Coogan Kid //Licensed By Jackie Coogan// Patent Pending.
Flared composition head sewn to body. Lower composition arms. Cloth body and legs jointed with inside disks. Both arms are bent. Molded painted hair and painted brown eyes. Closed mouth. $100.00 head cracked; $400.00 in good condition.
Note: A standard dolly face head was used. See other Jackie Coogan in this section, with typical Jackie Coogan pageboy haircut.

15". Marks: none (Playthings, March 1920).
Tag on sleeve: Little Mary Mix Up, next line illegible//New York Evening Herald//Mfd. by E. I.
Horsman. (Cartoon character by R. M. Brinkerhoff. A booklet was furnished with every doll.)
Composition shoulder head and lower arms. Cloth body, upper arms, and legs, jointed with
inside disks. Molded painted hair, with pinhole into the head for hair ribbon. Painted blue eyes,
closed mouth. All original. $350.00 face rep.

14". Marks: E.I.H.//19 © 21.
Cloth label on pants: *Jackie Coogan Kid//Licensed by Jackie Coogan//Patent Pending.*
Composition shoulder head and short arms, molded painted hair and painted brown eyes, closed mouth. Cloth body and limbs, jointed with inside disks. Both arms are bent at elbow. All original. $400.00.
Note: Also see earlier version pictured in this section.

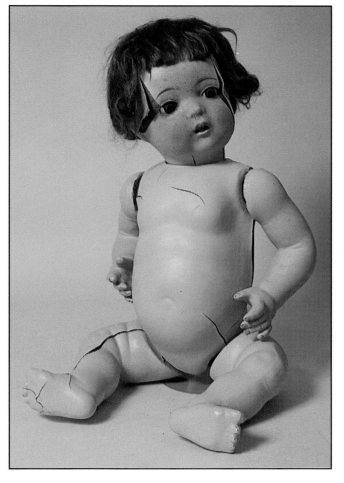

20". Marks: E.I.H. © A.D. Co.
All composition, fully jointed. Medium brown original mohair wig. Gray celluloid sleep eyes, open mouth with two upper teeth. $50.00; $350.00 good condition.
Note: *Playthings, May 1920: Adtocolite Babies. Our wonderful full composition baby in four sizes, both painted hair and with wigs and moving eyes.*

Baby Horsman

Most composition dolls intended to be toys have always been mass produced. This meant that makers were watching the "bottom line," trying to keep production costs low. Profit margins were narrow and competition keen. The same style body and limbs were used for many dolls, and even bisque character heads were sometimes mounted on stock bodies (see Averill's Bonnie Babe etc.). There were always a few exceptions to the rule. Such an exception was Baby Horsman. A totally new body and limbs were created for this doll. While many composition babies have similar cloth bodies, this one is different. The seat is much deeper so that it can sit better and the front is well rounded. While the arms are disk jointed at the shoulders, they are very loosely stuffed and floppy. The curved cloth legs are also stuffed very loosely towards the joints. That this was done intentionally is confirmed by a full-page display ad in a 1923 issue of *Toys and Novelties*, which stressed the "soft, cuddlesome feeling of a real baby." The intention definitely was to create a very realistic, special baby. This idea is reinforced by a quote in the advertising copy: "Baby Horsman's hands are the dimpled hands of a baby." Most unusual is the head of this 24" character baby. While most good quality, higher priced composition

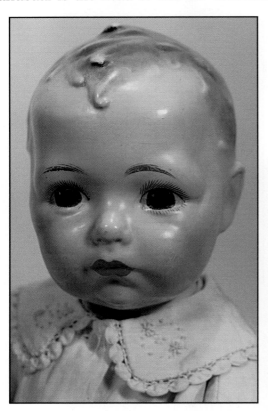

dolls had sleep eyes, this one has eyes that are artistically painted with extra detailing such as "rays" on the irises and multi-stroke brows. The quality in the modeling of the features is exceptional, beautifully portraying the mood of a pensive looking child. Baby Horsman may have been created in response to the tremendous success of the Bye-Lo Baby.

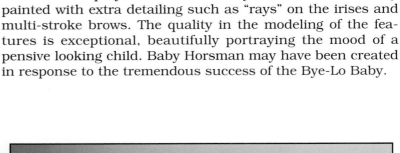

24", Baby Horsman (Playthings, January 1923). Marks: E.I. © H C. (designed by Edith Hitchcock).
Composition flange head and hands, cloth body and limbs, very loosely stuffed, disk jointed at shoulders, stitched hip joints. Molded painted light brown hair, painted blue eyes, closed mouth. Re-dressed. (For picture of body construction see Baby Horsman and variants.) $350.00.

Baby Horsman and variants.
14", 20", and 24", all are marked E. I. © H. Co.
Since the construction of the two smaller dolls diverges so widely from the advertising claims (soft and cuddly - small doll, particularly, stuffed very firmly), it is uncertain that they were sold as Baby Horsman. 14", $150.00; 20", $200.00; 24", $350.00.
Note: The 14" baby's head was cut off at the top and glued back to facilitate insertion of the sleep eyes. This was not done for the 20" size, indicating that the small doll is of an earlier date.

16". Marks: E.I. © H. Co.//E. I. Horsman//Inc. (head: Baby Horsman mold).
Composition shoulder head and full arms, jointed at shoulders, composition legs to above the knee, cloth body, stitched hip joints. Molded painted blond hair and blue eyes. Closed mouth. Re-dressed. $180.00.

19". Marks: E.I.H. © A.D.C. (Toys and Novelties, April 1922).
Composition shoulder head and arms to below the elbow. Cloth body and straight legs. No shoulder joints, stitched hip joints. Molded painted blond hair and painted blue eyes, closed mouth. All original. $350.00.

20". Marks: E.I.H. © Co. Inc. Ca. 1924.
Dress tag: Horsman// Doll//Voice Patented// By B. E. Lloyd.
Cardboard tag on underwear: To make eyes move. Should eyes stick, pressure applied equally on the eyes with the finger tips will correct this. if eyes are fastened, remove pin from back of head.
Composition shoulder head and arms to below the elbow, no shoulder joints. Composition legs to above the knee, stitched hip joints. Cotton stuffed cloth body and upper limbs. Brown mohair wig. Gray celluloid sleep eyes, open mouth with two upper teeth, celluloid tongue. All original. $350.00.

20". Marks: E.I.H. © Co. Inc. Ca. 1924.
Data identical to previous doll. $350.00.

17", Tynie Baby. Marks: none. Composition flange head and short arms, cloth body and limbs, stitched hip joints. Molded painted blond hair and painted blue eyes. Closed mouth. Doll came in long christening gown of very cheap material that was very dirty and totally disintegrated. Arms have been slipcovered. $150.00.

21", Tynie Baby. Marks: © 1924//E.I.H. Co. Inc. (Copyright 1924).
Composition flange head and full arms jointed at shoulders. Cloth body and all cloth legs with stitched hip joints. Molded painted blond hair, tin sleep eyes, closed mouth. Re-dressed. $180.00 faded.

16". Marks: Horsman.
Composition flange head and limbs, legs curved, jointed at shoulders and hips, cloth body. Molded painted hair and green celluloid sleep eyes, open mouth. Re-dressed. $100.00.

22". Marks: E.I.H. Co. Inc. (Baby Dimples, Toys and Novelties, September, 1927).
Composition flange head and arms, jointed at shoulders, bent legs to above the knee. Cloth body and upper limbs, stitched hip joints. Molded painted blond hair, gray tin sleep eyes, open mouth with two upper teeth, molded tongue. All original (no dress). $350.00.

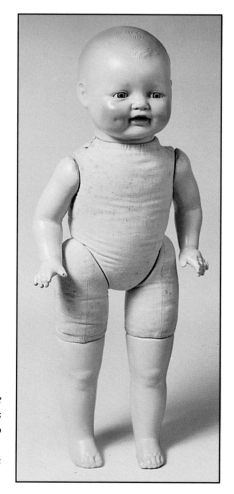

21". Marks: E.I.H. © Co. Inc.
Composition flange head, arms, and legs to above the knee. Cloth body and upper legs, jointed at shoulders and hips. Gray tin sleep eyes, open mouth with two upper teeth. All original. $200.00.
Note: Obviously, a Baby Dimples head was used for this straight leg doll.

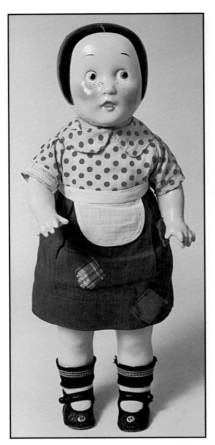

18". Marks: ©//1925//M.N.S.
Dress tag: Horsman//Doll//MFD in U.S.A.
Sleeve tag: Ella Cinders//Trade Mark Reg. U.S. Pat. Off.//
Copyright 1925//Metropolitan Newspaper Service. (Ella Cinders, Playthings, July, 1928).
Composition flange head, arms, and legs to above the knee. Firmly stuffed cloth body and upper legs, jointed at shoulders and hips. Painted black hair with painted middle part, painted blue eyes, open/closed mouth with white line for teeth, freckles across nose. All original. $600.00.
Note: From the famous comic strip by Bill Conselman and Charlie Plumb.

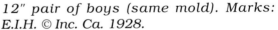

12" pair of boys (same mold). Marks: E.I.H. © Inc. Ca. 1928.
Composition shoulder heads and limbs, cloth bodies, jointed at shoulders and hips. Molded painted hair and painted eyes, closed mouths. Left: original clothes, old shoes/socks. Right: Re-dressed. $125.00 each.

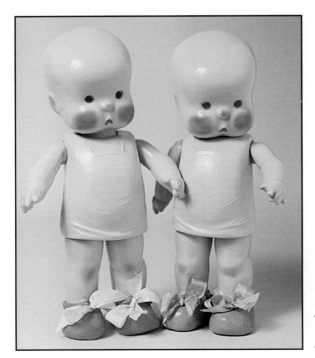

10" pair of HEbee-SHEbees, cartoon characters created by Charles Twelvetrees (Playthings, April, 1926). Marks: none.
All composition, fully jointed. Molded painted shirts and blue and pink slippers. Slippers have wire loop in front for insertion of ribbon. No molded or painted hair. Blue irises and pupils, closed mouth. $350.00 each fair.

20". Marks: E.I. © H. Co.//E. I. Horsman//Inc. Ca. 1928. Composition shoulder head, arms, and legs to above the knee. Cloth body and upper legs. Jointed at shoulders, stitched hip joints. Mohair wig, gray tin sleep eyes, open mouth with two teeth and celluloid tongue. All original except bow, shoes, and socks. $250.00.

Two Rosebud dolls.
20". Marks: Rosebud. Ca. 1930.
Tag on orange dress: Rosebud//MF'D in U.S.A.
Composition head, shoulder plate and limbs, fully jointed. Cloth body firmly stuffed with cotton.
Left: Blond human hair wig.
Right: Brown mohair wig.
Gray tin sleep eyes, paint upper and lower lashes, real upper lashes, multi-stroke brows. Open mouth with four upper teeth, dimples in cheeks. All original. $350.00 each.

Horsman's Patsy Competition

Horsman had bought the composition doll line of Louis Amberg & Son in 1930, including a 14" all-composition girl with molded hair and a jointed waist. In the November 1930 issue of *Playthings*, Horsman announced that their Peggy was made in three sizes, 12", 14", and 20" (the 14" Peggy pictured was no other than the Amberg twist waist doll). All three featured drill holes in their heads to hold a stick pin with hair ribbon. Obviously, Horsman was trying to compete with popular Patsy line.

Apparently, the Peggy dolls did not sell as well as expected, as they were not featured the following year. The April 1931 issue of *Playthings* carried another Horsman announcement, illustrated with a doll that looked much more like the Effanbee Patsys. The article stated "Babs is the smallest, then comes Sue, then Jane, and Nan is the largest." (Compare sizes: Patsy, Jr., Patsy, Patsy Joan, Patsy Ann.)

14", Peggy. Marks: Amberg//Pat. Pend.// L.A. & SD. Ca. 1928. $250.00.
20" Peggy Ann. Marks: none. $350.00.
Dress tag front: Peggy Ann.
Dress tag back: Horsman//Doll//MF'D. U.S.A.
12", probably sold by Horsman as Peggy Jr. Marks: IT. $350.00.
Two smaller dolls: All composition, fully jointed. 14" jointed waist.
Large doll: Cloth body, swivel shoulder plate.
All three dolls have pin holes in their heads.
Stickpin keeps hairbow in place.

This picture accompanied the second Horsman announcement (April 1931).
Note that fabric, trim, and style of outfit is identical to that of 11½" Babs seen in this section (pg. 273 left photograph).

Close-up of Babs seen in the previous illustration. If all Horsman Patsy look-alikes had no identification marks on the dolls themselves, collectors would do well to commit to memory the configuration of the waves framing the face and chin dimple, to be able to recognize Horsman look-alike dolls of this series.

11½". Marks: none (Babs, Playthings, April 1931).
All composition, fully jointed molded painted brown hair and blue tin sleep eyes, closed mouth. All original. $200.00.
Note: Also see previous comments on Patsy competition.

17". Marks: none (Jane, Playthings, April 1931).
All composition, fully jointed, molded painted hair and blue tin sleep eyes, closed mouth, dimple in chin. Redressed. $250.00.
Note: This would be the Patsy Joan equivalent. Patsy and Patsy Ann size not pictured. See previous introductory comments on Patsy competition.

Two 13", Peterkins. Marks: E.I.H. © Inc.
(Toys and Novelties, June 1929).
Composition flange head and limbs, jointed at shoulders and hips. Cloth body. Molded painted hair and eyes, closed mouth.
Left: all original, tagged outfit.
Right: Re-dressed and repainted. White, $150.00; Brown, $400.00.

11". Marks: ©//Horsman. 1930s.
Box lid: Baby//Buttercup//Kantbreak//Hard Rubber Head.
All rubber, fully jointed. Molded painted dark brown hair, gray tin sleep eyes, open mouth with round hole and drink and wet mechanism. Original clothes and box. (box contained homemade layette.) $250.00.
Note: Hard rubber head, but included for completeness (Effanbee's Dydee very popular at this time.)

27". Marks: none on doll (Shirley Temple look alike).
Silver and blue paper tag (with rearing horseman in middle of shield): A//Horsman // Doll.
Composition head, shoulder plate, arms, and legs, cloth body. Jointed at shoulders, stitched hip joints. Blond mohair wig retains its original set. Brown tin sleep eyes, open mouth, four upper teeth. All original. $350.00.

Left: 23". Marks: Sister//1937 Horsman.
Right: 21". Marks: Brother//1937 Horsman.
Composition flange heads, arms, and straight legs to above the knee, jointed at shoulders. Cloth body and upper legs, stitched hip joints. Molded painted hair (Sister with top knot) and brown sleep eyes. Sister had metal eyes, Brother's are celluloid with unusually large irises. Both have closed, very small mouths. Re-dressed. $350.00 each fair.

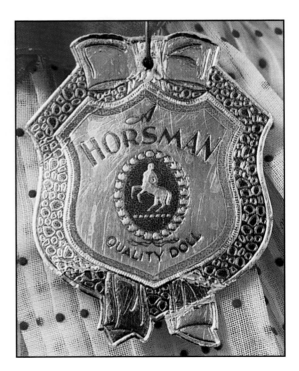

Whatsit Dolls Get Big Publicity Send-Off

"Whatsit Dolls are truly different! There are two distinct models, each with a different facial expression. They are produced under a special license, and will be featured in the *Whatsit*, a newspaper by and for boys and girls, with a circulation of over three million copies. Further promotional efforts by the Whatsit licensor will consist of an extensive nationwide publicity campaign by radio, newspaper, and other media" (*Toys and Bicycles*, May 1937). (The two dolls' names were Naughty Sue and Roberta. See next two illustrations.)

As of this date, no further information was available on the Whatsit campaign. It may have been a reaction to Effanbee's very popular *Patsytown News*, a promotional piece in the shape of a newspaper for children.

14". Marks: Naughty Sue//1937 © Horsman.
Original tag accompanying doll read as follows: Whatsit (followed by drawing of two stick figures) Dolls// by children//for children//A Genuine Horsman Doll.
Back of tag: A Gift//From Whatsit To you//Send this tag with your name and address, and we will mail for FREE a beautiful Whatsit Stamp Album with a complete collection of 96 Whatsit stamps designed by children for children. Be sure to write you name and address plainly. Whatsit Design Club, 277 Park Avenue, New York City.
All composition, fully jointed. Molded painted brown hair with molded top knot for tying on bow. Painted blue eyes to side and up. Open/closed mouth, molded tongue. Bent right arm. Re-dressed (original Shirley Temple dress). $400.00.

14". Marks: Roberta//© 1937 Horsman.
Had same double sided tag as Naughty Sue (Whatsit).
All composition, fully jointed. Molded painted brown hair
with middle part and braids curled into buns over ears.
Puckered, closed mouth. Brown sleep eyes have been
oiled. Re-dressed. $400.00.

15". Marks: "C" Jeanie//Horsman.
Composition flange head, arms, and tied-on swinging
legs. Cloth body with mama crier, old clothes and
shoes. Molded painted brown hair with slight top
knot, bangs in front, creating a definite part horizontal
to forehead. Molded, curly hair in back of bottom of
hairdo. Very small closed mouth. Tin sleep eyes,
never had lashes. $150.00.

12". Marks: JO-JO//© 1937 Horsman.
All composition, fully jointed. Girl has original brown
mohair with two pigtails (over molded hair) and
brown tin sleep eyes. Boy has molded paint dark
brown hair and blue tin sleep eyes. Both have closed
mouth. Contemporary clothes with new shoes and
socks. $150.00 each.

24" and 28". Marks: none (Playthings, September 1938).
Paper hang tag: Horsman's Sweetheart//A Horsman Art Doll.
All composition except for arms which are made of hard rubber. Fully jointed. Brown mohair wigs, green sleep eyes, open mouths with six upper teeth. All original. $700.00 each.

11". Marks: none. Late 1940s.
Paper tag: A//Genuine//Horsman//Art Doll.
Composition flange head, arms to above elbow, and bent legs to above knee with stitched hip joints. Cloth body. Original red mohair wig, blue tin sleep eyes, closed mouth. All original. $200.00.
Note: Similarity to Alexander's Bitsy, but much cheaper quality.

13". Marks: none.
Paper tag: Horsman//Bright Star//Quality Doll. 1940s.
All composition, fully jointed. Medium brown mohair wig, gray sleep eyes, open mouth with four upper teeth. All original. This doll came in several sizes. $200.00.

21". Marks: none. 1940s.
Paper label: A//Genuine//Horsman//Rosebud//Doll.
Brown composition swivel head and shoulder plate, jointed arms and tied on, swinging "uni" legs, cloth body with mama crier that still works. Black mohair wig, brown sleep eyes, open mouth with four upper teeth. All original. $400.00.

18". Marks: Horsman//Doll.
Paper tag: A//Genuine//Horsman//Art Doll.
Brown composition flange head and tied-on lower limbs. Cloth body and upper limbs. Ma-ma voice still works. Black mohair wig over molded hair, brown sleep eyes, closed mouth. All original.
$350.00.

12". Marks: none. Ca. 1948.
Campbell Kids.
All composition, fully jointed, with molded painted shoes and socks. Molded painted brown hair, painted black eyes, closed mouths. All original. $350.00 each.

IRWIN & CO.
NEW YORK CITY

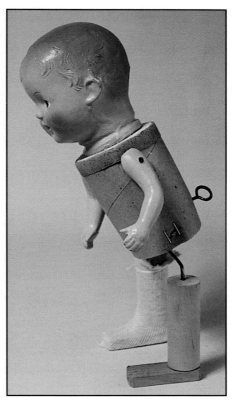

*13", Mechanical Toddler. Marks: Gold Doll (E. Goldberger) (Playthings, November 1932, Ad placed by Irwin).
Composition flange head has been glued to a cardboard cylinder which is the body and hides the walking mechanism. Wooden legs and feet are mounted on rods. Molded painted yellow hair and painted blue
eyes, closed mouth. All original (composition arms). $150.00.*
*Note: The Playthings ad illustration showed another toddler with a different head as well as a teddy
bear. The ad further claimed that they were offering 12 different characters. Each doll had a round paper
tag pinned to their chest, calling them Darling Toddlers.*

IDEAL NOVELTY & TOY CO.
BROOKLYN, NEW YORK

Ideal Novelty & Toy Co., of Brooklyn, NY, was founded by Morris Michtom in 1906. Ideal had started
small, and for some years produced teddy bears and other stuffed toys.

Two of the earliest dolls advertised by Ideal in 1910 were Mr. Hooligan, a character from the comic
strip *Happy Hooligan*, created by Frederick Burr Opper and Snookums, from the comic strip *The Newlyweds*, by George McManus. Ideal claimed that the dolls were made with "Ideal unbreakable heads."
Actually, those heads were probably made in Germany, as they are constructed of papier mache composition. Both featured plush bodies, just like Horsman's Billiken, the sales success of the day. The
earliest Ideal doll made of domestic glue base composition and available for examination was Baby
Mine, advertised in *Playthings*, June 1911.

By 1913, Ideal was carrying an extensive line of dolls. As other enterprises, they were offering original
designs and those copied from German bisque character dolls. In 1915, Ideal concluded a licensing
agreement for the production of the Uneeda Kid, well known advertising symbol of The National
Bisquit Company.

That same year, Ideal was granted a patent for a special eye mechanism which could be inserted into a doll's head through the neck opening. Up to now, in order to insert sleep eyes, the top of the head had to be cut off and reglued after insertion. This necessitated the use of a wig. These new eyes could not only close but they also "winked and blinked." This was another exclusive that helped Ideal become a leader in the doll industry (see separate chapter on doll eyes).

While Georgene Averill, of Averill Manufacturing Co., had invented and popularized the basic design of the mama doll (see chapter on mama dolls), Ideal made their own special contributions in this area. In 1923, they advertised a line of mama dolls called Flossy Flirt. The name derived from the fact that Flossy Flirt's sleep eyes could not only wink and blink, but they also moved from side to side.

During this period, Ideal was the first American company to produce dolls with rubber limbs. Vanity Flossy, another mama doll, which was introduced in 1927, had rubber arms and a cupped right hand. With it she could hold a mirror or brush. Some of the Flossies had rubber legs with squeakers in them. Babies with rubber arms and eventually rubber legs were produced as well. In the 30s, when Effanbee's all-rubber Dy-Dee Baby was a big sales leader, Ideal featured Betsy Wetsy, an all-rubber doll.

Ideal's biggest success was the Shirley Temple doll, produced under license from Fox Films Corp., and designed and modeled by famous doll sculptor, Bernard Lipfert. Introduced in 1934, she was still listed in their 1939 catalog. She was made in seven sizes

Ad from the January 1910 issue of Playthings, placed by Ideal. Pictured in the ad is Mr. Hooligan, a character from the comic strip Happy Hooligan, by Frederich Burr Opper. Mr. Hooligan is not an American-made composition doll. His head was probably produced in Germany. The picture is included here for completeness sake, as Mr. Hooligan was one of the first dolls assembled and sold by Ideal. At this time, Horsman's Billiken was all the rage. Billiken, too, had a plush body. $500.00.
Note: The ad indicated that "we can furnish heads to manufacturers and complete dolls to jobbers." It also mentions, Snookums, the Newlywed doll.

14". Marks: none. Snookums from the cartoon The Newlyweds, by George McManus (Playthings, January 1910).
Papier mache composition head, painted features, open/closed mouth with one painted tooth. Molded top knot at peak of head and one in back. Plush body and limbs with felt mitten hands and boots. Jointed at shoulders and hips. $600.00.
Note: This is not an American-made composition doll. The head was probably made in Germany. It is included here for completeness sake, as it is one of the first dolls Ideal assembled and sold.

and dressed in copies of the costumes Shirley wore in her movies. Just like Effanbee's Patsy doll, Shirley was a trendsetter and had many imitators. During the 30s, Ideal created other dolls of movie stars such as Judy Garland and Deanna Durbin. While popular, none of them were as successful as the Shirley Temple dolls. During the 30s, Ideal entered into other licensing agreements with various firms like Walt Disney. They also produced dolls for mail order companies like Sears, and smaller firms such as Arranbee and Vogue. In fact, according to the Colemans, Ideal was one of the few companies that produced their own composition parts. For many of the smaller companies, "manufacturing" dolls actually meant assembling them from parts purchased elsewhere.

The production of composition dolls ended around 1950 and plastics became the preferred material for dollmaking. Ideal remained a leader in the toy industry for many years to come.

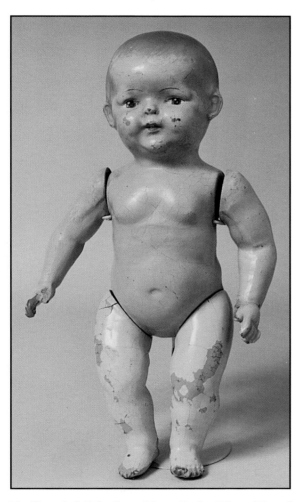

Muff and doll both sold as Baby Mine (Playthings, July 1911).
12" doll. Marks: Ideal//Baby Mine.
Romper tagged: Baby Mine//Ideal//Made in USA.
All composition, jointed at shoulders and hips only, with steel springs. Painted eyes and hair, open/closed mouth with two upper teeth.
7" x 5" x 13" muff marked: Ideal Baby Mine//Trademark//U.S. Pat. 41179//Doll Muff. Doll, $150.00; Muff, $80.00.
Note: Notation on ad "By special permission of Margaret Mayo, Playwright, who originated the 'Baby Mine' comedy." Mask face on muff is made of celluloid and is not of the same mold as the composition doll's head.

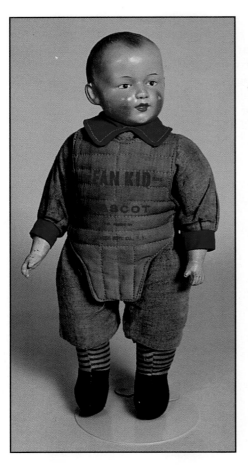

14", Fan Kid. Marks: none.
Vest: FAN KID//Trade Mark//Mascot//Pat. Applied for// Strauss Mfg. Co. NY (Playthings, July 1912).
Composition flange head and short arms, cloth body and limbs, jointed with inside disks. Striped stockings and black cloth boots are part of leg casing. Molded paint hair and blue eyes, concave pupils. Open/closed mouth with molded tongue. All original. $250.00.

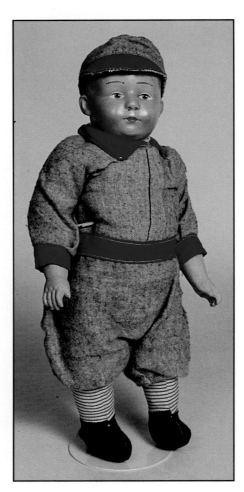

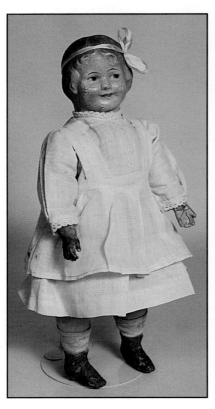

14". Marks: none (Playthings, June 1912) this may be their Naughty Marietta. Composition flange, short arms and brown boots. Cloth body and limbs jointed with outside disks. Molded brown hair with depression all around the head to accommodate ribbon. Blue painted eyes, open closed mouth with two painted teeth. Seems all original. $50.00 poor condition.

11½". Marks: none (presumed to be Ideal, identical uniform as Fan Kid).
Composition flange head and short arms, cloth body and limbs, jointed with outside disks. Red striped stockings. Black boots are also sewn in. Molded painted brown hair and blue eyes, closed mouth. Original uniform including cap. $175.00.

15". Marks: none (Playthings ad March 1913, Baby Betty).
Composition flange head, short arms, and well modeled legs to above the knee. Cloth body and upper limbs, jointed with inside disks. Molded painted and striated, brown hair. Blue painted eyes, open mouth. $50.00 poor condition; $150.00 average.
Note: Identical head as doll in Scots costume, except for open mouth.

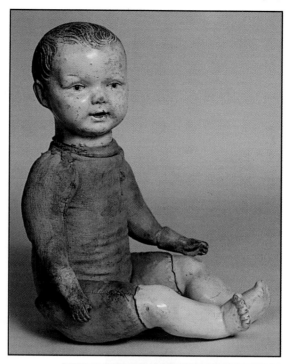

15". Marks: none (Farmer Boy, Playthings, June 1914). Composition flange head has molded red cap. Molded painted brown hair, painted blue eyes. Mouth is puckered as if he were whistling (no actual opening). Composition arms to above the elbow and legs with bare feet to above the knee. Cloth body and upper limbs, jointed with inside disks. Original clothes. $350.00.

17". Marks: none (Playthings, March 1913).
Composition flange head, short arms and molded white boots. Cloth body and limbs jointed with outside disks. Molded painted, striated hair and painted blue eyes, open/closed mouth. Original clothes. $150.00.
Note: This head was also used for Arctic Boy, Tiny Toddler, Baby Betty (various 1913 ads).

13". Marks: none (Playthings, June 1915, In the ad his name is Bronco Bill, and he is dressed as a cowboy).
Composition flange head, short arms and molded brown boots. Cloth body and limbs, jointed with outside disks. Molded painted brown hair and blue eyes. Closed, puckered mouth. Old clothes. $125.00.

Three Uneeda Bisquit Dolls, 11", 15", and 23" (Various Playthings ads 1915, patent granted December 8, 1914. By special arrangement with The National Bisquit Company).
All have composition flange heads and lower arms. Molded, painted hair and painted blue eyes, closed mouths, molded boots. Cloth bodies and upper limbs, jointed at shoulders only with outside disks. Exception: 11" molded lower torso and molded hat, re-dressed. Other two: All original. (Only one original cracker box.) 11", $450.00; 15", $450.00; 23", $650.00.
Note: Advertised as "Two dolls in one for the price of one. Remove the raincoat and you have another doll — a fine ROMPER BOY." Modeled after Fiammingo Head.

Right: 16". Marks: none (Playthings, June 1915).
Composition shoulder head and short arms, cloth body, upper arms, and legs stuffed with excelsior and jointed with outside disks. Molded painted blond hair with molded ribbon depression, individually rocking, blue sleep eyes, closed mouth, re-dressed. $50.00 (fair condition).
Note: Contemporary body but head did not come on this body assembly.
Left: 15". Marks: none.
Same head as above but composition flange head, short arms and molded boot. Body, upper arms, and legs stuffed with cork. Jointed at shoulders and hips with inside disks. Striped stockings are the leg casing. Re-dressed. $150.00.

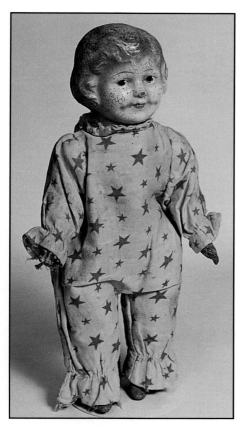

14", Zu-Zu Kid. Marks: none, made by Ideal under license from National Bisquit Co. (Playthings February 1916). Composition flange head, short arms, and brown boots. Cloth body and limbs jointed with inside disks. Molded painted brown hair, painted blue eyes. Open/closed mouth with four painted teeth. Original clown suit. Pointed hat of same material missing and Zu-Zu Cracker box. $150.00 fair.

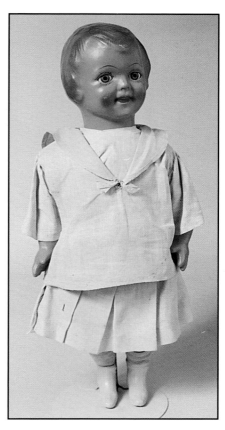

16". Marks: none (Playthings, May 1913). Identical head mold and construction to girl in white sailor outfit, except for painted eyes. Redressed. $150.00.

15", Sailor Girl. Marks: none. Cloth tag: Ideal Novelty & Toy// Moving Eyes//Trade Mark, Pat. August. 10-15//Made in USA. Composition flange head and arms to inch above elbow, molded white boots. Separate socks are glued into boots. Cloth body and limbs, jointed with inside disks. Individually rocking gray tin sleep eyes, open/closed mouth with four upper, painted teeth. Molded painted light brown hair. All original. $250.00.

15". Marks: none (has individually rocking Ideal eyes).
Composition flange head, short arms, and molded brown boots, cloth body, jointed at shoulders and hips with outside disks. Original brown mohair wig over molded hair, blue tin sleep eyes, open/closed mouth with two painted upper teeth. Old clothes. $125.00.

12". Marks: IDEAL US of A, Dough Boy (Toys and Novelties, February 1918). All composition, fully jointed with steel springs. Molded painted hair and blue eyes, closed mouth. Original felt hat. $350.00.

21", Baby. Marks: none, but has individually rocking sleep eyes patented by Ideal. Also, pictured and identified as Ideal, McDonald Bros., Minneapolis, Christmas Catalog of 1919.
Composition flange head and short arms. Cloth body and limbs, bent legs, jointed with inside disks. Molded painted light brown hair with prominently molded, high tuft of hair in front. Gray sleep eyes, open mouth. Redressed. $150.00.

6", head only, Ideal. Marks: none.
Identical head mold as doll shown for previous 21"
baby with painted eyes. $35.00 head only.

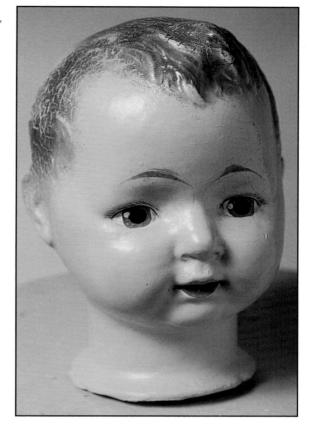

13". Marks: Ideal//US Of A.
Composition flange head, short arms,
and molded brown boots. Cloth body,
upper arms and legs, jointed at shoul-
ders and hips with outside disks. Light
blond mohair wig, blue tin sleep eyes
rock individually. Open/closed mouth
with two painted upper teeth, re-
dressed. $50.00.

17". Marks: Ideal (in diamond) U S of A. Ca 1918.
Composition shoulder head and short arms. Cloth body, upper
arms and legs stuffed with cork, jointed at shoulders and hips
with inside disks. Molded painted light brown hair and blue,
individually rocking eyes, open/closed mouth with four painted
teeth. Re-dressed. $150.00.

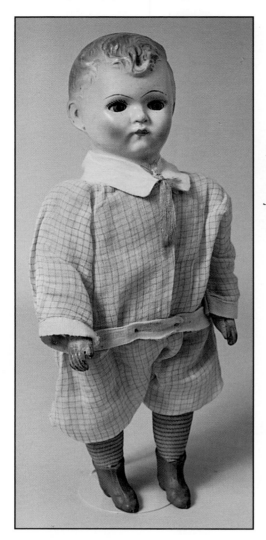

13", Boy. Marks: none (but identified as Ideal doll in McDonald Bros. Co., Wholesale Catalog, Minneapolis, December 1919). Composition flange head, short arms, and molded boots. Cloth body, upper arms, and legs stuffed with excelsior and jointed with outside disks. Molded painted brown hair and blue, individually rocking eyes, closed mouth. Original romper suit. $250.00.

17". Marks: Ideal//US OF A.
Composition shoulder head and short arms. Cloth body, upper arms and legs, stitched hip joints. Molded hair. Must have had wig, no hair color. Blue tin sleep eyes, closed mouth. $50.00 fair condition.

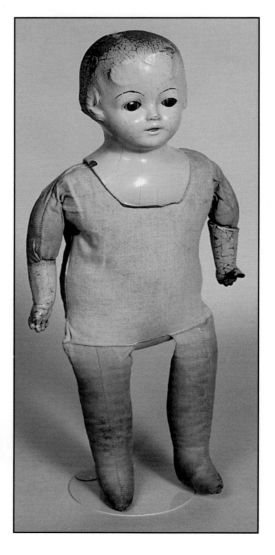

18", Walker. Marks: Ideal (in diamond) and U S of A. Composition shoulder head and lower arms. Cloth body and limbs jointed with inside disks at shoulders and metal outside disks at hips with walker mechanism. Dark brown mohair wig, blue tin sleep eyes rock individually. Open/closed mouth with four painted teeth. Slip, panties, and dress may be original. $250.00.

28". Marks: none.
Composition flange head and short arms, cloth body, upper arms, and legs, jointed with inside disks at shoulders. At hip level, same walker mechanism as girl in previous picture. Molded painted hair with two very distinctive front curls. Blue tin sleep eyes also rock individually, closed mouth and double chin. Re-dressed. $150.00 fair.
Note: A January 1918 Playthings ad pictured a Peggy baby doll with identical head (two front curls definitely verifiable).

16", Soozie Smiles (Playthings, February 1924). Marks: none. Tag is photographic copy of original and reads: 1. Soozie Smiles//is one of the "Ideal" doll//family of one hundred beauti//ful doll brothers and sisters//they all talk, walk, sleep//and are hard to break -

2. My name is//Soozie Smiles//Reg. U.S. Pat. Off.//My dear little friend//if you are good and happy//I smile to you and call "mama"//If you cry, I cry also.//See what//a funny face I make when I cry//Just turn my face around and pull//my hat down to my neck -//Ideal Toy & Novelty Co.//Made in U.S.A.//Pat. Pend.//Ideal//Talking walking sleeping dolls.

Composition flange head with two faces, one smiling and sleep eyes, and one crying with painted eyes. Short composition arms. Cloth body with full cloth legs and stitched hip joints. All stuffed with cotton. All original clothes, including hat, shoes and socks. $400.00.

Note: Playthings, February 1916, Baby Bi-Face, same head, but painted eyes on both sides and a cork stuffed body and dressed as baby in short, white dress, bonnet, and sweater.

13½". Marks (in dotted circle): *Genuine//Twinkie Doll//Copyr. 1916//Eye Pat.//Twinkies Specialty (1920s).*
Composition flange head with individually rocking and also flirting eyes, made of glue base composition. Closed, smiling mouth, molded painted brown hair. Celluloid hands. Cloth body and limbs stuffed with cotton and jointed with inside disks. Flannel body and limb casing is also doll's suit. Felt shoes and vest can be removed. Seven metal bells attached to points on vest. $350.00.
Note: 1916 patent date refers to eye mechanism only. Having individually rocking eyes identifies this doll as having been made by Ideal. It may have been sold by somebody else.

13". Marks: *Ideal (This is Hush-A-Bye-Baby, see* Playthings, *September 1925).*
Composition flange head and short lower arms. Cloth body and straight legs. No shoulder joints, stitched hip joints. Molded painted yellow hair, blue tin sleep eyes, closed mouth, re-dressed. $150.00.
Note close resemblance of this doll to Arranbee's bisque head Dream Baby.

Frequently, a popular doll was sold with varying names. In 1926, Ideal announced the introduction of Suck-A-Thumb baby. This doll had soft rubber arms and cloth legs. The following year, this same doll was called Smiles and had so-called flirty eyes. They moved from side to side in addition to winking and closing. In 1930, the doll was introduced with soft rubber legs as well as arms and was called Tickletoes.

Suck-A-Thumb, the baby with the non-flirting eyes, cloth legs, and rubber arms was used as a premium by various companies using such names as Cuddles and Honeybunch.

16". Marks: Ideal US OF A (diamond shape). This is Smiles (Playthings, July 1927).

Composition flange head, cloth body, and bent legs, rubber arms to within one inch of shoulder joint. Cloth upper arms are glued into rubber part. Stitched hip joints. Molded painted blond hair. Gray tin flirty eyes that rock individually. Open mouth with two painted upper teeth. All original, including pacifier. $80.00 (fair condition).

Note: Identical head as Smiles.

16". Marks: Ideal US of A (This is Tickletoes, Playthings, June 1930).
Composition flange head, cloth body, rubber arms, and straight legs to above the knee, jointed at shoulders, stitched hip joints. Molded painted blond hair and blue metal eyes that also move from side to side. Open mouth with two painted upper teeth. All original. $350.00.
Note: Though the hang tag shows a doll with bent legs, the model pictured here has straight legs.

19", Vanity Flossie (See 1927 Sears Roebuck catalog, illustrated in Toys and Novelties, January 1927). Marks: Ideal (in diamond) U S of A.
Composition flange head, rubber lower arms, composition lower legs. Cloth body and upper limbs stuffed with cotton, jointed at shoulders, stitched hip joints. Dark blond, marcelled mohair wig, blue tin sleep eyes that also can move from side to side. Open/closed mouth with two upper painted teeth. Right hand is cupped so that it can hold objects. Contemporary clothes. $250.00.

20", Flossie Flirt (mama doll). Marks: Ideal.
Composition flange head, short arms, and legs to above the knee. Cloth body with arms tied on and stitched hip joints. Dark brown mohair wig over molded hair. Brown tin sleep eyes that also move from side to side. Open/closed mouth with two upper painted teeth. All original, including shoes and socks. $250.00.

Two Carry Joy Dolls, 16" and 20". Marks: Ideal//US //Of A.

Heart-shaped paper tag on large doll: "Carry Joy"// Reg. U.S. Pat. Off.//Ideal//Talking//Walking// Sleeping//Winking. 16" Carry Joy came with rectangular tag pictured separately.

Composition flange heads and short arms. Cloth body, upper arms, and full legs with stitched hip joints. Blue tin sleep eyes also wink individually. Open/closed mouths with painted upper teeth. Dark brown mohair wigs. Both dolls are all original. Large doll came with her original gray cardboard box which has no markings whatsoever. Small, $200.00; Large, $250.00.

Note: Head molds not identical.

MOTHERS: We want to make your little girl happy with a beautiful Sleeping doll; at the same time we want to acquaint you with the low prices and superior service at our stores.

"Carrie Joy" is an unbreakable doll, 20 in. tall. She sleeps, winks, walks, talks and can turn her head. She has real ha wears a pretty lace-trimmed dress, bor also underclothes, shoes and stockin Your little girl will love "Carrie Joy" than any other doll she has ever **READ OUR WONDERFUL OFFER ON**

Front of original coupon offering Carry Joy as a premium for buying $10.00 worth of merchandise. Unfortunately, the name of the store is not indicated.

Note: Tag mentioned 20", though doll received was 16" tall. Dress shown on tag is identical to that worn by the 16" doll.

SAVE THIS VALUABLE CARD

HOW TO GET THIS LOVELY DOLL FOR ONLY 99c

When you buy at our stores, the amount of your purchase is punched on this card.

Keep this card until you have bought only $10.00 worth of goods. Then return this card to us with only **99c.** and receive one of these charming $3.00 dolls.

Cordially yours,

NAME ....

ADDRESS ....

Back side of coupon offering Carrie Joy as a premium.

18". Marks: Ideal U S of A (in diamond).
Composition flange head, rubber limbs, cloth body and upper limbs, jointed at shoulders, stitched hip joints. Squeeker in rubber legs. Blond mohair wig, gray tin sleep eyes, open/closed mouth with four painted upper teeth. All original. $150.00 rubber fair condition.

298

21". Marks: Ideal US of A in diamond).

Dress tag front: Ideal Dolls Talk Walk Sleep Wink//Eyes Pat. U.S.A.//Aug. 10, 1915//"Flossie//Flirt" Watch My//Eyes Roll //As I Walk.

Back of tag: "Flossie Flirt" is an "Ideal Doll,"//Made in U.S.A. under the most sanitary conditions//"Flossie Flirt" is the strongest composition doll // in the world//Always Insist On Getting A Genuine "Ideal Doll."

Composition flange head. Composition arms and legs are replacements, originals were rubber. Cloth body and upper legs, jointed at shoulder, stitched hip joints. Original reddish brown mohair wig, gray tin sleep eyes that also move from side to side (flirt) and wink independently. Open mouth with four upper teeth. Original clothes, old shoes and socks. $150.00.

17", Peter Pan (The Household Magazine, November 1929). Marks: Ideal (in diamond) US OF A.

Paper heart tag: Peter Pan//Reg. US Pat. Off.//Patent Pending//Ideal.

Composition flange head and hands, cloth (flannel) body and limbs. Body and limb casings are part of clothes, but slippers, vest, collar, and hat are removable. Molded painted light yellow hair and gray tin sleep eyes. Close mouth. $260.00.

Note: In the above ad, the Peter Pan doll was used as a premium. For four subscriptions to The Household Magazine, one could get the doll.

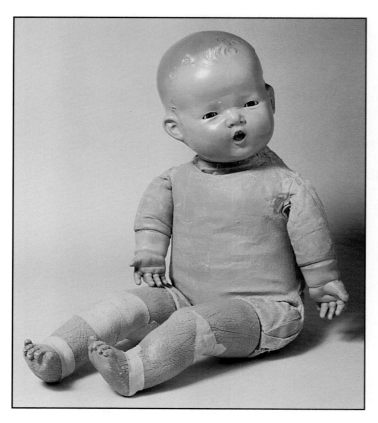

22", Snoozie. Marks: © B. Lipfert (Playthings, November 1933).

Composition flange head, rubberized, stuffed cloth body, short rubber arms and legs to above the knee. Celluloid sleep eyes. Molded painted hair, open mouth with two upper teeth and metal tongue, pierced nostrils. Rubber legs have been patched. $80.00 fair condition. Note: The ad copy stated that "Snoozie lies on her back wide awake, with her baby-like glass (really celluloid) eyes wide open. But lay her on her right side and she goes to sleep peacefully." Such a mechanism is not present on the doll pictured, but has been examined on another 22" doll. Doll in ad has open/closed mouth.

17", Snoozie. Marks: By B. Lipfert (Playthings, November 1933).

Composition flange head, short rubber arms, composition legs to above the knee are original. Cloth body (not rubberized), stitched hip joints. Molded painted hair and gray tin sleep eyes (no special eye mechanism). Open mouth, metal tongue, two upper teeth. Pierce nostrils. $250.00.

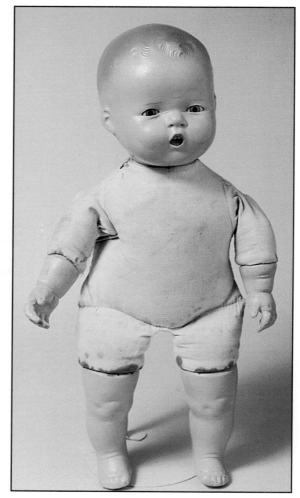

13". Marks on head: Shirley Temple//13.
Body: Shirley Temple//13.
Original pin: The World's Darling. Genuine Shirley Temple.
An Ideal Doll .
All composition, fully jointed, blond mohair wig, hazel
sleep eyes. Open mouth with six upper teeth. All original.
Nancy and David Carlson collection. $850.00.

16". Marks on head: Shirley Temple//
Ideal//Novelties And Toys Corp.
Body: Shirley Temple//16.
Dress tag: Genuine//Shirley Temple//
Doll Dress//Trade Mark Registered//
Ideal Novelties And Toy Co.//NRA
Code//Made in U.S.A.
All composition fully jointed, blond mohair
wig, hazel sleep eyes, open mouth with
six upper teeth. All original. Nancy and
David Carlson collection. $850.00.

18". Marks: Shirley Temple//18 (on head and body)
Captain January outfit.
All composition, fully jointed. Original blond mohair
wig, hazel sleep eyes, open mouth with six upper
teeth. All original. Shirley Temple trunk 20 x 9 x 9".
Doll, $850.00; trunk $200.00.

12". Marks: none. This is Suzette an I-De-Lite doll, 1936. All hard rubber, fully jointed. Blond mohair wig, celluloid sleep eyes, open mouth with two upper teeth. All original. Kathy Evans collection. $350.00+.

Note: Though not made of composition, the doll is included for completeness sake. Looking very much like composition, it can be mistaken for it. However, the doll is much heavier than a comparable 12" example made of composition would be.

12", Mortimer Snerd and Fanny Brice (Baby Snooks). Marks: Ideal Doll//Made in USA (1939 Ideal catalog), designed by J. L. Kallus.

Composition heads and hands, wooden bodies, woven wire mesh flexible limbs with wooden shoes. Molded painted hair, eyes, and open/closed mouths. Fanny has molded hair loop. Both are all original. $250.00 each.

Note: Mortimer Snerd was one of ventriloquist Edgar Bergen's puppets. Fanny Brice, famous comedian, played Baby Snooks character on stage and radio.

9" from nose to rear, 8" height. Marks: Ferdinand W.D. Ent.//Ideal Novelty//& Toy Co// Made in USA, has stenciled bee on back (Playthings ads 1939). (W.D.— Walt Disney.) All composition, fully jointed. Molded painted eyes, open/closed mouth (originally held several flowers in his mouth). $100.00 fair, flower missing.

12". Marks: Ideal Doll//Made in USA (designed by J. L. Kallus) Shown in 1939 Ideal catalog as Otto the Clown.

Composition head and hands, wooden body and shoes, woven wire mesh flexible limbs, original clown suit. Molded painted reddish hair and painted blue eyes, white face make-up, four blue dots, open/closed mouth with two molded painted teeth. $250.00.

21". Marks: Ideal (Dopey).
Composition flange head and hands to wrist (hands have only four fingers). Cloth body and limbs. No hip joints. Bald head, painted blue eyes, jointed jaw, molded painted tongue. Original clothes. Cap is a replacement. $800.00.

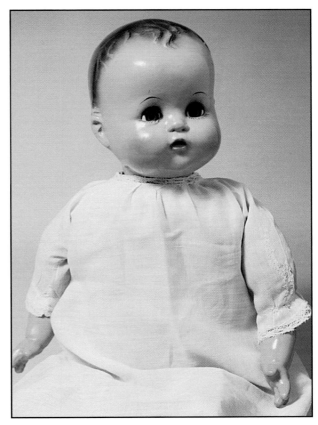

18". Marks: Ideal.
Composition flange head, lower arms and bent legs. Cloth body and upper limbs with stitched joints. Molded painted brown hair, gray sleep eyes, closed mouth. Re-dressed. $95.00.

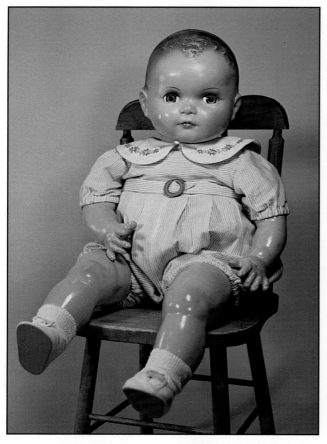

23". Not marked (head: Brother Coos mold). Mark seems to have been rubbed out.
Molded painted hair same as Sister, also brown sleep eyes and closed mouth, composition head, shoulder plate, and limbs, cloth body, re-dressed. $250.00.

24". Marks: Ideal Doll//Made In USA (Brother Coos head mold).
Original brown mohair wig over molded painted hair, brown sleep eyes, closed mouth. Composition head on composition shoulder plate, cloth body, composition limbs (bent legs), re-dressed. $250.00.

7½" and 11". Marks on both: "Pinocchio"//Des. & © by Walt Disney//Made by Ideal Novelty & Toy Co. Marks on heads: © P. WDP//Ideal Doll//Made in U.S.A. (Playthings, September 1939).
Composition heads and bodies, wooden segmented limbs.
7½": Molded hat with applied band, oilcloth collar and cut out, blue felt bow, black eyes. $350.00.
11": Felt hat with applied, blue band, molded, paint white collar, tied rayon ribbon bow, blue eyes. $450.00.

20″. Marks on head: © P. WDP//Ideal Doll//Made in USA.
Marks on front: "Pinocchio"//Des. & © By Walt Disney//
Made by Ideal Novelty & Toy Co.
Composition head, body, and gloved hands, wooden seg-
mented limbs. Real bow, felt hat. Molded painted black hair
and painted blue eyes, open/closed mouth with tongue.
$800.00.
Note: Smaller sizes have knob hands.

8½″. Marks: Jiminy Cricket//Des. & ©
By Walt Disney//Made By Ideal Novelty
& Toy Co.//Long Island City (Play-
things, May 1940).
All wood, segmented, felt hat brim, col-
lar and ribbon tie. $400.00.

13″. Marks on back only: 13.
Cloth tag: Ray//An Ideal Doll.
This is Magic Eye Cinderella (see Jan Foulke's 12th
Blue Book).
All composition, fully jointed. Blond human hair
wig, blue, flirty sleep eyes, open mouth with four
upper teeth. All original, including metal crown.
$400.00.

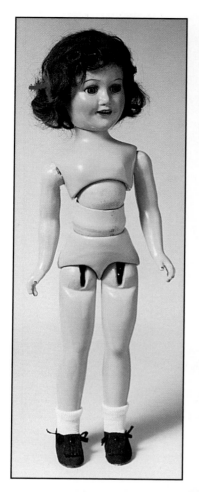

21". Marks on head: 21//
Deanna Durbin//Ideal Doll.
Marks on body: Ideal doll//
Made in U.S.A.
All composition, fully jointed
plus two waist joints. Dark
human hair wig, blue sleep
eyes, open mouth with six upper
teeth. All original. $800.00+.

15". Marks: 15//Deanna Durbin.
On back: 15//Ideal Doll.
Metal button: Deanna Durbin Doll//A Universal
Star//Made by Ideal Novelty & Toy Co., Long
Island City//New York. Paper tag: "An ultra fine
product//an//Ideal Doll //made in U.S.A.
by//Ideal Novelty & Toy Co.//Long Island
City//New York (tag is double sided).
All composition, fully jointed, dark human hair wig,
blue sleep eyes, open mouth with four upper teeth.
All original, including hair ribbons and original box.
Also came with picture of the star. 1939 Ideal cata-
log stated: "An autographed picture comes with
each Deanna Durbin Doll." $750.00 (complete set).

15". Marks on head and back: Ideal Doll.
Pin: "She's A Doll//Deanna Durbin//A Universal Star" (Playthings, October 1938 and 1939 Ideal catalog).
All composition, fully jointed. Brown human hair wig in original set, decorated with sprig of flowers on each side. Gray sleep eyes, open mouth with four upper teeth. All original. $350.00, repair right cheek.

Gabby, Gulliver, and King Little (Playthings, December 1939).
20", Gulliver. Marks on head: Deanna Durbin //Ideal Doll.
Back: Ideal Doll//21 (the latter backwards).
All composition fully jointed. Dark brown human hair wig, painted brown eyes, open mouth with six upper teeth, all original. $500.00.
10", Gabby: Marks on back: Ideal Doll//© P.P.P.I.//Made in USA. Front: "Gabby"//© by Paramount Pictures Inc. 1939//Made by Ideal Novelty & Toy Co. Inc. (designed by J. L. Kallus).
Composition head and upper torso (which is the blouse). Wooden lower body and segmented wooden limbs. Molded painted brown hair and black eyes, closed mouth. $350.00.
13", King Little with crown (designed by J. L. Kallus).
Same markings and construction as Gabby, except front is marked King Little and his molded coat ends in a real, shaped piece of cloth. $350.00.
Note: Deanna Durbin did not play Gulliver in this film, as it was a full-length cartoon feature.

18", Judy Garland as Dorothy from The Wizard of Oz. Marks: 18//Ideal Doll//Made In USA.
All composition, fully jointed. Dark human hair wig. Brown sleep eyes, open mouth with six upper teeth. All original. $1,200.00.

15". Marks on head: 15//Ideal Doll.
Body: 16//USA.
Judy Garland as Dorothy from The Wizard of Oz (1939 Sears Christmas catalog).
All composition, fully jointed. Brown human hair wig (has been cut). Brown sleep eyes, open mouth with six upper teeth. Re-dressed. $350.00 re-dressed, hair cut.

20". Marks: none. She is Toddling Sue. See Ideal catalog, June, 1939.
All composition fully jointed. Original blond mohair wig over molded hair, blue sleep eyes, open mouth with two upper teeth. All original. $150.00.

JUNEL NOVELTY INC. NEW YORK

11". Marks: none.
Hang tag: Junel//A Quality Product//MFR//Junel Novelty Inc.//New York.
Box Label: Novelty//Costume Dolls//Made by //Junel Novelties, Inc.//New York.
Boy's box: No. 26/17 Style: Mexican Boy.
Girl's box: No. 26/15 Style: French.
Good quality, all composition, fully jointed. Original mohair wigs, blue painted eyes, closed mouths. All original. $60.00 each.

ALBERT KAHN & CO.
NEW YORK CITY
1920 – 1927

Advertised unbreakable Kanko dolls, dressed dolls, walking and dancing dolls (*Coleman II*, pg. 607).

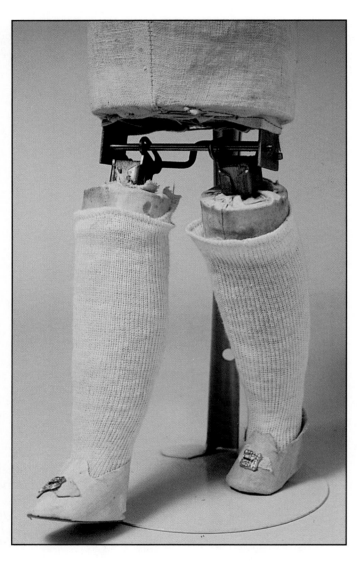

18″. Marks: T. T. Co.
Original metal button and celluloid streamers: Standard of Merit//The Kanko//Doll//Made in USA// Walking//Dollie.
Metal plate on underside of walking mechanism marked Kanko-Walking Doll//MF'R'D By Albert Kahn //N.Y.//Pat. Pend.
Composition shoulder head and short arms. Cloth body, full legs, and upper arms jointed at shoulders. Walking mechanism is mounted on a wooden platform on the underside of the body. Dark brown mohair wig, gray tin sleep eyes, open mouth. All original. $275.00 rare, complete condition, though faded.
Note: String threaded through mouth is tied to eye mechanism. It was supposed to keep the counter- weight of the eye mechanism from hitting the head during shipment.

KNICKERBOCKER TOY CO., INC.

Manufacturers of dolls and stuffed toys, Knickerbocker Toy company was incorporated February 16, 1927, and went out of business in the mid-80s (J. Axe, *Doll News*, Spring, 1992).

9", Matador. Marks: ©//Walt Disney//Knickerbocker Toy Co.
Paper tag front: Made Under Sanitary Laws//Knickerbocker Toy Co., Inc.//New York.
Paper tag back: Walt Disney's//Ferdinand//The//Bull.
All composition jointed only at the shoulders. Painted black hair and eyes. Open/closed mouth with painted upper and lower teeth. Molded painted black shoes. All original. Ray and Betsy Baker Collection. $500.00.
Note: For this doll, the Dopey mold (from the set Snow White and the Seven Dwarfs) has been used. Like the dwarfs, the matador's hands have only four fingers.

Snow White and Seven Dwarfs.
15", Snow White. Marks: © Walt Disney//1937.
Large paper tag front: Snow White//by//Walt Disney.
Back: America's//Premier Line of//Stuffed Toys //Walt Disney's//Mickey Mouse//and//Donald Duck//Manufacturers//Knickerbocker Toy Co., Inc.//New York City//©.
All composition, fully jointed. Molded painted black hair with molded blue hair bow in front. Brown painted eyes, closed mouth. All original.
9" dwarfs. Marks: © Walt Disney//Knickerbocker Toy Co.
Round paper tag: Walt Disney's Snow White and the Seven Dwarfs.
Back Side: America's//Premier Line of//Stuffed Toys//Walt Disney's Mickey Mouse//and//Donald Duck//Manufacturers//Knickerbocker Toy Co., Inc.// New York City.
All composition, jointed only at shoulders. Hands have only four fingers, molded painted brown boots. All dwarfs have same head mold except for Dopey. He also is the only one who has no beard and has an open/closed mouth with two painted teeth. Others have closed mouths. All have no hair. All original clothes.
Original boxes marked Knickerbocker Toy Co.// New York//Trademark followed by ink stamp of individual dwarf's name.
Snow White box label illegible.
Note: various facial expressions were created in the painting of features.

17", Pinocchio (Playthings, August 1939).
Marks on head: Pinocchio//Knickerbocker Toy Co.//©//Made In USA//Walt Disney Toy Product.
Paper tag front: Walt Disney's Pinocchio.
Paper tag back: Made Under Sanitary Laws//Trade Mark// Knickerbocker//Toy Co. Inc.//New York.
All composition, fully jointed. While there is a molded indication of hinges at elbows and knees, there are no actual hinges. All original. Molded painted black hair and blue eyes, closed mouth. $800.00.
Note: Knickerbocker also had a Jiminy Cricket.

7½" long, 7" high, ca. 1940.
Marks on head and body: FIGARO ©//D. PR.
Knickerbocker Toy Co.//Made in USA.
All composition, fully jointed, including the tail.
(This is Pinocchio's cat.) $1,000.00.

KESTNER COPY

11", all composition baby, light blue knit
suit/cap.
Composition socket head, fully jointed, but
on much later body (head ca. 1915, looks like
Kestner copy). Molded painted light brown
hair and blue eyes. Open/closed mouth.
$50.00 fair.

KEWPIE TYPE

20", Kewpie-type. Marks: none.
All composition, fully jointed. Molded painted dark brown hair
and big, blue eyes, closed mouth. Hair bow stapled on. All
original including shoes/socks. $150.00.

K AND K TOY CO., INC.
NEW YORK

K and K Toy Co., Inc., New York (Geo. Borgfeldt & Co. sole agents). See: Geo. Borgfeldt & Co.
Though many dolls were made by this company for Borgfeldt over a long period of time, not many, apparently, were identified with the K and K mark.

18", Rosemarie, ca. 1929. Marks: K and K Co. Inc. (Geo. Borgfeldt) Medallion on original box labeled: Rosemarie //Reg. U.S. Pat. Off.//Doll//Made by K and K Toy Co., Inc//New York.
Composition shoulder head and limbs, jointed at shoulders and hips, cloth body. Blond mohair wig, green celluloid sleep eyes, open mouth with four upper teeth. All original. $300.00.

22". Marks: K and K Toy Co. Inc. (Geo. Borgfeldt). Ca. 1928. Composition shoulder head and limbs, cloth body. Jointed at shoulders and hips. Blond mohair wig, celluloid eyes, open mouth with four upper teeth. Old clothes. $250.00.

L.D. CO.

16". Marks: L. D. Co.//1914.
Composition flange head, velour body and limbs, felt mitten hands and boots, stuffed with excelsior, jointed at shoulders and hips with inside disks. Elaborately molded light brown hair, painted blue eyes, open/closed mouth with two upper teeth. $150.00.

15", Boy. Marks: L. D. Co. 1915.
Composition flange head, lower arms and molded brown, flat heeled boots. Cloth body/limbs, jointed with outside disks. Re-dressed. Molded, painted, and striated hair, painted blue eyes, closed smiling mouth. (Could not be Liberty or Lyon Doll Co. One started in 1918 the other 1917, according to Coleman. Teddy Girl has same mark and is marked even earlier, 1914.) $120.00.

MADAME LOUISE DOLL CO., INC.
405 DENISON BLDG.
SYRACUSE, NEW YORK

Mrs. Marguerite L. Davis (nee Lemonier), wife of Dr. John L. Davis, was the owner of the Madame Louise Doll Company. From 1939 through 1943, she advertised a line of religious dolls in *Playthings* magazine. A cardinal doll and bishop doll were illustrated with an announcement in *Toys and Bicycles*, in the June 1939 issue. Apparently, the same dolly face all composition doll was used throughout. During WW II, this doll was also offered dressed as nurse's aide, civilian defense doll, army nurse, and Red Cross personnel of different nations. In addition, the March 1943 ad announced "In tribute to the American Women in Our Armed Forces, Madame Louise has created three dolls that have become sensational sellers — Wave, Marine Girl, and WAAC dolls." The last year in which the Madame Louise Doll Company was listed in the Syracuse Business Address Directory was 1947.

19". Marks: none on doll.
Original box label: Madame Louise Doll. Co., Inc.//405 Denison Building//Syracuse, N. Y. //Refugee.
All composition, fully jointed, blond mohair wig, blue sleep eyes, open mouth with four upper teeth. All original including bundle containing an extra dress. $450.00.
Note: The August 1941 announcement in Playthings stated that "a complete change of outfit, including shoes, socks, kerchief, dress etc." was in the bundle.

THE CARDINAL AND BISHOP DOLLS made by Madame Louise Doll Co., Inc., Syracuse, N. Y., offer new opportunities for your doll department. The cardinal is dressed in a black robe, high quality lace supplice, purple sash, a purple mozetta and a black biretta, lined with purple and with seams of purple thread. The bishop has a black robe with red buttons on the front, red sash, high quality lace supplice, a red silk mozetta and a red biretta.

TOYS *and* BICYCLES—June, 1939

Illustration and text from "Blue Ribbon Toys of 1939" report in Toys and Bicycles, June 1939.

Illustration from Playthings, April 1942, report on the New York City Toy Fair. The accompanying text read as follows: "Red Cross dolls of different nations were among the outstanding numbers in the Toy Fair display of the Madame Louise Doll Co., Inc. On the top row at the left of the picture are two dolls, replicas of those sent to Mrs. Winston Churchill, wife of England's Prime Minister" (refers to two Refugee dolls). Note that two sizes of dolls are pictured.

Full page ad, Playthings, March 1943.

MAIDEN AMERICA TOY CO.
NEW YORK CITY

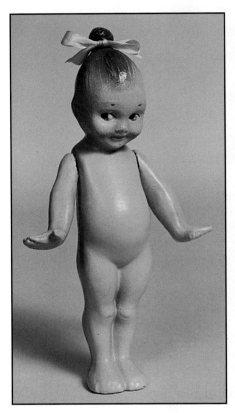

8", Maiden America. Marks: none.
Label on foot: Des. Pat.//8-24-15//© 1915.
All composition, jointed at shoulders only. Molded top knot. Blue painted eyes, closed mouth. Originally, came with wide red, white, and blue ribbon around body, tied into a big bow in back. $85.00.
Note: This doll was heavily advertised in Playthings and Toys and Novelties between 1915 and 1919, and seems to have been intended as a mascot or good luck charm as well as a toy. Although the makers meant to exploit a national theme in their promotions, no evidence was found in the numerous ads, that the doll was ever given as a premium for the purchase of war bonds.
In Toys and Novelties, April 1918, pages 19 – 34, thirteen toy traders, instead of advertising their products as usual, had used this space to endorse the purchase of U.S. Liberty Bonds. A full page advertisement of the Maiden America doll was to the left of this special insert. This proximity may have given rise to the idea that the doll was given as a premium for the purchase of Liberty Bonds.

McCALL, PEGGY

13", Peggy McCall Sewing Manikin with original box, instruction booklet, and pattern. Marks: None on doll.
All composition, removable arms. Molded painted blond hair and painted blue eyes. Molded, painted black shoes. $100.00.

Toys and Novelties, March 1943.
Display ad placed by Dritz-Traum Company,
Inc., showing larger size kit.

"Peggy" Sewing Box

"Peggy," the Fashion Model sewing box is made in 3 sizes to retail at $2, $3 and $5. The latter set is illustrated. In this set "Peggy" is 13 inches high, and each set contains two McCall patterns designed and made especially to fit "Peggy." All boxes are carried out in red, white and blue—patriotic design. In the $5 box also are 3 pieces of fabric, wool, knitting needles, package of sewing needles, tape measure, thimble, thread and needle threader, as well as a descriptive booklet carrying a message to young Americans who are just learning to sew. Because of the great interest in home sewing which is now apparent, this new line of sewing boxes, put out by the DRITZ-TRAUM COMPANY, INC., will be of special interest to toybuyers. Attractive displays showing Peggy fully dressed, as pictured, are obtainable.

Toys and Novelties, August 1942.

METROPOLITAN DOLL CO.
NEW YORK CITY
1924 – 29

Made various kinds of dolls, some of which were designed by Ernesto Peruggi (*Coleman II*, pg. 834).

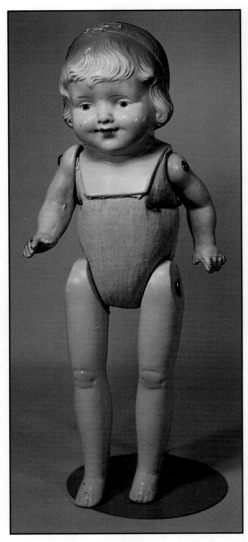

19". Marks: Metropolitan//Doll.
Composition shoulder head and limbs, cloth body, pin jointed at shoulders and hips with outside metal disks. Molded, painted blond hair and painted blue eyes, closed mouth. $100.00.
Note: All composition, interchangeable legs. Because of this feature, they have been flattened on both sides at the upper end.

21". Marks: Metropolitan Doll.
Composition shoulder head and arms, cloth body and legs, pin jointed. Molded painted brown hair and painted blue eyes. Closed mouth. All original. Nancy and David Carlson collection. $180.00.

MITRED BOX CO.
NEW YORK CITY
1911 – 1917

In the January and March 1912 issues of *Playthings*, The Mitred Box Company presented their Yankee Doll line, which, ironically, consisted entirely of composition dolls modeled after German examples. Of four dolls pictured, one was a ball-jointed dolly face doll with painted eyes and a wig; the second an all composition boy with molded, short hair and black boots (copy of a turtlemark celluloid doll); third an all composition baby, apparently a Heubach copy; and fourth an all composition coquette girl, which was, obviously, also a Heubach copy.

Of these four dolls, only the Heubach copy all composition baby was not available for examination. Of the three checked, only the socket head for the ball-jointed doll bore identification marks. But all three dolls had one factor in common: their composition socket heads ended in a rounded-off, wooden neck piece into which a hook had been screwed to hold the stringing.

This wooden neck piece construction is very distinctive and has only been located on three other composition dolls. One is the all-composition baby which was a copy of the famous German K*R #100 doll. While the K*R #100 was copied by many American firms, Hahn & Amberg (later Louis Amberg & Son) seem to have been the only ones that ever advertised an all composition version (*Toys and Novelties*, April 1910). (Therefore, this doll has been placed in the Amberg section.)

Two more unmarked dolls have been located with this neck socket construction. One, an all-composition girl with elaborately modeled hair and bow and an open/closed mouth, is also a Heubach copy (popularly known as the singer). She seems to be a companion to the all-composition coquette and has, therefore, been placed into this section. The other doll examined was a two-face one. A Louis Amberg & Son ad of April 1912 (*Playthings*) mentioned "The Doll With Two Faces, Laughing and Crying." For this reason, the 12" two-face baby with identical neck construction has been attributed to Amberg and is pictured in the Amberg section.

Because of their distinctive, identical construction, Amberg and Mitred Box may have been using the same supplier for these socket heads (Denivelle?). Additional research may shed more light on this matter.

It is hoped that the Heubach copy baby seen in the Mitred Box ad will become available for examination at some future date. (Also see Elektra, socket heads with flat wooden neck piece, into which the hook for stringing is screwed.)

5" (head only). Marks: Yankee Doll//Made In USA (Playthings, January 1912).
Solid dome composition socket head with wooden neck piece and hook feature. Molded eyebrows, decal eyes, open/closed mouth with four molded painted teeth. $30.00 head only.
Note: This head would have been mounted on a ball-jointed body.

321

14". Marks: none (Playthings, March 1912).
Composition socket head, body, and limbs, fully
jointed. Molded boots and socks. Molded painted
brown hair, and blue hair ribbons. Painted blue
eyes. Doll on left has a closed mouth, doll on right
open/closed mouth. Re-dressed. $350.00 each.
Note: Description of special socket heads in introductory paragraph.

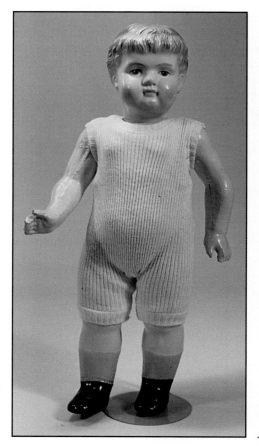

13". Marks: none (Playthings, January 1912).
Composition socket head, body, and limbs (slanted hip),
fully jointed. Molded painted hair and painted blue
eyes, closed mouth. Molded boots and ribbed socks.
(Copy of German turtlemark celluloid doll.) $250.00.

MODERN TOY CO., INC.
BROOKLYN, NEW YORK
1914 – 1926

Manufacturers of dolls, stuffed toys, and novelties. Their 1916 ad showed a picture of their "New and Sanitary Doll Factory," a five-story, large corner building. The building had the following inscription: "Modern Toy Co., Inc.//Makers of Modern Dolls."

16", Babbit Cleanser Boy. Marks: none (Playthings, February 1916).
Composition flange head and hands, appropriate old cloth body and limbs, inside joints. Molded painted hair with middle part, painted blue eyes, molded lids, closed mouth. $250.00.
Note: Doll in ad is dressed in white suit and visor cap, capital "B" on front of cap and on tips of collar. Dark belt. Round pin-on button reads "Babbit Cleanser." Doll in ad is holding a box of Babbit cleanser (molded white boots).

Left: 19". Marks: M.T. Co.
Composition flange head and short arms. Cloth body, upper arms, and legs, jointed with inside disks. Molded painted hair with molded loop for hair ribbon. Painted blue eyes, closed mouth, re-dressed.
Right: 17". Marks: none.
Same construction as girl but open/closed mouth with molded tongue and two upper painted teeth, no hair loop. Re-dressed. $200.00 each.

14". Marks: M.T. Co. Ca. 1916.
Composition flange head and short arms, cloth body, upper arms, and legs, jointed with outside disks. Molded painted hair and painted blue eyes. Open/closed mouth with three painted lower teeth. All original except cap. $150.00.

MOLLY-'ES

Moll-'es was the trade name used by Molly Goldman of Philadelphia, Pennsylvania. Molly Goldman designed and made doll clothes which she sold under her own name; but she was also a supplier for many of the large New York doll companies. Raggedy Ann and Andy dolls were made by the firm for some time. Molly Goldman also bought dolls, dressed them and sold these creations under her own name. A *Playthings* ad of October 1939, announced and pictured the Glamour Girls of 1940, a set of beautifully dressed debutante type dolls. Babies and dolls in ethnic costume could also be found in her line of products.

14" (without turban). Marks: none.
Paper hang tag: A Thief of Bagdad//Creation.
Back side: Authentic//Dolls//Inspired By//Alexander Korda's//
"Thief of Bagdad"//I Am The Sabu//Created By//Molly-'es.
All composition, fully jointed. No hair, painted brown eyes, closed mouth. All original. Face has been restored. $250.00 (restored).
Note: This is one of a set of five dolls which Molly Goldman created for this theme. The others were a composition princess and three men. The latter were cloth dolls with mask faces in colorful costumes and turbans.

Front of tag.

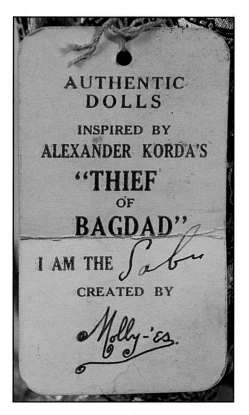

Back of tag.

MONICA DOLL STUDIOS
HOLLYWOOD, CALIFORNIA
1941 – 1952

The Monica Doll Sudios were owned by Mrs. Hansi Share.

The Monica dolls were the first and only composition dolls ever to have rooted hair. A different composition formula was used in their production (not wood pulp).

A 1941 announcement stated that the Monica dolls were available with composition or cloth bodies. They were first introduced in a 20" and 24" size. A *Toys and Novelties* ad of March 1947, listed 15", 17", and 20" sizes. Package inserts indicated that the dolls were given individual names. They were sold by such prestigious stores as Neiman Marcus and F.A.O. Schwarz.

An announcement on page 204 in the October 1949, issue of *Toys and Novelties* stated "Just added to the Monica Studios line of dolls the all-plastic Marion doll, made in Hollywood, has the same patented process of rooting human hair in the scalp that Monica has had. In addition, she has moving eyes."

20". Marks: none.

Paper hang tag: Monica//Doll//Hollywood.

Made by Monica Doll Studios (Various Toys and Novelties and Playthings ads 1941 – 1949).

All composition fully jointed. Blond human hair rooted into the scalp (only composition doll to have this feature). Painted blue eyes with rays scratched into iris and two highlights. Closed mouth. Original outfit (hair in original setting). $600.00.

Inside of paper hang tag read as follows: "My Dear Doll Mother: You will love to include me into your family, not only because I am beautiful and good, but because you can do so much with me. My real human hair grows right out of my head ...it is not a wig glued on...so you can comb and curl it as much as you like without spoiling it.

My clothes zip and snap on and off, just like yours, so that you can always keep me in fresh dresses.

In any case I will keep you very busy.

Monica "

MAMA DOLLS

Some dolls have been included here that are noteworthy for one or the other reason: an unusual hairdo or character face, rare originality, popularity, etc. As the name indicates, all had mama voice boxes inserted into their stuffed cloth bodies. In rare instances, these criers are still in working order. Manufacurers of these dolls are not known, 1920s – 1930s.

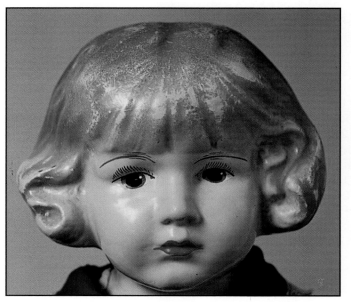

18". Marks: none.

Composition shoulder head and full arms, legs to above the knee. Cloth body, jointed at shoulders, stitched hip joints. Molded painted hair and painted blue eyes, closed mouth, re-dressed. $250.00.

26". Marks: none.
Composition shoulder head, full arms, and legs to above the knee. Cloth body and upper legs. Jointed at shoulders, stitched hip joints. Original, brown human hair wig, gray tin sleep eyes, open mouth with four upper teeth. All original except for hair ribbon. $250.00. Note: While contemporary hats and bonnets have survived, few dolls are seen with their original hair ribbons in place. Many original illustrations show mama dolls with wide ribbons as demonstrated here.

24". Marks: none. Late '20s. Composition shoulder head, arms, and legs to above knee. Jointed at shoulders, stitched hip joints. Mohair wig, gray celluloid over metal sleep eyes, open mouth with two painted upper teeth. All original. $300.00.

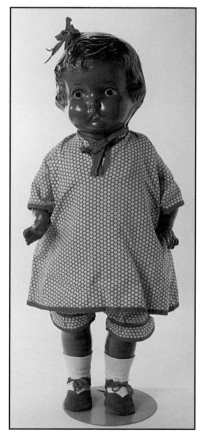

24", Brown Mama Doll. Marks: none.
All original including shoes, socks, and hair ribbon (a piece of red trim).
Composition shoulder head, full arms, and legs to above the knee. Cloth body is crudely stuffed with excelsior with stitched hip joints. Arms jointed with long pin turned around on itself on one side. Molded painted black hair with molded loop and brown eyes, closed mouth. $300.00.

28". Marks: none.
Composition shoulder head, full arms, and legs to above the knee. Cloth body and upper legs stuffed with excelsior. Jointed only at shoulders, stitched hip joints. Molded painted brown hair with molded ribbon loop, painted blue eyes, closed mouth. Contemporary clothes. Repainted. $150.00.

26". Marks: none.
Composition flange head, full arms (sometimes tied-on), and legs to above the knee. Cloth body and upper legs, jointed at shoulders, stitched hip joints. Molded painted blond hair, gray tin sleep eyes, open mouth with four upper teeth, redressed. $150.00 (more if original clothes).
Note: These large, Lovums type (Effanbee) toddlers were very popular during the '30s. Their quality is usually excellent.

MUTUAL NOVELTY CO.
NEW YORK, NEW YORK

25". Marks: none (Parisienne, French Flapper, or Cigarette Doll. U. S. Design Patent No. 67031, April 14, 1925 Toys and Novelties, April 1925). All composition, fully jointed, including knees and elbows, molded slippers. Painted black eyes, gray eye shadow. Black floss wig with braids coiled over ears (has no ears). Drill hole into mouth for insertion of cigarette (painted wooden peg). All original. Slippers repainted. $400.00.

NEW DOLL CO.
NEW YORK or
1913 – 1915

NATURAL DOLL CO.
NEW YORK
1914 – 1930

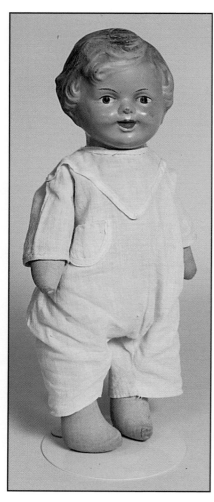

12". Marks: N. D. Co.//For//JRM Co. (Copy of German doll and Fiamingo head).
Composition flange head and short arms, cloth body, upper arms, and bent legs, jointed with inside disks. Molded painted blond hair and painted blue eyes, closed mouth. Old romper. $125.00.

13½". Marks: N. D. Co.
Composition flange head, cloth body stuffed with sawdust, unusual wire joints on outside (this may be a replacement body). Molded painted brown hair and painted blue eyes. Open/closed mouth. Old romper. $80.00.

10". Marks: N. D. Co.
Composition flange head and short arms. Cloth body and limbs, jointed with outside disks. Molded painted brown hair and painted blue eyes, closed mouth. All original red/green felt outfit including slippers. $50.00 (fair condition).

August, 1920 PLAYTHINGS

PHYLLIS MAY

Original New Toy Creation

The Phyllis May Doll is the latest and most delightful addition to the New Toy family.

These dolls are composition head; stuffed body—come with painted hair and eyes and also with mohair wigs; human hair curl wigs and sleeping eyes. They are dressed in a reproduction of the original Phyllis May dress and cap, in both plain colors and flowered designs, and wear sox and slippers. A tag bearing the Phyllis May verse is fastened to the belt of each doll.

Phyllis May is a little girl from story-book land, made popular in the New York Evening Mail by Miss Hazel Drikker. So interested did the children become in this new character that they began making requests for a Phyllis May Doll. Naturally, it was the New Toy Company who first saw the possibilities of such a doll, and this line promises to be one of the most popular ever produced.

Ready for Immediate Delivery.

NEW TOY CO., Inc.

Fifth Ave. Bldg., New York

Factory: Newark, N. J.

Kindly mention PLAYTHINGS when writing to advertisers

NEW TOY CO., INC.

Display ad Playthings, August 1920.

PATSY TYPE

19". Marks: none.
All composition, fully jointed. Molded painted brown hair, gray tin sleep eyes. Open mouth with four upper teeth. Contemporary outfit came on doll.
$200.00.
Note: Same construction as Patsy: bent right arm, protruding abdomen.

PILGRIM PAIR

12", Pilgrim Pair (before 1920).
Marks head: N - 4 (the 4 is printed backwards)
Back: AMB://N -4 (backwards) (all markings not very clear).
All composition fully jointed. Socket head with cardboard pate. Head was made by the pouring process and was not dipped, airbrushed only. Body and limbs were dipped and seem to have very little paint on top of that (layer all crackled). All parts are made of the early glue base composition. Blond and dark brown mohair wigs glued directly to the head, painted blue eyes, open/closed mouth with two painted teeth. All original. The outfits have been all hand sewn. No machine stitching whatsoever. Yet, outfits seem well designed. $350.00 pair.

QUAN QUAN CO.
LOS ANGELES and
SAN FRANCISCO, CALIFORNIA

10". Marks: none. This is Ling Ling (Antique Trader, May 31, 1989).
All composition with bent legs, fully jointed. Cap and pom pons are glued to head. Black eyes, closed mouth. All original. $90.00.

**QUADDY PLAYTHINGS MFG., CO.
NEW YORK CITY, NEW YORK
and
KANSAS CITY, MISSOURI
1916 – 1917**

16". Marks: none.

Original tag read: Peter Rabbit/Quaddy - Pat. Jan. 30, 1917 (see design patent No. 50,236, January 30, 1917, granted to Harrison Cady of Brooklyn, N. Y., Assignor to Thornton W. Burgess, of Springfield, Mass.). Composition flange head, cloth body and limbs jointed with outside disks. Ears and back of head were painted brown and molded to resemble fur. Painted black eyes to the side with long black eyelashes. Open/closed mouth with painted long whiskers on each side. All original clothes except for bow tie and socks. $300.00.

Note: This Peter Rabbit was a storybook as well as a cartoon character. He was originally one of the animals in Mr. Burgess' famous children's stories illustrated by Harrison Cady. In 1920, he became the title character in Mr. Cady's Sunday comic strip for the New York Tribune.

JESSIE MCCUTCHEON RALEIGH
CHICAGO
1916 – 1920

Jessie McCutcheon Raleigh was not a dollmaker but a businesswoman and entrepreneur who had considerable success with a Good Fairy Statuette (a good luck symbol) introduced in 1915. The statuette had been designed for her by Grace Bliss Stewart and modeled in clay by Josephine Kern.

The production of composition character dolls started in 1917 and was aimed at the high end of the market. Mrs. Raleigh did not use the already existing glue base or wood-pulp composition but had her own formula developed by a Dr. W. P. Dun Lany. This new material was advertised as being light weight, but actually was not. It was reported that the painting of the doll's facial features was done by art students. In 1919, dolly-faced dolls with sleep eyes and mohair or human hair wigs in elaborate outfits were added to the line. Three types of body/limb assemblies had been created for this doll. In 1918, Butler Bros. claimed to be sole distributors of the Raleigh dolls. Their wholesale catalog carried four pages of Raleigh dolls in 1918 and two pages in 1919. However *Playthings* and *Toys and Novelties* ads placed by the Raleigh firm in 1917, 1919, and 1920, do not mention this relationship.

At the end of World War I, increasing competition from domestic composition dolls and German imports caused difficulties, and the company was taken over by the Pollyanna Co. (A. Fleetwood, N. Y., representative) in 1920.

It is interesting to speculate why the Raleigh company succumbed to competition. The basic reason may have been that Mrs. Raleigh was not that familiar with the New York City centered doll industry (she was in Chicago). She had a special composition material developed for her that was rather heavy, at a time when the New York city dollmakers were already using wood pulp composition that was much lighter than the earlier glue base composition and Mrs. Raleigh's special formula. While her character dolls had beautifully modeled faces and hands, the feet of these all-composition children were not level. The dolls could not stand unaided.

By 1920, the American toy industry had made great strides and competition was stiff in every respect. Mrs. Raleigh definitely had created artistic dolls. One can only regret that the company did not survive for a longer period of time.

Jesse McCutchen Raleigh had special bodies and limbs designed for her dolls (see next four examples).

13". Marks: none.
All composition, fully jointed with steel springs. Hands molded into fists. Molded painted, brown hair, painted blue eyes, open/closed mouth, re-dressed. $350.00.

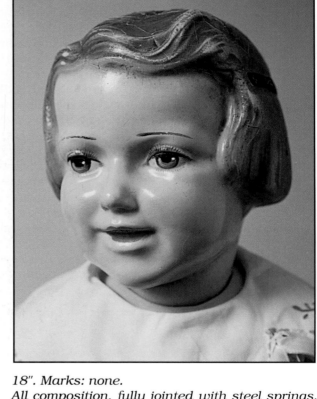

18". Marks: none.
All composition, fully jointed with steel springs. Molded painted hair with black barette on left side. Brown eyes well painted and highlighted, vertical upper and lower eyelashes, open/closed mouth with four upper molded painted teeth, re-dressed. $800.00.

11", Goldilocks. Marks: none (Ladies' Home Journal, December 1919).
All composition, fully jointed. Blond mohair wig over molded hair. Painted brown eyes, open/closed mouth with two painted upper teeth. All original, including shoes and socks. $350.00.
Note: Print of Three Bears on jumper front.

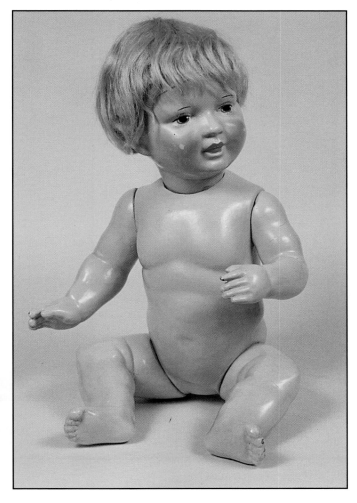

18", Raleigh Baby, 1919. Marks: none. All composition fully jointed. Bent legs. Blond mohair wig. Brown painted eyes, open/closed mouth with two upper painted teeth. Vertically painted upper eyelashes. $450.00.

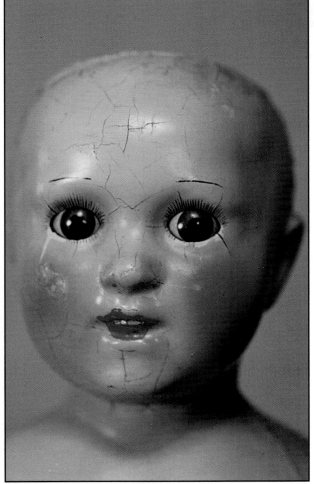

Close-up of 24", sleep eye dolly face doll. For body types, see next three illustrations. Since these dolls are never marked, it is important to memorize their tightly painted, vertical eyelashes, thin brown eye brows and shape of painted mouth with four painted, upper teeth. Also, their cheek blush was airbrushed onto the surface. Most other composition dolls had their cheek blush applied under the skin paint, which produced a softer looking blush. $80.00 (poor).

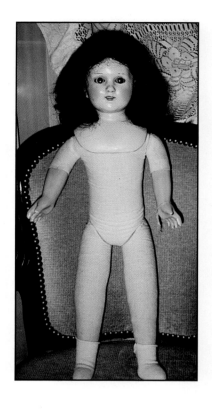 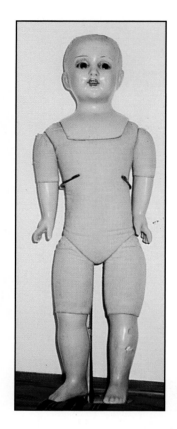 

Three types of body construction for Raleigh sleep eye, dolly face dolls, 24" tall (all composition doll 22"). Once studied, these bodies should be easy to recognize, as their design, shape, and tight jointing is different from contemporary composition dolls (human or mohair wigs).

Half page ad, Toys and Novelties, March 1920. This ad shows two examples of elaborate and fancy outfits in which the dolly faced children were dressed.

RABBITS

16", Rabbits. Marks: none.
Composition shoulder heads, cotton stuffed
cloth bodies with brown flannel arms and
boots, body and legs one piece, i.e., they
cannot sit down. Stitched shoulder joints.
Painted features. Heads have been
restored. Original clothes except for bows.
$100.00 each.

16½". Marks: none.
Composition shoulder head, cloth body and legs
one piece, cloth arms, loose shoulder joints. All
original. $100.00.

REGAL DOLL MANUFACTURING CO.
NEW YORK CITY and JERSEY CITY, NEW JERSEY
1919 – 1930+

Various trade ads from the 1930s mention Trenton, New Jersey, as their factory location. Regal succeeded the German American Doll Co. in 1919. Kiddie Pal and Kiddie Joy were registered trademarks. In 1926, they made newborn baby dolls designed by Ernesto Peruggi.

Their trade ads from the early '30s consistently show mama dolls and babies as well as Patsy-type children.

They produced various style trousseau sets during this period for which an all-composition Patsy look-alike and Maizie were used.

27". Marks: none.
Paper tag: Our Lindy//America's Pride//MFD by Regal Doll Mfg. Co//N.Y.C.//Copyright Reg. 83336. Ca. 1928.
Composition shoulder head, molded painted hair, painted blue eyes, open/closed mouth with painted teeth, cloth body. One-piece twill flier's suit with plush collar. Leather mittens, leather boots, and belt. All original. Collection of Sterryl Shirran. $800.00.

Right: 19", Kiddy Pal Dolly (so marked on original box). Marks: none.
Composition shoulder head and short arms tied on. Composition legs to above the knee. Cloth body and upper limbs stuffed with excelsior. Elaborately molded painted blond hair and blue eyes, open/closed mouth, all original clothes. $200.00.
Left: 22". Marks: Kiddie Pal Dolly//Regal Doll Mfg. Co. (Toys and Novelties, January 1930).
Composition shoulder head and full arms, composition legs to above the knee. Jointed at shoulders, stitched hip joints. Cloth body and upper legs stuffed with cotton. Molded painted blond hair blue eyes. Open/closed mouth with two upper painted teeth. Contemporary clothes. $200.00.

26". Marks: Kiddy Pal Dolly//Regal Doll MFG. Co. Inc. Illustrated in 1928 Butler Brothers catalog.
Composition shoulder head and limbs, cloth body, jointed at shoulders and hips. Molded painted blond hair, blue tin sleep eyes, open mouth with two upper teeth. Redressed. $200.00.

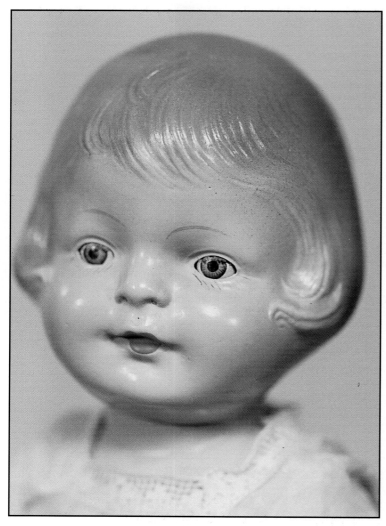 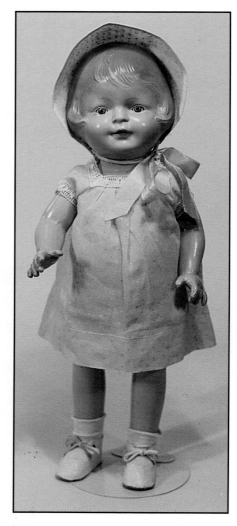

15". Marks: none (Playthings, April 1931. Doll's name is Maizie.)
All composition, jointed at shoulders and hips only. Molded painted blond hair, gray tin sleep eyes,
closed mouth. All original, including shoes and socks. $150.00.

REPUBLIC DOLL & TOY CO.
NEW YORK CITY
1919 – 1921

Two sitting figures 6½" and 9" tall.
Larger one marked Kweenie//Republic Dolls//152-56 Wooster St. New York.
All composition, no joints. Molded painted reddish hair (smaller one has no hair paint and may have had a wig). Black eyes with painted lashes all around the eye lid, closed mouth. Both are holding a ball. For the small one, the suit paint has been carried across the feet to make it look like bathing slippers. $50.00; $40.00.

SANTA CLAUS

20", Santa Claus, 1930s. Marks: none.
All composition, fully jointed, molded cap and full white beard. Blue eyes, closed mouth. All original suit of red flannel trimmed with white plush fabric, black oilcloth belt and boots. Pack made of same fabric as suit. $500.00.

SCHOEN & YONDORF CO. (SAYCO DOLL CORP.) NEW YORK CITY 1907 – 1950+

In 1922, Ignatz Schoen, formerly of Schoen Toy Manufacturing Co., and Myer Yondorf were partners. Myer Yondorf had previously been with E. Goldberger and the New Toy Manufacturing Co. (*Coleman I & II*). In 1926, they advertised a set of dancing comedy dolls representing Hal Roach's *Our Gang*. They had identical construction as Dancing Katharina pictured in this section. The ad further mentioned "soft, cuddly novelty toys, mama and baby dolls." Apparently, they did not mark many of their dolls, as so few can be identified. Their trade name Sayco was registered in 1924.

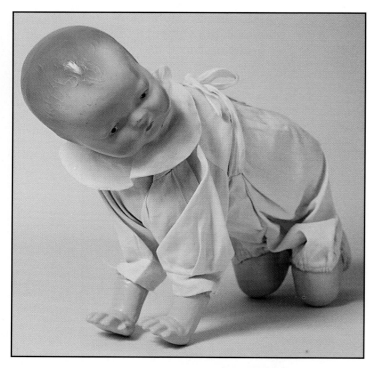

12", Dancing Katharina. Marks: none (Playthings May 1925).
Composition shoulder head and short arms tied on. Upper torso covered with cloth. Metal wind-up mechanism, metal legs and feet. Original felt costume. Original blond mohair wig with braids. Painted blue eyes, closed mouth. $200.00+.

16", Creeping Baby. Marks: none (Playthings 1926 – 27). Composition flange head and lower limbs, cloth body. Limbs connected by metal rods. Molded painted blond hair and blue eyes, closed mouth, original romper. Picture on original ad shows little girl holding ribbon tied under the arms. When pulled forward, the arms and legs move back and forth. Original ad also shows the following poem: "I'm Not So Helpless Any More, Just Watch Me Creep Across The Floor. No Cry for Mama or for Daddy, Because I Help Myself Already. Just Take the Ribbon, Pull Me Slight And I Will Follow You, All Right!" $150.00 (fair condition).

18". Marks: none (may have been sold by Sayco).
Composition flange head. Soft stuffed cloth body and limbs. Plush cap is removable. Body covering is also the suit. Molded painted, curly dark brown hair, brown sleep eyes that can also move from side to side. Closed mouth. $250.00.

21", Baby Coquette. Marks: none. (McMaster's catalog, September 20, 1992, #159 doll with original paper tag.) Composition flange head, hands, and bent legs to above the knee. Cloth body and upper limbs. Molded painted brown hair and gray sleep eyes that also move from side to side. Closed mouth. All original. $300.00.

18". Marks: none.
Paper hang tag: Sayco//Doll.
All composition, fully jointed. Light brown original mohair wig, blue sleep eyes, open mouth with two upper teeth. All original. $200.00.
Note: Doll has Princess Elizabeth type head, also used by Arranbee and others.

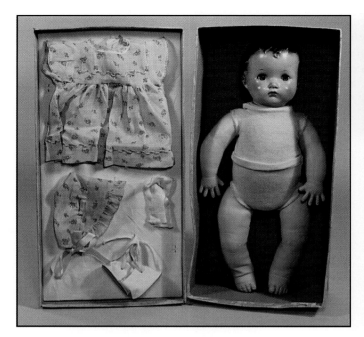

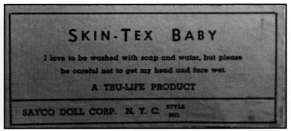

15". Marks: SAYCO (on back of head).
Box label reads: SKIN TEX BABY//I love to be washed with soap and water, but please be careful not to get my head and face wet. //A TRU - LIFE PRODUCT//SAYCO COLL CORP. N.Y. C. STYLE//No.
Closed mouth, brown sleep eyes, black molded, painted hair. Jointed arms, neck (flange). Latex body perfect. $100.00.
Wardrobe, stapled to inside cover of box, consists of dress, matching bonnet, white rayon socks, and a pair of white lace booties (oilcloth).

SHAKER

13", Shaker Sister. Marks: none. 1930s. May have been done by Shakers.
All composition, jointed only at shoulders and hips. Original, blond mohair wig over molded hair with center part and molded bow (so-called Snow White type). Painted blue eyes closed mouth. Fine woven straw bonnet has glued fabric lining, paper edging. Pleated satin ruffle was attached with running stitch by hand. Lace trimmed cotton combination and half slip, cotton socks, and oil cloth shoes. Dress has detachable collar trimmed with tatting. On the dress, only the sleeve seams and skirt hem were machine stitched, the rest was constructed by hand. All fabric edges are raw and have been pinked. There are no buttons. Garments are held in place with stick pins. $150.00.

SNOW WHITE LOOK-ALIKE

13". No marks.
Molded, painted blond hair with blue hair bow in front, closed mouth, blue painted eyes. Jointed at hip and shoulders. Head and body one piece. Clothes factory made and contemporary but not original. $90.00.

12". No marks.
Molded, painted dark hair with blue bow in front, brown painted eyes, open/closed mouth with white line between lips as indication of teeth. Jointed at shoulders and hips. Body and head one piece. Re-dressed. $90.00.

STEWARDESS

14". Marks: none.
Jacket and cap marked Stewardess. All original.
All composition, fully jointed. Blond human hair wig, gray tin sleep eyes, closed mouth. $250.00.

THE ALBERT SCHOENHUT COMPANY
PHILADELPHIA, PENNSYLVANIA
1872 – 1935

The Schoenhuts were manufacturers of quality wooden toys and dolls. From small beginnings, they had rapidly expanded and become very successful with their unique toy products. After having been in business for almost 50 years, by the late 1920s, this had changed. Now, composition dolls held a major market share. Effanbee's very successful Patsy had been introduced two years earlier. The economic down turn caused by the onset of the Depression was affecting Schoenhut doll sales. All three events may have influenced the company's decision to produce a composition doll, the only one they would ever make. It was designed by Harry Schoenhut and introduced in their 1930 catalog.

While she has a small, pouty mouth like Effanbee's Patsy and a tiny nose, her curly hair style contributed to creating a very different looking and appealing doll. The same holds true for her body construction. While she has almost identical arms to Patsy's, her flat bellied torso and legs are of different design. Also of note is that the doll has a traditional so-called socket head, whereas for the Patsy types, the head is wide open at the neck and swivels on a protrusion that is part of the torso.

13". Marks: Schoenhut Toys Made in U.S.A. (round paper label on back).
All composition, fully jointed. Molded painted reddish blond hair, slightly intaglio, painted blue eyes, closed mouth. Collection of Ruth and Bob Zimmerman.
Note: The doll was strung in the manner of the Schoenhut animals. The elastic runs from leg to head to leg (arm to arm) and is held in place with a small nail at each end. Dresses were styled in the Patsy (Effanbee) manner (see 1930 Schoenhut catalog, pg. 22). $400.00+.

TAIYO TRADING COMPANY INC.

Successors to Takito, Ogawa & Co., and the Tajimi Co., New York City and Chicago.

16". Marks: H. B. Co. (Playthings, June 1919).
Composition shoulder head and full arms nailed to body. Wooden body, legs, and feet. Simple walker mechanism: When one foot is put down and pressure applied to the doll in a forward motion, the other leg moves on. Black mohair wig over molded hair, painted light brown eyes, closed mouth. All original. $250.00 each.
Note: The ad stated "...This beautiful little doll...is typical of the popular character portrayed by Fay Bainter in the big New York theatrical success East Is West. This play opened at the Astor in New York on December 25, 1918, and stayed for 680 performances. The wording suggests that the doll-makers did not have permission to use the Fay Bainter name for the doll.

3-IN-1 DOLL CORPORATION
NEW YORK, NEW YORK

A full-page ad in *Toys and Novelties* of August 1947, announced the three-face Trudy as "The Most Amazing Doll Creation In A Decade." Trudy's head was mounted on a wooden dowel that extended into the body. A knob on top permitted the turning of the head to make the different faces appear. Her hair was attached to the hood or bonnet. Trudy came dressed in a felt outfit of overalls and jacket with attached hood and matching shoulder bag or a fleece sleeper with attached hood. According to the ad, the 14" doll was also available with composition limbs and dressed in print dress with matching bonnet, white socks, and shoes which could be removed. A 20" size Trudy was available as well, also in print dress and with composition limbs. The dolls had a paper tag which read "An Elsie Gilbert Creation//Sleepy//Weepy//Smily//Trade Mark of the//Three In One//Doll Corp.//Patents Pending."

14", Trudy. Marks: none.
All original green felt overalls and yellow jacket with matching hood and shoulder bag. Original tufts of blond mohair. $350.00.

14", with ears. Marks: none.
Composition head with painted blue eyes and closed mouth. Cloth body and limbs with stitched hip and shoulder joints. All original outfit. Replaced hair. $200.00.

TERRY LEE CO., INC.
LINCOLN, NEBRASKA
1946 – ca. 1960

The original Terri Lee doll was designed and sculpted by Maxine Sunderman Runci, niece of the owner, Mrs. Gradwohl. The Terry Lee dolls were very different from contemporary composition dolls, with their distinctive faces and well designed and executed clothes. They met with instant success. The Terri Lee dolls were made of composition for one year only, from 1946 to 1947. After that date, they were produced of hard plastic. (For further information on the Terri Lee dolls see *Fashionable Terri Lee Dolls*, by Peggy Wiedman Casper.

17". Marked on back: Terry Lee//Pat. Pending.
All composition, fully jointed, with hole between left thumb and forefinger to hold a daisy (daisy not original). Blond, synthetic, very stiff hair, painted brown eyes, closed mouth. All original. $400.00. Rare! Coat tagged: Terry Lee. Outfit pictured in original advertising as No. 2060/1948 (See: Illustration 60, pg. 71 Fashionable Terry Lee Dolls).
Original booklet entitled "The True Story of Terry Lee Toddler//Terri Lee."
Inside reads as follows: I am not a doll but a real little girl. I was born while my father was overseas and he never came back, so I am a "war" baby like so many of you. My mother is a sculptor so she made this figure of me to be your playmate. I love to stick clay on things while she is modeling.//My wardrobe is very complete just like yours and I am going to become a very important little girl for I will forecast fashions for you — things you will love to wear. I will also forecast hair styles, for my wig maker is a professional hair stylist. My hair is different from other dolls. You may comb it if it becomes tangled, dampen each curl with a piece of cotton moistened with water, make waves and pin curls, and tie a net around my head just like your mother does yours, until my hair is perfectly dry. Then a spray of brilliantine and I'll be just like new. Or, if you wish, you may curl my hair with a curling iron.//I hope you will love me for I'll love you."

17". Marks on back: Terry Lee//Pat. Pending.
Dress label at neck: Terri Lee.
All composition, fully jointed. Blond, synthetic, very stiff wig, painted brown eyes, closed mouth. All original clothes (bought separately), replaced shoes and socks. Left hand rebuilt. $250.00 (fair).

THE TOY SHOP
NEW YORK CITY
1920S – 1930S

The Toy Shop sold a general line of baby and mama dolls as well as stuffed animals and teddy bears. Their January 1926 *Toys and Novelties* ad stated "We manufacture all our dolls complete from toes to head." They also claimed to be mama doll specialists and were offering "a complete line of white and colored dolls."

15". Marks: none on doll.
Paper tag: Aunt//Jemima//Manufactured//only by//The //Toy Shop//New York.
Composition shoulder head and short arms. Cloth body and limbs. No shoulder joints, stitched hip joints. Brown leg fabric, stuffed with cotton. Body/arm fabric is white and stuffed with excelsior. Molded painted black hair and brown eyes. Closed mouth. All original except for red bandanna.
Note: The Toy Shop first advertised this doll in Toys and Novelties, June 1923, stating "By special permission and under arrangements with the Aunt Jemima Mills Company, St. Joseph, Mo." Aunt Jemima was featured every year through 1926. The doll can also be seen in the Sears catalogs of 1924, 1925, and 1930. Aunt Jemima was again pictured in the 1931 Sears catalog. This time, she had composition legs. Over the years, the dolls were available in sizes 14", 18½", 20", and 24". $150.00 (fair condition).

TIP TOP TOY CO.
NEW YORK CITY
1912 – 1921

Manufacturers of "unbreakable dolls, stuffed animals, and speciality toys." Their early ads showed the usual assortment of German bisque copies (in composition) and also German bisque dolls.

Their 1920 – 1921 catalog (Strong Museum, Rochester) featured mostly novelty Kewpie dolls on pedestals. The catalog also stated that "good materials are taken into the Tip Top factories in Manhattan, Brooklyn, Jersey City, and Hoboken."

24". Marks: TTT Co. 86. Ca, 1918.
Composition flange head and short arms. Cloth body and limbs jointed with inside disks. Celluloid sleep eyes, open mouth with two upper teeth. Human hair wig is a replacement. Old clothes.
$200.00.
Note: Unusually large size for a cork stuffed body doll.

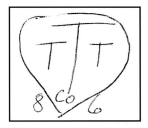

TOBIE

10½". Marks: Tobie//Copyright//1932.
Head and body molded in one piece. Jointed at shoulders and hips. $200.00.

TOY PRODUCTS MANUFACTURING CO.
NEW YORK CITY
1925 – 1930

Made dolls for jobbers and quantity buyers. Member of the Doll Parts Manufacturing Association. In 1930, they advertised their We dolls, a line of mama and baby dolls. Each doll carried a paper tag that pictured a mama doll and baby and was inscribed We dolls.

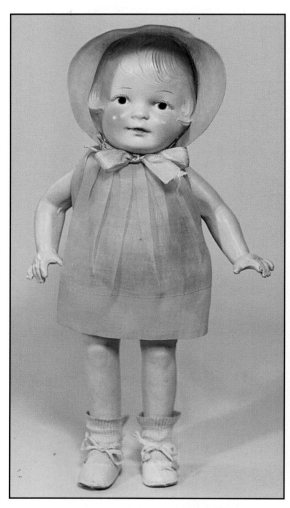 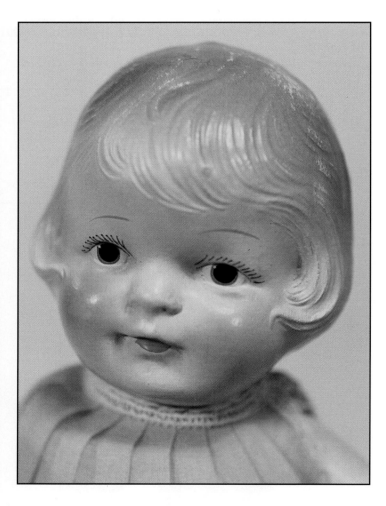

15". Marks on back: TOY PRODUCTS//MFG. CO. INC.
Molded painted Patsy-type hairdo, blue painted eyes, closed mouth, jointed at shoulder/hips with steel springs, body and head one piece. All original outfit, including shoes and socks. Same head mold as Maizie by Regal Doll Mfg. Co. $150.00.

TREGO DOLL MANUFACTURING CO.
NEW YORK CITY
1918 – 1921

Valentine Treat was president of the company. Like so many other firms during this period, they sold domestically made composition copies of German ball-jointed bisque dolls.

19". Marks: Trego//Made in USA.
Composition socket head on wood and composition ball-jointed body. Original black human hair wig. Brown celluloid sleep eyes. Open mouth with two upper teeth. Redressed. $300.00.

22". Marks: TREGO//Made in USA.
Composition socket head on composition ball-jointed body. Dark brown human hair wig, gray celluloid sleep eyes, open mouth with four upper teeth. Old sailor outfit. $200.00.

TRION TOY CO., INC.
BROOKLYN, NEW YORK
1911 – 1921

A double page ad in *Toys and Novelties*, February 1919, stated that 18,000 doll heads were being made daily for their character dolls. This was accompanied by a picture showing workers putting doll heads into endless rows of trays (crate and barrels full of doll heads shown in foreground), with the notation, "Skilled workers in Trion factory have splendid light and air."

1915 ads pictured a little girl in sailor dress with side-glancing eyes as Little Rascal, and also a molded hair girl with hair bow was called Sunny. In June of 1919, a Reiman, Seabrey Co. ad seemed to imply that they were sole representatives.

  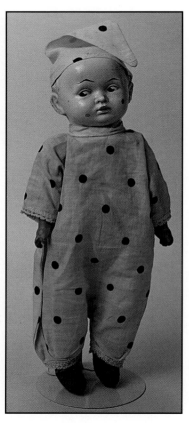

17". Marks: C//Trion Toy Co.//1915. This is Happy (Toys and Novelties, January 1916).
Composition flange head and short arms, cloth body, upper arms and legs, jointed with outside disks. Molded brown boots. Molded painted blond hair and painted blue eyes. Open/closed mouth with two upper molded painted teeth. All original. $150.00.

13½". Marks: Trion Toy Co. His name is Cheery (Playthings, December 1916).
Composition flange head with molded red hat. Cloth body and limbs (note extremely short arms, stump hands), jointed with outside disks. Painted blue eyes, open/closed mouth with white line between lips for teeth, dimples in cheeks. Copy of original outfit. $100.00 (fair condition).

14". Marks: Trion Toy Co. //1915 (Playthings, February 1917).
Composition flange head and short arms, cloth body, upper arms and legs, jointed with outside disks. Black sewn on boots. Entire head is painted white, black eyes painted like a comma on its side, closed mouth. Red dot on right cheek and blue dot on left. White dot on nose. Original suit and cap. In March 1917 ad, this doll is shown wigged, dressed as a little girl with straw hat. $150.00.

13". Marks: Trion Toy Co.
Composition flange head and short arms. Cloth body, upper arms and legs, sewn on black boots, jointed with outside disks. Molded painted blond hair and painted blue eyes, closed mouth. All original felt outfit. $150.00.
Note: This doll was definitely dressed and sold by the Averill Mfg. Co. as part of their Madame Hendren line of dolls dressed in felt costumes (Averill ad in Playthings, June 1916). Doll pictured there (costume patented June 15, 1915).

TYNIE BABY TYPE

13". Marks: none. Tynie Baby type with three rust colored pigtails tied with original green rayon ribbons. Original romper.
Composition flange head and hands, cloth body and bent legs, stitched hip joints. Molded painted reddish hair and painted blue eyes, closed mouth. $80.00.

UNMARKED DOLLS

All dolls listed in this section are from the early period of American dollmaking (1910 – 1920) and further exemplify the wide range of very attractive dolls available during this decade. Several very interesting character faces are included, besides a most fascinating variety of molded hair styles. (Names of manufacturers for these dolls not available.)

22". Marks: none.
Composition flange head and arms to below elbow, crude cloth body and limbs jointed with outside cardboard disks. Faintly molded blond hair and blue eyes, open/closed mouth. Re-dressed. Doll is very faded. $300.00.

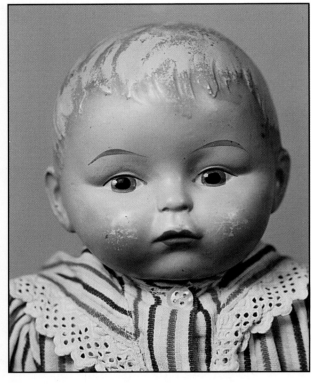

16", Pouty Boy in striped blouse. No marks. Ca. 1915.
Composition flange head and hands. Cloth body and limbs, inside joints. Molded painted hair and blue eyes, closed mouth. Old clothes. $200.00.

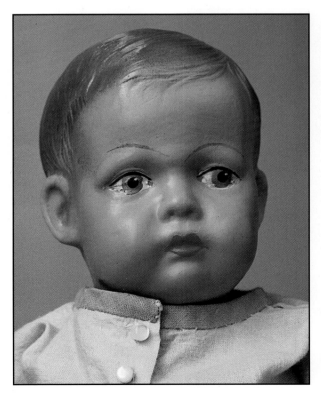

14". No marks (copy of German doll and Fiamingo head).
Composition flange head and short arms. Cloth body and bent baby legs, jointed with outside disks. Molded painted brown hair and blue eyes, closed mouth. Re-dressed. $150.00.

14". Marks: none. Ca. 1915.
Composition flange head and short arms. Cloth body and limbs. Arms jointed with inside disks, bent legs with outside disks. Molded painted brown hair and painted blue eyes, closed mouth, re-dressed. $150.00.

22". Marks: none.
Composition flange head and short arms, cloth body, upper arms, and legs, jointed with outside disks. Molded painted brown hair and painted blue eyes, closed mouth. Original romper. $250.00.

23", Girl with elaborate hairdo and surprised look. Marks: none.
Composition flange head and short composition arms. Cloth body stuffed with cork and arms and bent legs with excelsior. Molded painted brown hair and black eyes, open/closed mouth. Old white dress. $250.00.

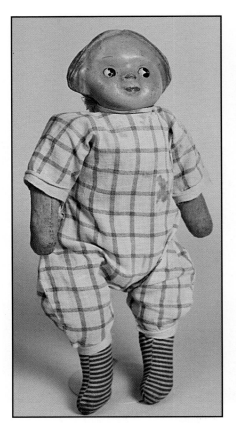

11". No marks (similar doll pictured in Playthings 1911). Composition flange head, cloth body and limbs, jointed at shoulders and hips. Stump hands, bent legs with striped, sewn in stockings. Molded painted hair with middle part and hair hanging down straight all around. All black eyes painted in "lying-on-its-side" heart shape, closed mouth. Romper probably original. $90.00.

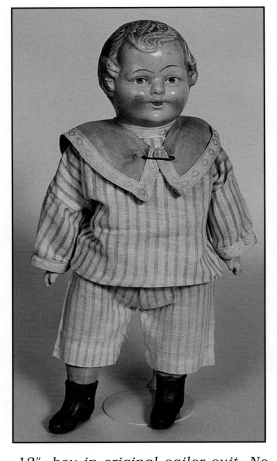

12", boy in original sailor suit. No marks. Ca. 1915.

Composition flange head and short hands. Cloth body, upper arms, and legs, jointed with outside disks. Molded brown composition boots. Molded painted brown hair and blue eyes. Closed mouth. $80.00.

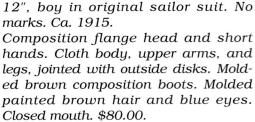

14", boy in all original white sailor suit. No marks. Ca. 1915. Composition flange head and short arms. Cloth body, upper arms, and full legs, jointed with inside disks. Molded painted brown hair and blue eyes, closed mouth. Shoes added. $125.00.

15", girl, molded hair with middle part. No marks. Composition flange head, cloth body and limbs, jointed with outside disks, stump hands. Molded painted hair, painted blue eyes, closed mouth. Re-dressed. $80.00.

19", girl. Marks: none. Ca. 1915. Composition flange head and arms to below elbow. Cloth body and limbs, jointed with inside disks. Molded painted red hair and brown eyes. Open/closed mouth with two painted upper teeth. Re-dressed. $150.00.

13". Marks: none. Ca. 1915. Composition flange head and arms to below elbow. Cloth body jointed with inside disks. Bent legs. Old romper. Molded painted curly brown hair and blue eyes. Closed mouth. $125.00.

Left: 15"; right: 14".
Composition flange heads and short arms. Cloth bodies, upper arms and legs jointed with inside disks. Molded painted blond hair and painted blue eyes, closed mouths. Wire staple for ribbon loop for 15" doll. 14" doll has bent legs. Old clothes. Left, $80.00 (fair condition); right, $125.00.

13". Marks: none.
Composition flange head, short arms to below the elbow and molded, white flat heeled boots. Cloth body, upper arms and legs jointed with outside disks. Molded painted brown hair and painted blue eyes, closed mouth. All original. $150.00.

Left: 9". No marks.
Composition flared head, cloth body and limbs jointed at shoulders and hips with outside disks, stump hands, bent legs. Molded painted hair and blue eyes, open/closed mouth. Original romper. $80.00.
Right: 9½". No marks (K*R 100 Look Alike).
Composition flared head, cloth body and limbs, jointed at shoulders and hips with inside disks, stump hands, bent legs. Molded painted hair and blue eyes, open/closed mouth. Original romper. $80.00.

16". Marks: none.
Composition flange head and short arms. Cloth body, upper arms, and full legs, jointed with inside disks. Molded painted light brown hair and painted blue eyes, closed mouth. Old clothes. $80.00.

16". Marks: none.
Composition flange head, short arms and molded brown boots. Cloth body and limbs jointed with outside disks. Molded, striated, blond hair with two molded hair loops, painted blue eyes, closed mouth. Cotton socks are tucked into boots and sewn on. Re-dressed. $100.00.

13". Marks: none.
Three dolls with identical heads from the same mold. All three are dressed in homemade clothes that seem to have been made for them when they were played with and are, therefore, historical documents in their own way. Note different states of preservation. The stockings are part of their leg casings. They have different color stripes: brown/blue, all blue, and all brown. $80.00 each.

12". Marks: none.
Composition flange head, cloth body and limbs, jointed with outside disks. Molded painted brown hair and blue eyes, closed mouth. Old clothes. $70.00.

10", boy in Russian style gray suit. Marks: none.
Composition flange head and hands. Cloth body and limbs jointed with outside disks. Sewn on black cloth boots. Painted blue eye, closed mouth, re-dressed. $70.00.

18". Marks: none.
Composition flange head and short arms. Cloth body, upper arms, and full legs, jointed with inside disks. Molded painted brown hair and blue eyes, painted to the right. Closed mouth. Re-dressed. $125.00.

18", girl with dark human hair braids. Marks: none.
Composition shoulder head and arms to below the elbow. Cloth body and limbs, jointed with inside disks. Gray celluloid sleep eyes, closed mouth. Original dark brown human hair wig. Re-dressed.
$125.00.

5½". Marks: none.
Brown figure with molded shoes, bloomers, hair bow, and finger to mouth. Painted all black eyes look to her right side.
$40.00.

UNEEDA DOLL CO.
NEW YORK CITY
1917 – 1930+

Carried a general line of composition dolls. In 1927, they were reported as making dolls for jobbers, mail order houses, and stores.

14". Marks: none on doll.
Paper hang tag: Beauty Quality//A//Uneeda//Doll//Uneeda Doll Co. Inc.//N.Y.C.//Made in U.S.A.
All composition, jointed only at shoulders and hips. Molded painted brown hair, inset celluloid eyes with floating pupils, closed mouth. All original including box. $150.00.

Display ad from the September 1948 issue of Play-things. The Carmen doll shown seems the same type as used by R & B, Mary Hoyer, and others: a 14" all-composition doll with slim waist that is fully jointed and has sleep eyes.

Display ad from September 1936 issue of Playthings. The ad mentioned that Sweetums drinks her bottle and has composition head, arms, and legs, soft life-like body, and sleeping eyes.

UNCLE SAM TYPE

17", Uncle Sam type. Marks: 3 0 B. Ca. 1919. Composition flange head and short arms. Cloth body, upper arms, and legs with sewn in black boots, jointed with outside disks. Molded painted hair and painted blue eyes, open/closed mouth with two painted upper teeth. All original except flag. $125.00.

VOGUE DOLL INC.
MEDFORD, MASSACHUSETTS
1922 – PRESENT

Vogue Doll Inc. was founded by Mrs. Jennie Graves.

She sold dolls dressed by her and bought from other sources. The first doll used for this purpose was an 8" bisque headed example purchased from Armand Marsaille in Germany called Just Me. When these were no longer available, Mrs. Graves changed over to a 8" all-composition doll named Toddles (name has been found ink stamped on some of their shoe soles; *Ginny An American Toddler Doll*, A. G. Mandeville, pg. 16). These little dolls were dressed in adorably styled and executed copies of children's fashions but also were issued in series named Nursery Rhymes, Fairy Tales, Bridal Party, Military Group, etc. Virginia Graves Carlson, the daughter of Mrs. Graves, was the designer of these doll fashions.

An 8" all-composition baby with curved legs was also available.

Mrs. Graves also dressed larger dolls, as seen in this section. They were not marked. These larger dolls came dressed in formal bridal gowns as well. Some, dressed in little girl's fashions, carried matching purses containing a mirror, powder, and a powder puff. They were called Make-Up dolls.

By 1950, hard plastic took the place of composition, and the company went into their most productive period with the 8" hard plastic Ginny dolls.

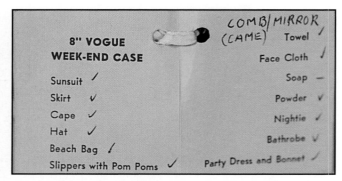

8" VOGUE WEEK-END CASE		COMB/MIRROR (CAME)	
		Towel	✓
Sunsuit	✓	Face Cloth	✓
Skirt	✓	Soap	—
Cape	✓	Powder	✓
Hat	✓	Nightie	✓
Beach Bag	✓	Bathrobe	✓
Slippers with Pom Poms	✓	Party Dress and Bonnet	✓

Inside of booklet tied to round, clear container.

7½". Marks on head and body: Vogue.
All composition, fully jointed. Blond mohair wig over molded, curly hair, painted blue eyes, closed mouth. All original. Came with weekend case (round plastic case, 6¼" diameter. See separate illustration for list of contents and "weekend case" name). $400.00.

8". Marks on head: Vogue. Marks on body: illegible. All composition, fully jointed. Blond mohair wig over molded hair, painted blue eyes, closed mouth, all original. $300.00.

7½". Marks: Vogue (head and body).
Cape tagged: Vogue, Inc.
All composition, fully jointed. Original blond mohair wig, painted blue eyes, closed mouth. All original including shoes, socks, and box. $400.00.

19". Marks: none. Sold by Vogue Doll Co. (Doll Reader, November 1983, pg. 122, Identical doll and outfit reported as tagged: "Vogue Dolls Inc.//Medford Mass.").
All compostion, fully jointed. Blond mohair wig, brown sleep eyes, open mouth with four upper teeth. All original outfit made of fake lamb fur and trimmed with red felt, red oil cloth shoes. $400.00.

19". Marks: none.
All composition, fully jointed. Mohair wig, brown sleep eyes, open mouth with four upper teeth. All original. Wool coat and hat trimmed with red felt. $400.00. original, plain white dress.

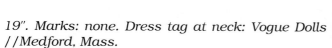

19". Marks: none. Dress tag at neck: Vogue Dolls //Medford, Mass.
All composition, fully jointed. Blond mohair wig with braids, blue sleep eyes, closed mouth. All original outfit, including shoes and socks. $450.00.

13", W.A.A.C (Shoe sole ink stamped WAAC-ETTE).
13", W.A.V.E.S.
Marks: none (have been reported with Vogue, Inc. label).
All original. All composition, fully jointed, blond mohair wigs, blue and brown sleep eyes, open mouths with two upper teeth. $300.00 each.

11". Marks: none.
Ink stamp on sole of shoe: Dora Lee.
All composition, fully jointed, blond mohair wig, blue sleep eyes, closed mouth. All original. $190.00.

LOUIS WOLF & CO. SONNEBERG/THUER. NURNBERG/BAVARIA, BOSTON, AND NEW YORK 1870 – 1930+

They were importers, producers, and distributors of dolls. In 1928, they merged with Bing, forming the Bing-Wolf Corp. Averill Manufacturing Co. became associated with Bing Wolf (Coleman II).

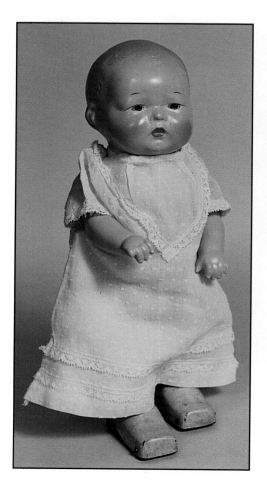

12". Marks: illegible. This is Toddling Toodles (Playthings, July 1925).
Marked on stationary wind-up key: Waterbury Clock Co.
Composition shoulder head and full arms attached to metal torso with wind-up mechanism inside. Metal legs and feet. Feet have two rollers each inside them. Molded painted blond hair and painted blue eyes. Closed mouth. Re-dressed. (Doll in ad picture is dressed similar style.) $250.00.

W.D. CO.

11", Topsy/Turvy, black/white.
Both heads marked W. D. Co.
Composition shoulder heads and full arms, pin jointed. Straw stuffed, crude body. Molded painted hair and eyes. Closed mouth. Re-dressed. $180.00.

WOODTEX CO.
NEW YORK CITY
1922 – 1923+

The first *Coleman Encyclopedia* lists this company as having made dolls' heads, arms, and legs in a range of sizes. *Composition Dolls*, Vol II by P. & P. Judd, shows a picture of a doll marked "Woodtex," which has identical above-the-knee jointed legs as the doll illustrated here. The Judd doll, however, has a cloth torso with slanted hip joints. This unusual above-the-knee jointing has only been seen on the two dolls discussed here. From this fact the assumption is that the unmarked doll illustrated here was made by Woodtex. The only puzzle piece that does not fit into this theory is the Coleman's date of 1922 – 1923 for the existence of the Woodtex Company, as slim cloth body type dolls with slanted hip joints were not produced until about 1928. The most logical explanation for this would be that the Woodtex Company may have been in existence longer than 1923.

WHISTLER

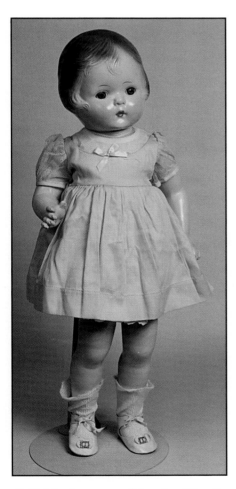

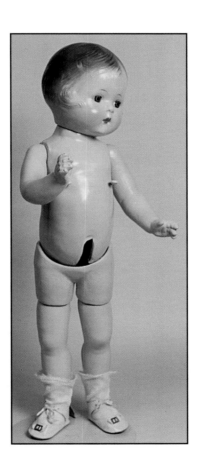

24". Marks: none (May be Woodtex Co.), Patsy-type.
All composition, fully jointed with unusual lower torso/upper leg section. Molded painted brown hair, gray tin sleep eyes, closed mouth, re-dressed. $300.00.

17", Whistler.
Marks: none. Ca. 1915. Composition flange head and short arms. Cloth body and limbs, jointed with outside disks. Molded painted brown hair and blue eyes. Closed puckered mouth. Re-dressed. $150.00.

WONDERCRAFT CO.
NEW YORK

11". Marks: Pat. Pending (on inside of dress). Paper label on bottom of feet: Bobbi-Mae// Swing "N" Sway Doll//Inspired by//Sammy Kay//Painted Pending//Manufactured by// Wondercraft Co.//New York (Anderton I, pg. 329) (Playthings, June 1948).
All composition. Dowels mounted on top of legs and neck have been threaded onto cross bars that let head and body sway independently when tapped. $200.00.

11", Denny Dimwit. Marks: none. By Permission of the Famous Artists Syndicate, ca 1948, The Chicago Tribune, and Denny Dimwit from Winnie Winkle, The Breadwinner, by Branner, Original box decorated with panels from the cartoon strip (Anderton/II, pg. 652).
All composition. Leg and neck dowel is threaded onto metal cross bar that lets head and mid-section sway independently when tapped. Molded painted tufts of hair and painted black eyes. Open/closed mouth with two painted teeth. $250.00.

WORLD WAR I SOLDIERS AND NURSES

18", WWI Soldier. Marks: none.
Composition shoulder head and short arms. Cloth body, upper arms, and full legs, jointed with inside disks. Molded painted brown hair and blue eyes, open/closed mouth. All original clothes including white shirt, undershirt, and long underwear. $300.00.

14", WWI Military with flag. Marks: none.
Composition flange head and hands, cloth body, upper arms, and legs, jointed with outside disks. Curly mohair glued directly onto molded painted hair, painted blue eyes, open/closed mouth. Blue and red uniform is made of felt, as is the beige hat with leather hat band. Black oilcloth belt. One-star flag came with doll. $150.00.

15", WWI Nurse. Marks: ©L.
Composition flange head and short arms, cloth body, upper arms, and full legs, inside joints. Molded painted light brown hair and blue eyes, closed mouth. All original uniform except for slippers. $80.00 (very faded).

16", WWI Nurse. Marks: none (pictured in McDonald Bros. Co. catalog, Minneapolis 1919; Illustrated Price Guide, Erhardt, pg. 84).
Composition shoulder head nailed to cloth body, full composition arms pin jointed, all cloth legs jointed with outside disks. Molded painted blond hair and painted blue eyes, closed mouth. All original clothes. $200.00.

13", WWI Nurse with flag sash. No marks. Composition flange head and lower arms. Cloth body, upper arms, and full legs, inside joints. Blond mohair wig over molded hair, painted blue eyes, closed mouth. All original uniform including head piece and slippers. $200.00.

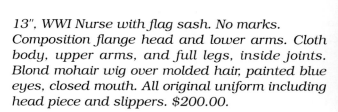

THE ZAIDEN TOY WORKS
NEW JERSEY and NEW YORK
1906 – 1930+

Mr. David Zaiden developed and produced composition dolls and sold various other products. During his career, he was associated with many New York area doll companies and agencies at different times (see *Coleman Encyclopedia*). Early display ads indicate that his production consisted of copies (in composition) of German bisque headed dolls. No evidence was found that Mr. Zaiden produced other than the mechanical dolls during the 20s.

He was granted various patents for mechanical dolls:

No. 1,368,592 dated February 15, 1921, for an electric shoulder action shimmy doll (not pictured).

No. 1,382,708 dated June 28, 1921, for a shoulder action shimmy doll with spring wound mechanism.

No. 1,423,383 dated July 1922, for a hip action shimmy dancer.

No. 1,452,134 dated April 17, 1923, for a gyrating mechanism at navel level of doll.

No. 1,411,825 dated April 4, 1922, for a doll that can dance and can move her right arm up and down at elbow level (rigid shoulder, normally jointed left arm) (not pictured).

Mr. Zaiden's shimmy dancers were still advertised in 1930.

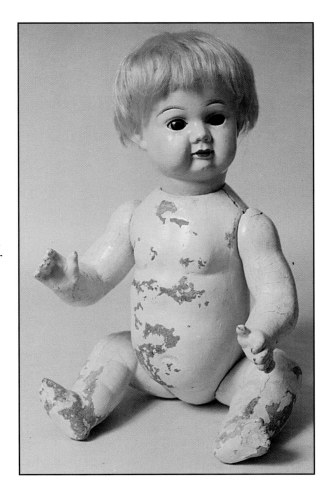

17". Marks on head: Colonial Toy Mfg. Co. Body: Colonial Toy Mfg. Co.//Zaiden//Doll. All composition, fully jointed. Gray sleep eyes, closed mouth. Metal pate, original blond mohair wig. Copy of German bisque baby. $100.00 fair.

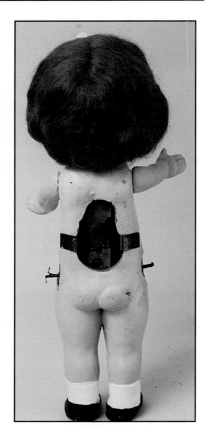

16". Marks: none (assumed to be made by Zaiden. Was unable to locate ads or patent for eye mechanism).

All composition, jointed at shoulders only with steel spring. Wind-up mechanism inserted into doll through cut-out in back. Note protrusions through holes at hip level. Skirt would be attached to protrusions, and they would move up and down when wound. Mechanism also connected to metal eyes. When wound, in addition to the shaking hips, the eyes will move from center to one side and back to center (eyes do not sleep). Wig is a replacement, closed mouth. Painted lower and upper lashes. $150.00.

Note: All mechanical dolls in this section show identical construction; i.e., wind-up mechanism was inserted through opening in back and covered with a piece of cloth or metal plate.

12½" Shimmie Dancer (Playthings, June 1921). Marks: none. All composition. Painted, black eyes, closed mouth. Arms are mounted on metal bar which is connected to a wind-up mechanism inside the body. When wound, bar and arms move up and down alternately. Molded hair is not painted, and there is evidence that the doll had a wig. Original clothes missing. $150.00 (fair condition).

13". Marks: none (Playthings, June 1921 and various other ads during ten-year period).
All composition, jointed at shoulders only with steel spring. Same hip mechanism as doll on page 378, upper left. Original brown mohair wig, metallic head band with rhinestone decoration. Painted black, pupilless eyes and closed, smiling mouth. Brown wool skirt with metallic straps is also original. Molded painted blue socks and black slippers. $200.00.

16". Marks: none (Playthings, March 1929; photographic illustration was used for this doll and is recognizable). All composition, jointed only at shoulders. Painted brown eyes, open/closed mouth with four painted teeth. Painted silver slippers. Original costume and mohair wig. Cut-outs at belly button and chest level accommodate protrusions which are attached to bra and skirt. Movement at chest: from side to side. Motion at belly button level describes a circle. When wound, moving bra and skirt give the impression that the doll is shimmying. $300.00.

18". Marks: none.
All composition, jointed at shoulders only. For description of double action mechanism, see brown dancer. Dark brown mohair wig decorated with ribbon and feathers. Painted blue eyes, open/closed mouth with white line between lips. Painted gold sandals. All original. $300.00.

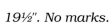

19½". No marks.
All composition, jointed at shoulders only with steel spring. Left arm is bent at right angle. For description of double action mechanism see brown dancer. Blond mohair wig decorated with metallic ribbon. Painted brown eyes, open/closed mouth. Painted black slippers. All original. $300.00.

NUMBERS FOUND ON GLUE-BASE COMPOSITION HEADS

Many early heads by Fleischaker & Baum (Effanbee) were marked with numbers. Some were dressed and sold by the Averill Mfg. Co., and now some have been identified that were sold by the Louis Amberg & Son and Gem Toy Co.

Effanbee

19" Baby, crude body, mold/painted tongue/teeth . . . . .7c.
14" Baby Huggims, 1915 Effanbee catalog 24
20" Boy with broad smile, open/closed mouth 2/teeth, (came on wrong body — may have been baby?) .27c.
14" Billy Boy, Sober Grumpy, 1915 catalog 34
11" Baby, original long white gown/cap 52
15" Boy, straight legs, black cloth boots 54
12" Betty Bounce, 1915 catalog 70
11" Betty Bounce, molded hair loop 70
14" Merry Sunshine Kid, Smiling Grumpy 104
15" Aunt Dinah, 1915 catalog, Smiling Grumpy, reversed 106
20" Merry Sunshine Kid, Smiling Grumpy 108
14" Baby, slightly bent legs, nurser mouth . . . . .124 N
13" Johnny Jones, 1915 catalog, Copy K*R #114 152
15½" Johnny Jones, 1915 catalog, Copy K*R #114 or Deco 152 156
22" Johnny Jones, 1915 catalog, Copy K*R #114 158
12" Pouting Bess, 1915 catalog, Heubach face 162
15" Pouting Bess, 915 catalog, Copy K*R #114 166
14" Grumpy, 1915 catalog, DECO 174
13" Boy, Russian suit/striped trim, blue 303
15" Whistler, original sailor suit, Fiamingo copy 364
14" Baby, bent legs, closed mouth, painted eyes 455
30" Carnival boy 802

Amberg

13½" Pouty Pet girl, original advertising 494
14½ Pouty Pet boy, different hairdo 494
15" Boy, replaced body, picture Coleman II, pg. 33 but listed there as marked L.A.&S. 784

Dolls Dressed by Averill Mfg. Co.

15" Boy, red/green Dutch outfit, Fiamingo copy 334
14" Boy, yellow/brown Dutch outfit, Sober Grumpy 34

Gem Toy Company

17" Boy, gray teddy bear body, head marked Gem//491, 9 not clear could be 481, has a pouty expression 491

BIBLIOGRAPHY

General Reference Books/Periodicals

Anderton, Johana Gast. *Twentieth Century Dolls from Bisque to Vinyl*.
 More Twentieth Century Dolls, from Bisque to Vinyl.

Axe, John. *Collectible Patsy Dolls and Patsy-Types*.
 Effanbee: A Collector's Encyclopedia, 1949 – 1983.
 The Encyclopedia of Celebrity Dolls.

Blum, David. *A Pictorial History of the American Theater, 1860 – 1960 (1950)*.

Boardman, Gerald. *The Oxford Companion to American Theater (1984)*.

Burdick, Lorraine. *Child Star Dolls and Toys* (Second printing 1970).

Carlson, Nancy. *The Elegance of Effanbee*.

Coleman, Dorothy S., Elizabeth A., and Evelyn J. *The Collector's Encyclopedia of Dolls, Vol I and II*.

Corson, Carol. *Schoenhut Dolls: A Collector's Encyclopedia*.

Doll News. United Federation of Doll Clubs, 1976 – 1997.

Doll Reader. Harrisburg, PA: Cumberland Publishing, Inc., 1976 – 1997

Ellenburg, Kelly M. *Effanbee: The Dolls with the Golden Hearts*.

Foulke, Jan. Blue Books. Focusing On #1 – *Effanbee Composition Dolls*.
 Focusing on #2 — *Treasury of Madame Alecander Dolls*.
 Focusing on #3 — *Gebrueder Heubach Dolls*.
 Kestner, King of Doll Makers.
 Simon & Halbig Dolls, The Artful Aspect.

Gale Research Co. *Something about the Author, Vol. 17 and 19*; Michigan, 1979.

Horn, Maurice (ed.). *The World Encyclopedia of Comics*.

Hoyer, Mary. *Mary Hoyer and Her Dolls*.

Izen, Judith. *Collector's Guide to Ideal Dolls*.

Izen, Judith and Carol Stover. *Collector's Encyclopedia of Vogue Dolls*.

Judd, Polly & Pam. *Composition Dolls, Identification & Price Guide, Vol I & II*.

Lackman, Ron. *Same Time...Same Station, an A – Z Guide to Radio*. 1996.

McKeon, Barbara Jo. *Rare and Hard to Find Madame Alexander Dolls*.

Mandeville, Glenn A. *Ginny...An American Toddler Doll*.

Moyer, Patsy, Ed. *Patsy & Friends Newsletter*.

Pardella, Edward R., *Shirley Temple Dolls and Fashions*.

Schoonmaker, Patricia N. *Effanbee Dolls The Formative Years 1910 – 1929*.
 Patsy Doll Family Encyclopedia, Vol. I and II

The Effanbee Patsy Family and Related Types, ©1971.

Shoemaker, Rhoda. *Composition Dolls, Cute and Collectible, Vol I – IV.*
The Antique Trader Weeksy's Book of Collectible Dolls. Edited by Kyle D. Husfleon (Reprints from four years.) The Babka Publishing Co., Dubuque, Iowa (1976).

United Federation of Doll Clubs. *Doll News.* 1976 – 1997.

Wiedman Casper, Peggy. *Fashionable Terri Lee Dolls.*

Articles

"What Type of Doll Will Sell Best in 1927?" *Toys and Novelties,* February 1927, pg. 131.

"The Development of the American Doll." *Toys and Novelties,* January 1927, pg. 341.

"Phenominal Sale of American Walking and Talking Dolls." *Playthings,* January 1922, pg. 267.

"Dolls — Made in America." *Fortune Magazine,* December, 1936, pg. 103.

"Effanbee's Unlikely Duo – W.C. Fields and Charlie," Don Jensen, *Doll Reader,* October 1990.

Old Catalogs and Reprints

Adams, Margaret. *Collectible Dolls and Accessories of the Twenties and Thirties* from Sears Roebuck & Co. Catalogs.

Averill Manufacturing Co. catalog, ca. 1925.

Kringle Society of Dolls. Marshall Field & Company, 1914.

E.I. Horsman, catalog, ca. 1915, Strong Museum, Rochester.

Fleischaker & Baum, Dolls Ancient & Modern (1915 catalog – reprint).

Ideal Dolls, Ideal's catalog from 1930, reprinted 1987 by Lorraine Burdick.

Playthings, 1910 – 1950 (trade magazine).

The A. Schoenhut Company Catalog, 1930. (Reprinted by Schoenhut Collector's Club, 1996.)

Tip Top Toy Co. catalog, Strong Museum, Rochester.

Toys and Novelties, 1910 – 1950 (trade magazine).

INDEX

ABOUT THE AUTHOR

Ursula Mertz has been a doll collector since 1975. Composition dolls have become a full-time commitment. From 1976 to 1986, she had a repair business, specializing in partial restorations of composition and other painted surface dolls. Among her customers were collectors from throughout the United States. Her visual arts background and consequent knowledge of color theory and paint mixing enabled her to very successfully match her restorations to old painted surfaces, an art practiced by few.

It was this hands-on experience in doll repairs that gave Ursula an opportunity to study composition dolls inside out and develop proper maintenance procedures for them. It also was helpful in developing the technical information, presented in this book.

At the same time, Ursula has been a dealer specializing in composition dolls and selling at various large doll shows. This has given her an opportunity to examine and evaluate great numbers of composition dolls.

Ursula has mounted doll exhibits on various themes at the local and national level and she continues to lecture on various composition doll subjects. Throughout her career, she has written numerous articles for both *Doll News* and *Doll Reader*. She is presently the author of the column "American Doll Showcase" in Doll Reader.

The author is a member of UFDC (United Federation of Doll Clubs) and has been very active in this organization for many years. At their annual convention in Anaheim, California, in July 1997, she was given their annual national Award of Excellence for Protection and Preservation of Dolls.

Ursula is married to Otto J. Mertz, able photographer for the majority of photographs in this book and well known to readers of the "American Doll Showcase" column. In fact, the whole family became involved. Daughter Linda, and son-in-law, Paul, helped with the proofreading of the manuscript for this book. What are her plans for the future? "Much remains to be done in the area of composition doll research," she commented.

COLLECTOR BOOKS

Informing Today's Collector

For over two decades we have been keeping collectors informed on trends and values in all fields of antiques and collectibles.

BOOKS ON DOLLS

4631 **Barbie Doll** Boom, 1986–1995, Augustyniak $18.95
2079 **Barbie Doll Fashion,** Vol. I, Eames....................................$24.95
4846 **Barbie Doll Fashion,** Vol. II, 1968–1974, Eames $24.95
4847 The **Barbie Doll Years,** 2nd. Ed., 1959–1996, Olds.................$17.95
3957 **Barbie Exclusives**, Rana $18.95
4632 **Barbie Exclusives**, Book II, Rana...$18.95
4557 **Barbie,** The First 30 Years, 1959–1989, Deutsch.....................$24.95
3873 **Black Dolls**, Book II, Perkins...$17.95
1529 Collector's Ency. of **Barbie Dolls**, DeWein/Ashabraner $19.95
4882 Coll. Encyc. of **Barbie Doll Exclusives & More**, Augustyniak....$19.95
2211 Collector's Encyclopedia of **Madame Alexander Dolls**, Smith ..$24.95
4859 Collector's Guide to **Barbie Doll Paper Dolls**, Mieszala $16.95
4861 Collector's Guide to **Tammy**, Sabulis/Weglewski $18.95
4863 Collector's Guide to **Vogue Dolls,** Izen/Stover.....................$29.95
4707 Decade of **Barbie Dolls** & Collectibles, 1981–1991, Summers $19.95
5039 **Doll Values,** Antique to Modern, 2nd Ed., Moyer $12.95
1799 **Effanbee Doll** Encyclopedia, Smith $19.95
4571 **Liddle Kiddles,** Identification & Value Guide, Langford...........$18.95
5047 **Madame Alexander** Collector's Dolls Price Guide #23, Crowsey..$9.95
4873 **Modern Collectible Dolls,** Id. & Value Guide, Moyer $19.95
3826 Story of **Barbie**, Westenhouser $19.95
1513 **Teddy Bears & Steiff** Animals, Mandel $9.95
1817 **Teddy Bears & Steiff** Animals, 2nd Series, Mandel...............$19.95
2084 **Teddy Bears, Annalees's & Steiff** Animals, 3rd Series, Mandel..$19.95
1808 Wonder of **Barbie**, Manos $9.95
4880 The World of **Raggedy Ann** Collectibles, Avery $24.95
1430 World of **Barbie Dolls**, Manos $9.95

BOOKS ON TOYS, MARBLES & CHRISTMAS COLLECTIBLES

3427 **Advertising Character** Collectibles, Dotz $17.95
2333 Antique & Collectible **Marbles**, 3rd Ed., Grist $9.95
3827 Antique & Collectible **Toys**, 1870–1950, Longest $24.95
3956 **Baby Boomer Games**, Polizzi $24.95
3717 **Christmas Collectibles,** 2nd Edition, Whitmyer....................$24.95
4976 **Christmas Ornaments,** Lights & Decorations, Johnson $24.95
4737 **Christmas Ornaments,** Lights & Decorations, Vol. II, Johnson ..$24.95
4739 **Christmas Ornaments,** Lights & Decorations, Vol. III, Johnson .$24.95
4649 Classic **Plastic Model Kits,** Polizzi $24.95
4559 Collectible **Action Figures,** 2nd Ed., Manos $17.95
2338 Collector's Encyclopedia of **Disneyana**, Longest/Stern $24.95
4958 Collector's Guide to **Battery Toys,** Hultzman.......................$19.95
4639 Collector's Guide to **Diecast Toys** & Scale Models, Johnson $19.95
4653 Collector's Guide to **T.V. Memorabilia,** Davis/Morgan $24.95
4651 Collector's Guide to **Tinker Toys**, Strange $18.95
4566 Collector's Guide to **Tootsietoys,** 2nd Ed., Richter $19.95
4945 **G-Men & FBI Toys** & Collectibles, Whitworth $18.95
4720 Golden Age of **Automotive Toys,** Hutchison/Johnson $24.95
3436 Grist's Big Book of **Marbles**...$19.95
3970 Grist's Machine-Made & Contemporary **Marbles**, 2nd Ed. $9.95
4755 Hake's Price Guide to **Character Toy Premiums** $24.95
4723 **Matchbox Toys,** 2nd Ed., 1947 to 1996, Johnson...................$18.95
4871 **McDonald's** Collectibles, Henriques/DuVall $19.95
1540 **Modern Toys,** 1930–1980, Baker.......................................$19.95
3888 **Motorcycle Toys,** Antique & Contemporary, Gentry/Downs.....$18.95
4953 Schroeder's Collectible **Toys,** Antique to Modern Price Guide ..$17.95
1886 Stern's Guide to **Disney** Collectibles..................................$14.95
2139 Stern's Guide to **Disney** Collectibles, 2nd Series...................$14.95
3975 Stern's Guide to **Disney** Collectibles, 3rd Series $18.95
2028 **Toys,** Antique & Collectible, Longest $14.95

This is only a partial listing of the books on antiques that are available from Collector Books. All books are well illustrated and contain current values. Most of these books are available from your local book seller, antique dealer, or public library. If you are unable to locate certain titles in your area, you may order by mail from COLLECTOR BOOKS, P.O. Box 3009, Paducah, KY 42002-3009. Customers with Visa, MasterCard, or Discover may phone in orders from 7:00–5:00 CST, Monday–Friday, Toll Free 1-800-626-5420. Add $2.00 for postage for the first book ordered and $0.30 for each additional book. Include item number, title, and price when ordering. Allow 14 to 21 days for delivery.

Schroeder's ANTIQUES Price Guide

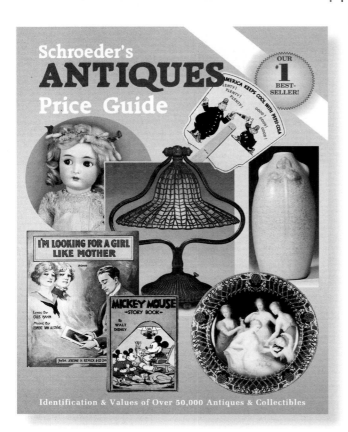

8½ x 11, 612 Pages, $12.95

. . . is the #1 best-selling antiques & collectibles value guide on the market today, and here's why . . .

- *More than 450 advisors, well-known dealers, and top-notch collectors work together with our editors to bring you accurate information regarding pricing and identification.*

- *More than 45,000 items in almost 550 categories are listed along with hundreds of sharp original photos that illustrate not only the rare and unusual, but the common, popular collectibles as well.*

- *Each large close-up shot shows important details clearly. Every subject is represented with histories and background information, a feature not found in any of our competitors' publications.*

- *Our editors keep abreast of newly developing trends, often adding several new categories a year as the need arises.*

If it merits the interest of today's collector, you'll find it in *Schroeder's*. And you can feel confident that the information we publish is up to date and accurate. Our advisors thoroughly check each category to spot inconsistencies, listings that may not be entirely reflective of market dealings, and lines too vague to be of merit. Only the best of the lot remains for publication.

Without doubt, you'll find
SCHROEDER'S ANTIQUES PRICE GUIDE
the only one to buy for
reliable information and values.

COLLECTOR BOOKS
A Division of Schroeder Publishing Co., Inc.